Golf
FOR
DUMMIES®
4TH EDITION

by Gary McCord

WILEY

Wiley Publishing, Inc.

Golf For Dummies®, 4th Edition

Published by
Wiley Publishing, Inc.
111 River St.
Hoboken, NJ 07030-5774
www.wiley.com

WILEY

About the Author

"Life is full of ups and downs, and it wouldn't be fun any other way." Living by this optimistic philosophy, **Gary McCord** persisted through years of mediocrity before finding success. An outstanding player, television announcer, instructor, author, speaker, and even movie actor, he has become a golf celebrity.

McCord is well known for enduring 23 years and 422 tournaments on the PGA Tour without nabbing a single victory. A man of good humor, he sported a "NO WINS" license plate for years to poke fun at his less-than-glamorous work as a professional golfer.

"Trapped in the headlights of bankruptcy," as he liked to put it, McCord pursued other avenues in golf and found himself launching a broadcasting career. He scored big when a CBS Sports executive tossed him a headset and asked him to do golf commentary — giving him only 15 minutes to prepare. McCord jumped in with no fear and impressed CBS with his performance. Twenty-five years later, he's still providing color commentary for CBS golf events. Fans and critics praise him for his knowledgeable perspective, refreshing humor, and sometimes irreverent wit toward a game known for taking itself too seriously.

Broadcasting changed his perspective on golf. Realizing that a better understanding of the golf swing would help his TV work, McCord studied the swing for two years. He emerged with knowledge, confidence, and an improved golf game.

McCord's own golf really came together as he began his career on the Champions Tour after his 50th birthday. In 1999, his first full season on that tour, he won two events — the Toshiba Senior Classic and the Ingersoll-Rand Senior Tour Championship — to finish 17th on the official money list with nearly $1 million in prize money. Since then, he has often finished in the top 30 on the money list while playing a limited schedule of 10 to 15 events per year.

When he isn't broadcasting or playing golf, McCord keeps busy with myriad other projects. He portrayed himself in and served as technical director for the golf movie *Tin Cup,* starring Kevin Costner, Rene Russo, and Don Johnson. He's also a writer. In addition to writing *Golf For Dummies,* he's the author of a collection of essays about his life on tour, *Just a Range Ball in a Box of Titleists.* His bestselling *Golf For Dummies* was released in DVD form in 2004.

McCord and his friend and CBS Sports colleague David Feherty became known to millions of golf fans and gamers as the voices of EA Sports' Tiger Woods PGA Tour video games. McCord also instructs and consults with more than 20 PGA Tour players.

Gary brings a sense of fun to everything he does and never takes himself too seriously. He and his wife, Diane, share the "ups and downs" of a busy life together at their homes in Scottsdale and Denver.

Dedication

I dedicate this book to spike marks, the wind just came up from the other direction, bad bounces, wrong yardage, rising barometric pressure, solar storms, dirt got in my eyes, yin and yang, the big bang theory, Brownian motion, dark energy, escape velocity, entropy, Newton's laws of motion, and a bad caddie. All the things we golfers can blame our erratic play on instead of ourselves, providing peace of mind in the unstable environment of this maniacal endeavor.

Author's Acknowledgments

To the game itself, golf. It's a clever game worthy of perspective. I'm not astute enough to unravel it all, but if you can get a good author, bingo, the game is easy. Thanks Kevin Cook for the time and effort he put into this 4th edition.

To my wife Diane, my mom Ruth, my sister Karen and her late husband Chris, my daughter Krista and her husband Mike, and my four granddaughters Breanne, Kayla, Jenae, and Terra: See what you can do with spell check!

And many thanks to the great golf team Wiley put together: Acquisitions Editor Stacy Kennedy; Senior Project Editor Chrissy Guthrie; Copy Editor Megan Knoll; photographers Erick Rasco and Matt Bowen; models Clayton Allen, Robin Anderson, Robert Gaier, and Swati Gunale; Technical Editor Emily Hallberg; and all the folks in Composition Services who processed the art and laid out the book like champions.

Publisher's Acknowledgments

We're proud of this book; please send us your comments at http://dummies.custhelp.com. For other comments, please contact our Customer Care Department within the U.S. at 877-762-2974, outside the U.S. at 317-572-3993, or fax 317-572-4002.

Some of the people who helped bring this book to market include the following:

Acquisitions, Editorial, and Media Development

Senior Project Editor: Christina Guthrie

(Previous Edition: Elizabeth Kuball)

Acquisitions Editor: Stacy Kennedy

Copy Editor: Megan Knoll

Assistant Editor: David Lutton

Technical Editor: Emily A. Hallberg, PGA

Editorial Manager: Christine Meloy Beck

Editorial Assistants: Rachelle Amick, Jennette ElNaggar

Art Coordinator: Alicia B. South

Cover Photos: © iStockphoto.com / Cary Westfall

Cartoons: Rich Tennant (www.the5thwave.com)

Composition Services

Project Coordinator: Patrick Redmond

Layout and Graphics: Joyce Haughey, Vida Noffsinger, Brent Savage, Tobin Wilkerson

Proofreaders: Cynthia Fields, John Greenough

Indexer: BIM Indexing & Proofreading Services

Photographers: Erick W. Rasco, Matt Bowen, Paul Lester, Scott Baxter Photography, Daniel Mainzer Photography

---

Publishing and Editorial for Consumer Dummies

Diane Graves Steele, Vice President and Publisher, Consumer Dummies

Kristin Ferguson-Wagstaffe, Product Development Director, Consumer Dummies

Ensley Eikenburg, Associate Publisher, Travel

Kelly Regan, Editorial Director, Travel

Publishing for Technology Dummies

Andy Cummings, Vice President and Publisher, Dummies Technology/General User

Composition Services

Debbie Stailey, Director of Composition Services

Contents at a Glance

Table of Contents

Introduction

● ●

1 can't believe this book is the 4th edition of *Golf For Dummies!* If it's the first golf book you've ever held in your hands, don't worry. I've read more of them than I can count, and this one's a particular favorite. To bring you this edition, I've gone back through everything I wrote in the first three, updating some material, writing a bunch more to keep up with this fast-changing game, and making everything even clearer and easier to follow.

Not to mention funnier!

Because golf, like life itself, can be hard but is ultimately enjoyable. Please remember that as you begin your adventure in the most maddening and wondrous game of all: Golf is fun. And the fun starts here.

About This Book

I've written this book for the rankest beginner, although I like to think that I have something to offer golfers at every level, even the pros. (Of course, my buddies on the professional tours will probably read this book just to see whether I can write a coherent sentence.) The guys I grew up with at San Luis Rey golf course in Southern California will check out *Golf For Dummies,* 4th Edition, to see whether I've used any of their funniest lines.

What you have here is no ordinary golf-instruction book. Most of the golf books you find in your local bookstore (or, increasingly, online) are written by professional players or teachers. As such, they focus solely on the golf swing. *Golf For Dummies,* 4th Edition, covers a lot more than the swing. This book ought to be the only one you need as you develop a golf dependency. (Feel free to consult a physician when you feel the first symptoms coming on — grinding your teeth, talking to yourself after missing a shot, punching the air after making one. These are the warning signs. But remember: This book is cheaper than a visit to the doctor.)

When I started out on the PGA Tour in 1974, I was full of fight and enthusiasm but lacked a basic knowledge of golf-swing mechanics. A warm panic would start to rise in me about ten minutes before I was due to tee off. My old friends Doubt and Dread would join me at the first tee. My brain would be racing, trying to figure out what *swing thought* (that one aspect of the swing that you meditate on to keep focused) to use that day. Most of the time, I'd be left with a thought like, "Keep the left elbow toward magnetic north on the downswing." Usually, that action resulted in a silly-looking slice into uncharted territory.

I swung the club that way for most of my career. So I know what it's like to play without knowledge or a solid foundation. Believe me, I'm a lot happier — and having a lot more fun — now that I know what I'm doing.

The reason I'm qualified to help you is that I have made a serious effort to become a student of the game. When I started working on golf telecasts for CBS, I didn't know much about the inner workings of the swing. But my new job forced me to learn. My odyssey led me to seek advice from some of the world's greatest teachers.

One of them was Mac O'Grady, a golfer I grew up with in Southern California. O'Grady had researched his method with passion since 1983. The result was a swing model that worked. I was lucky to study under O'Grady, and I can't thank him enough. But I don't cover Mac's model in this book; it's for advanced golfers. No one has ever called me advanced, so I'm gonna stick to basics.

Golf For Dummies, 4th Edition, puts you on track to becoming not just someone who can hit a golf ball but rather a real golfer. You'll soon discover the big difference between the two.

Conventions Used in This Book

To make the text even more accessible, I've used some handy conventions throughout the book:

- New words or terms are formatted in *italics* and accompanied by a definition.
- **Bold** text denotes the specific steps of processes that I've spelled out. It also highlights keywords in bulleted lists.
- Web site URLs are in `monofont`. When this book was printed, some Web addresses may have needed to break across two lines of text. If that happened, rest assured that I haven't put in any extra characters (like hyphens) to indicate the break. When using one of these Web addresses, just type exactly what you see in this book, pretending that the line break doesn't exist.

What You're Not to Read

The publishers and I have put this book together with your convenience in mind. Nice, huh? For that reason, I'm pointing out the text you don't have to read:

- ✔ When you see the Technical Stuff icon (shown later in this Introduction), you can skip that text if you want. It's not essential to understanding the rest of the book.

- ✔ The same goes for sidebars, which are scattered through the book, printed on gray backgrounds. Sidebars are extra added attractions. I've tried to make them fun and informative, but they aren't crucial to the rest of the book. Feel free to skip over them; you won't hurt my feelings.

Foolish Assumptions

Because you picked up this book, I assume that you're interested in golf. I also assume that you're not already a great golfer, or else you'd be out there making millions on the PGA Tour. Beyond that, I'm going to figure that you're a little like I was when I became a professional golfer.

Having said that, I'm assuming that you've probably dabbled with golf and want to get better. In my experience, most people give golf a try before they seek instruction. It must be an ego thing, kind of like those people who don't like to ask for directions when they get lost because they feel that it's an admission of failure. If that's you, think of me as your personal GPS: your Golfer Positioning System.

How This Book Is Organized

Golf For Dummies, 4th Edition, leads you through the process of becoming a golfer. Beginners need many questions answered as they take on the game. I've organized this book so that you take those steps one at a time and can flip to them anytime for quick reference. May this journey be a pleasant one!

Part I: Welcome to a Mad Great Game

Where do I play, and what's the course record? Wait a minute! First you need to know what this game is about. You need clubs. You need to know how to swing those clubs. You may want to take a lesson to see whether you like the game and then find golf clubs that fit you. In this part, I show you how to choose your clubs and give you some tips on the questions to ask before you make your purchase. Then I give you some ideas about what kind of golf courses to play. Picking up golf is a never-ending process of discovery, and it starts right here.

Part II: Getting Into the Swing

This part gets right to the point: I give you a close look at the workings of the golf swing and help with your mental preparation. You also get a good look at the short game, where most scoring takes place. I show you how to blast your way out of bunkers and how to develop a sound putting stroke.

Part III: Common Faults and Easy Fixes

In this part, I tackle the tough shots and help you deal with bad luck and bad weather. You'll develop many faults during your golfing life, and this part tells you how to fix most of them. You took a great first step by buying this book.

Part IV: Taking Your Game Public

In this part, you get the final touches of your education as a golfer. You discover how the rules were established, how to conduct yourself on the golf course, and the fine art of betting. You even get the do's and don'ts of golf-course etiquette. This part lets you walk onto any golf course and look like you know what you're doing. Because you *will* know what you're doing.

Part V: How to Be a Smart Golf Consumer

A sad fact of life is that you can't always be out on the course. In this part, I show you how to max out a day as a spectator and how to tap into the best of golf on TV, online, and in video games.

Part VI: The Part of Tens

This part contains the best-of, the most memorable, and some stuff that won't mean much to anybody except me. I just thought you'd enjoy knowing about it.

Part VII: Appendixes

Golfers have a language all their own. Appendix A lists the terms you want to add to your vocabulary. Appendix B lists some of the more popular golf organizations and resources, along with a select list of schools around the country.

Icons Used in This Book

As I guide you through this maze of golf wit and wisdom, I use several handy road signs. Look for these friendly icons; they point you toward valuable advice and hazards to watch out for.

This icon marks golf hazards to avoid or at least be aware of. Be careful!

This icon flags quick, easy ways to improve your game.

When you see this icon, be on the lookout for recommendations I swear by (follow them or I will never speak to you again) and important personal stories from my years of playing and covering golf.

This information may make your head spin; take two aspirin and get plenty of rest.

This icon flags information that's important enough to repeat.

Where to Go from Here

Feel free to flip through this book, picking your spots. It isn't designed to be read like a novel from cover to cover. If you're a complete novice, you may take a look at Appendix A first — get comfortable with the language. If you're a little more advanced and need help with a specific aspect of your game or swing, you can find that information in Chapters 6 through 10. The rest of the book helps you make that vital jump from "golf novice" to "real golfer."

As Frank Chirkinian, my former boss at CBS, said, "Golf is not a game; it's a way of life. If it was a game, someone would have figured it out by now."

Frank was right. But you *can* figure out how to get started in golf the right way and enjoy the game. That's what this book is for.

Part I
Welcome to a Mad Great Game

The 5th Wave   By Rich Tennant

"What? It helps me with my balance."

In this part . . .

This part explores the basics of golf: Why would anyone play such a crazy game? How did golf begin? What makes the sport special? In this part of the book, I describe a typical golf course. I also show you how to buy clubs and accessories that can help make you look like a pro. I discuss how to get into physical shape for good golf, where to take lessons, and how best to survive the lesson tee. In this part, you get a whirlwind tour, from the driving range all the way up to a full 18-hole course — including the penthouse of golf, the private country club.

Get ready; it's time to tee it up!

Chapter 1

Why Play Golf?

Golf is simple. You've got clubs and a ball. You have to hit the ball into a series of holes laid out in the middle of a large, grassy field. After you finish the 18th hole, you may want to go to the clubhouse bar and tell lies about your on-course feats to anyone you didn't play with that day. But if you're like most golfers, you play the game for much more than the chance to impress gullible strangers. You play for relaxation, companionship, and a chance to enjoy the great outdoors. Of course, you also encounter some hazards out there. This game is anything but straightforward.

How It All Began: Discovering Golf's Origins

Golf dates back to medieval Scotland, on the gloomy, misty east coast of the kingdom of Fife, where Macbeth ruled in the 11th century. Some historians say golf began when Scottish shepherds used their long, wooden crooks to knock rocks at rabbit holes. Their hobby became so habit-forming that the Scots of later centuries played "gowf" instead of practicing their archery.

The first printed reference to golf came in 1457, when Scotland's King James II banned "gowf" so that his subjects could concentrate on their archery — the better to beat the hated English on the battlefield. Golf was outlawed until 1501. After that, James's descendants, including his great-great-granddaughter Mary, Queen of Scots, embraced the game. (The original golf widow, she scandalized Britain by playing golf in the days after her husband, Lord Darnley, was murdered.)

The wooden golf balls of Queen Mary's day gave way to *featheries* — leather pouches stuffed with goose feathers — and then *gutty balls* made from gutta-percha rubber imported to Scotland from Malaysia in the 1850s. In 1860 one of the best Scottish golfers, Tom Morris of St. Andrews, helped organize the first Open Championship, the tournament that launched modern professional golf. Scottish pros immigrated to the United States, introduced Americans to the game, and the rest is history. And frustration. And fun.

Examining Why Golf Is Unique

You've probably heard that business leaders are constantly making huge deals on the course, advancing their careers. Well, "constantly" may be an overstatement — business leaders, like other players, spend much of their time on the course looking for wayward golf balls. But it's true that golf can help you climb the corporate ladder. That's one reason to play.

And it's about the 167th most-important reason. More-important reasons include spending time with friends, staying in shape, and enjoying some of the most beautiful scenery you'll ever see. (All tennis courts are pretty much the same, but each golf course is different from every other, and many are designed to show off their gorgeous settings.) Golf is a physical *and* mental challenge — it tests your skill and your will.

It's also a game for a lifetime. Your friends may play football and basketball in high school, but how many are still returning kickoffs or grabbing rebounds when they're 30, 40, or 60 years old?

The most important reason to play, though, is that golf is magic. It's maddening, frustrating, crazy — and totally addictive. After it becomes part of your life, you can barely imagine life without it.

Golf is also famously difficult. If it were easy, everyone would play the game. As I see it, two main factors are responsible for that:

- ✔ The ball doesn't move on its own.
- ✔ You have, on average, about three minutes between shots.

In other words, you don't react to the ball as you do in most sports. A baseball gets thrown, hit, and spat on. A football gets passed, tossed, kicked, and run up and down the field. A basketball gets shot, rebounded, and dribbled all over the place. But a golf ball just sits there, daring you not to lose it.

In most sports, you have only an instant to react to the action — your natural athleticism takes over, and you move to the ball. In golf, you get far too long to think about what you're doing. Thinking too much can strangle the soul and warp the mind.

Maybe golf would be easier if the ball moved and you were on skates. Then you could stop worrying and *react.* But if it were easy it wouldn't be golf, would it?

Breaking Down a Typical Course

Most golf courses have 18 holes, although a few, usually because of a lack of money or land, have only 9. The *19th hole* is golfspeak for the clubhouse bar — the place where you can reflect on your game over a refreshing beverage of your choice. (See Appendix A for the lowdown on golf jargon.) Courses beside the sea are called *links,* in honor of the parts of Scotland where the game began. (They were the link between beach and farmland.) Many people use "links" to mean any golf course, but we purists stick to the correct usage: A links is a course by the water.

Most golf courses are between 5,500 and 7,000 yards. A few monsters are longer, but leave those courses to the pros you see on TV. Start at the low end of that scale and work your way up.

Every hole is a par-3, a par-4, or a par-5. (Par-2s are for minigolf courses; the exceedingly rare par-6s tend to be gimmicks.) *Par* is the number of strokes a competent golfer should take to play a particular hole. For example, on a par-5 hole, a regulation par may consist of a drive, two more full swings, and two putts. Two putts is the standard on every green.

Three putts are too many. One putt is a bonus. The bottom line is that in a perfect round of par golf, half the allocated strokes should be taken on the greens. That premise makes putting crucial. (I talk about how to putt in Chapter 9.)

Obviously, a par-5 is longer than a par-4 (two full swings, two putts), which in turn is longer than a par-3 (one full swing, two putts). With rare exceptions, par-3s are from 100 to 250 yards in length; par-4s are from 251 to 470 yards long, barring severe topography; and par-5s are from 471 to 690 yards.

Many courses in the United States have a total par of 72, consisting of ten par-4s (40), four par-3s (12), and four par-5s (20). But you can find golf courses with total pars of anywhere from 62 to 74. Almost anything goes. Table 1-1 lists the yardages that determine par on a hole, for men and women. It's worth noting that these guidelines don't always refer to precise yardages, but rather to what the United States Golf Association (USGA) calls a hole's "effective playing length." A 460-yard hole that goes straight uphill, for example, may be a par-5 for men.

Table 1-1	Regulation Yardages	
	Women	*Men*
Par-3	210 yards or less	250 yards or less
Par-4	211 to 400 yards	251 to 470 yards
Par-5	401 to 575 yards	471 to 690 yards
Par-6	More than 575 yards	More than 690 yards

Source: United States Golf Association

That's the big picture. You often find several different teeing areas on each hole so that you can play the hole from different lengths based on your level of skill. The vast majority of holes have more than one teeing area — usually four. I've seen courses with as many as six different tees on one hole. Deciding which tee area to use can make you silly. So the tee areas are marked with color-coded tees that indicate ability to help you out:

- The **gold tees** are invariably the back tees and are for long-ball strikers or lower handicap players only.

- The **blue tees** are usually slightly ahead of the gold and make the holes shorter, but still plenty hard. Club competitions are played from these tees.

- The **white tees** are for everyday, casual play and are the right choice for most men, beginning golfers, and capable senior players. Stray from the white tees at your peril.

- The **red tees** are traditionally used by women or junior golfers, although many women I play with use the same tees I play.

Playing a Smart Game

Simply stated, the goal of golf is to get the ball into each of 18 holes in succession with the fewest number of shots, using no more than 14 clubs. After you hit the ball into all the holes, you add up your scores from each hole. The lower your total score, the better. That's it.

The game's charm lies in the journey. As you play, you find countless ways to get the ball into the hole in as few strokes as possible. Many outside stimuli — and many more inside your head — make golf one of the most interesting, maddening, thrilling, and just plain *fun* endeavors you'll ever find.

The best advice I can give you is to relax. Stay calm, make prudent decisions, and never hit a shot while contemplating other matters. You should play golf with complete concentration and no ego. The game tempts you to try feats of derring-do. To play your best, you must judge your talents and abilities honestly. You alone determine your success or failure: Should you try to make it over the water and go for the green that's 240 yards away? Or play it safe?

Don't get greedy — play the game one step at a time. Figure 1-1 shows a smart course of action. You start at the tee and hit your drive to Point A. From there, it's 240 yards to the green, with a watery grave lurking to the left. So you lay up to Point B, and go from there to the green via C. This approach doesn't always work — you may *aim* for Point B and still yank your second shot into the pond — but it's the smart play. And that's the key to good golf.

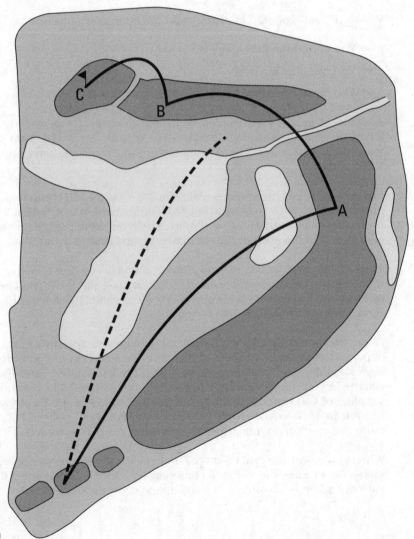

Figure 1-1:
A reasonable plan for playing a golf hole.

Score is everything. As you see in Chapters 8, 9, and 10, the most pivotal shots occur within 100 yards of the hole. If you can save strokes there, your score will be lower than that of the player whose sole purpose in life is to crush the ball as far as possible. So practice your putting, sand play, chips, and pitches twice as much as your driving. Your hard work will pay off, and your friends will be the ones dipping into their wallets (assuming you're wagering, as I discuss in Chapter 15).

Becoming a "Real" Golfer

What's a "real" golfer? The three essential characteristics are

- You understand the game.
- You can play it a little.
- You never dishonor its spirit.

Anyone can smack a ball aimlessly around a course. (I can already hear my fellow professionals saying, "Yeah — like you, McCord!") But that doesn't make you a real golfer. There's much more to this game than hitting a ball with a stick.

How can you start becoming a real golfer? It's easy: Read this book. You find everything you need to get started, from equipment to instruction to common problems, etiquette, betting, and more. I tell you about the pitfalls that beginners face (and I'm not just talking bunkers), and how to avoid them.

You need to start by buying golf clubs and balls. You don't have to shell out thousands of dollars to get started. You can start simple — use cheap equipment at first, and spend more if you enjoy the game. (Check out Chapter 2 for tips on what you need to get started.)

After you have golf clubs, you need to know how to grip the club: The *V* between the thumb and forefinger of your top hand should point to your right shoulder (for righties; reverse it if you're left-handed), and the golf club is more in your fingers and not so much in the palm of your hand. That seems simple, but you wouldn't believe how many beginners get it wrong — and complicate their voyage to the promised land of "real" golfers. (Chapter 6 has more information on this gripping — pardon the pun — topic.)

When you've got the grip down pat, along with the setup, you're ready to swing. Believe me, the swing isn't as easy as it looks. That's why I devote an entire chapter — Chapter 7 — to developing your own swing.

Knowing when to hit (and when *not* to), how to keep score, proper etiquette, and how to bet are integral parts of the game. You've probably heard about golf etiquette, handicaps, and one- and two-stroke penalties — and maybe even such goofy-sounding concepts as nassaus, skins, and barkies. If not, don't worry. The chapters in Part III give you the lowdown on these and other important topics.

Living the Golf Life

As any true golf nut can tell you, there's more to the game than playing it. You also have the fun of feeding your addiction by watching the sport in person or on TV, following it on the Internet, and playing virtual golf when the snow piles up outside. (See Part V for my guide to those off-the-course outlets.)

If the golf bug bites you, as it has bitten millions of others, that little sucker will have you living and breathing birdies, bogeys, barkies, and digital dimples — all the stuff that keeps golf nuts going when they're not actually out on the course, slapping balls who knows where.

Fun facts from golf history

✔ Dutch historians, including Steven von Hengel, have argued that golf originated in Holland around 1297. A form of the game called *spel metten kolve* (and also *colf*, which means "club") was popular in the late 13th century. *Colf* is believed to have been played mostly on ice.

✔ The first instruction book, written by Thomas Kincaid, appeared in 1687. Among his surprisingly sensible tips: "Maintain the same posture of the body throughout (the swing) . . . and the ball must be straight before your breast, a little towards the left foot." How did he know?

✔ In 1743, a shipment of 96 golf clubs and 432 golf balls made its way from Scotland to Charleston, South Carolina. Such a big order suggests it was intended for a group of golfers. Another golf club or society may have been organized in Savannah, Georgia, in 1796, only to be disbanded later. It would be another century before American golf got going for good.

✔ The first major tournament, the Open Championship, was held with only eight players at Prestwick Golf Club on the west coast of Scotland in 1860. Old Tom Morris finished second to Willie Park, whose prize was a year's custody of the Championship Belt and a purse of £0. That's right — zero pounds. In those days the honor of victory was supposed to be prize enough.

✔ America's first permanent golf club was formed in 1888 in Yonkers, New York. The St. Andrews Golf Club played on a three-hole layout that ended near a large apple tree. The club's golfers became known as the Apple Tree Gang. They hung their coats

(continued)

(continued)

on the tree before they teed off. According to legend, they finished play one day to find their coats stolen by a rival gang known for its disdain of fruit.

✔ In 1890, the term *bogey* was coined by Hugh Rotherham — only back then it referred to playing a hole in the perfect number of strokes, or a *ground score,* which we today call *par.* Shortly after the invention of the Haskell ball, which made reaching a hole in fewer strokes possible, bogey came to represent a score of one over par for a hole.

✔ The term *birdie* wasn't coined until 1898, emanating from Atlantic Country Club out of the phrase "a bird of a hole." This gap in terminology is no doubt attributed to the difficulty in attaining a bird, a fact that endures to this day.

✔ A match-play exhibition was held in 1926, pitting Professional Golfers Association members from Britain and America. Played in England, the home team dominated 13½ to 1½. The next year, at Worcester Country Club, the teams met again, only this time possession of a solid gold trophy donated by a wealthy British seed merchant named Samuel A. Ryder was at stake. Thus were born the Ryder Cup Matches.

✔ The Hershey Chocolate Company, in sponsoring the 1933 Hershey Open, became the first corporate title sponsor of a professional tournament. So blame the cocoa guys.

✔ A local telecast of the 1947 U.S. Open in St. Louis marked the advent of televised golf, a red-letter day in golf history if ever there was one. Now I could finally have a job.

Chapter 2

Choosing Your Weapons Wisely

*B*ritain's great prime minister Winston Churchill once griped that golf was "a silly game played with weapons singularly ill-suited to the purpose." Today's clubs are unrecognizable compared to the rather primitive implements used by Young Tom Morris (one of the game's early pioneers) and his Scottish buddies in the late 19th century, or even by Churchill half a century later. Yes, early golf equipment had more romantic names: Niblick, brassie, spoon, driving-iron, mashie, and mashie-niblick are more fun than 9-iron, 3-wood, 1-iron, 5-iron, and 7-iron. But today's equipment is much better suited to the purpose: getting the ball down the fairway to the green and then into the hole.

Nowadays, you have no excuse for playing with equipment ill-suited to your swing, body, and game. There's too much information out there to help you. And that's the purpose of this chapter — to help you get started as smoothly as possible.

How Much Is This Stuff Going to Cost?

Take one look at a shiny new driver made of super-lightweight alloys and other space-age materials. Beautiful, isn't it? Now peek at the price tag. Gulp! Each year, the hot new drivers seem to cost a few dollars more — many now retail for $400 and up. And that's just one club. You're going to need 13 more to fill up your golf bag, and the bag itself can set you back another $100 or more. Sure, Bill Gates and Donald Trump are avid golfers, but do you have to be a billionaire to play?

Not at all. Just as you can get a golf ball from the tee into the hole in countless ways, you can get the equipment you need, including the ball, in just as many ways.

The upscale approach

You may be planning to spend thousands of dollars getting started in this game. If so, let me have a word with you: Don't.

Of course, you can purchase a gleaming new set of clubs custom-fit to suit your swing. But if you're a beginning golfer, your swing is sure to change as you become more acquainted with this great game. A top-of-the-line set can cost more than a used car — why pay through the nose when your progress will soon render your custom fit obsolete? You can also opt for the high-tech golf balls that tour pros use — we get them free, but a dozen can cost you about $50. Again, that's a needless expense if you're a beginner.

Spending doesn't guarantee success. For that, you need a good swing. Still, you can rest assured that when and if you do shell out your hard-earned cash for today's name-brand golf gear, you aren't getting cheated. Golf equipment has never been better suited to its purpose.

Golf on a budget

Bear in mind that getting the most out of today's highest-priced equipment takes a pretty good player. Just as a student driver doesn't need a Maserati, beginning golfers can get their games in gear with the golf equivalent of a reliable clunker. In the old days, many golfers started out with hand-me-down clubs. They may have been Dad's or Mom's old set cut down for Junior to try. The young phenom may have graduated to a full set found at a garage sale, and if those clubs happened to fit the young whippersnapper's swing and physique, Junior may have made the school team. He may have even been on his way to a long, winless PGA Tour career, like me!

Today's version of the old garage sale, of course, is that virtual marketplace called the Internet. (I discuss many of the best golf Web sites in Chapter 19.) When you know what to look for (and I tell you throughout this chapter), you can find precisely what you need, either online or in a golf shop — often for a fraction of what *Messrs* Gates and Trump would pay. If you really keep an eye on costs, you can get started in this game for as little as $100.

Golf Balls: The Dimple Derby

Many technological advances have occurred in golf over the years, but perhaps nothing has changed more than the ball. It's no coincidence that the United States Golf Association (USGA) and the Royal and Ancient Golf Club (R&A) keep a tight rein on just how far a ball can go nowadays. If the associations didn't provide regulations, almost every golf course on the planet would be reduced to a pitch and putt. Everyone would be putting through windmills just to keep the scores up in the 50s.

For the record, here are the specifications the USGA imposes on Titleist, Callaway, TaylorMade, and the rest of the ball manufacturers:

- **Size:** A golf ball may not be smaller than 1.68 inches in diameter. The ball can be as big as you want, however. Just don't expect a bigger ball to go farther — it doesn't. I've never seen anyone use a ball bigger than 1.68 inches in diameter.

- **Weight:** The golf ball may not be heavier than 1.62 ounces.

- **Velocity:** The USGA has a machine for measuring how fast a ball comes off the face of a club. That's not easy, because impact lasts only 450 millionths of a second, and a good ball can zoom off the club at more than 170 miles an hour. When long-driving champion Jamie Sadlowski creams a drive, the ball takes off at an amazing 218 miles an hour!

  No legal ball may exceed an initial velocity of 250 feet per second at a temperature between 73 and 77 degrees Fahrenheit. A tolerance of no more than 2 percent is allowed, which means an absolute max of 255 feet per second. This rule ensures that golf balls don't go too far. (In addition to balls, the USGA now tests bouncy-faced drivers to keep a lid on distance.)

- **Distance:** Distance is the most important factor. For years the standard was the USGA's "Iron Byron" robot (named for sweet-swingin' Byron Nelson). No ball struck by Iron Byron could go farther than 280 yards. A tolerance of 6 percent was allowed, making 296.8 yards the absolute farthest the ball could go. Today the robot has some help from high-tech ball launchers in the USGA labs, and the upper limit has risen to 317 yards.

  Yeah, right. Iron Byron, meet the PGA Tour! Guys like Tiger Woods, Bubba Watson, Dustin Johnson, and their buddies just aren't normal — they regularly blast drives past 350 and even 400 yards!

- **Shape:** A golf ball must be round. An anti-slice ball on the market a few years ago was weighted on one side and failed this test. Nice try, though!

Even with these regulations, take a look around any golf professional's shop and you see many different brands. And upon closer inspection, you notice that every type of ball falls into one of two categories: Either the manufacturer claims that its ball goes farther and straighter than any other ball in the cosmos, or that its ball gives you more control.

Try not to get overwhelmed. Keep in mind that golf balls come in three basic types: one-piece, two-piece, and three-piece. (TaylorMade now offers a five-piece ball, the Penta.) You can forget one-piece balls — they tend to be cheap and nasty and found only on driving ranges. So that leaves two-piece and three-piece balls.

Don't worry; deciding on a type of ball is still easy. You don't even have to know what a two-piece or three-piece ball contains or why it has that many "pieces." Leave all that to the scientists. And don't fret about launch angle or spin rate, either. Today's balls are technological marvels, designed to take off high and spin just enough to go as straight as possible.

Go with a two-piece ball. I don't recommend a three-piece ball to a beginning golfer. Tour pros and expert players use such balls to maximize control. For many years, the best players used balls with covers made of *balata*, a soft, rubbery substance. Today, many high-performance three-piece balls have covers of something even better — high-performance urethane elastomer, which is a fancy way of saying "expensive superplastic." But you don't need that stuff. As a beginner, you need a reliable, durable ball. Unless you have very deep pockets, go the surlyn, two-piece route. (*Surlyn* is a type of plastic — the same stuff bowling pins are covered with — developed by the Dupont Corporation.) Most beginners use this type of ball. A surlyn-covered ball's harder cover and lower spin rate give you less *feel* — the softness that gives better players tactile feedback telling them how well they've struck the ball — which is why better players tend not to use them. But assuming you don't whack them off the premises, they last longer. They just may roll farther, too.

Golf balls used to come in three compressions: 80, 90, or 100. The 80-compression ball was the softest, and the 100 the hardest. When I was growing up, I thought that the harder the ball (100 compression), the farther it would go. Not the case. All balls go far when hit properly, but each one feels a little different. How hard or soft you want the ball to feel has to do with your personal preference. These days, you needn't worry about compression.

Here's a rule of thumb: If you hit the ball low and want to hit it higher, switch to a softer cover. Your drives will spin more and soar toward the stratosphere. If you hit the ball too high, switch to a ball labeled "low-trajectory."

Take all the commercial hype with a grain (make that a bowl) of salt. The most important factors you need to know when buying golf balls are your own game, tendencies, and needs. Your local PGA professional can help you choose the golf ball best suited to you.

Goosefeathers!

Early golf was played with a feathery golf ball — a stitched leather ball stuffed with boiled goose feathers. A feather ball cost three times as much as a club, and because feathery balls were delicate, players had to carry three to six balls at a time. The balls flew poorly in wet weather (a problem in Scotland), and were hard to putt because they weren't round. They were closer to egg shaped, in fact.

Although the feathery ball was a vast improvement over the wooden balls that preceded it, the gutta percha was an extraordinary breakthrough. In 1848, the Reverend Adam Paterson of St. Andrews introduced the gutta percha ball, or *gutty,* which was made from the sap of the gutta tree found in the tropics. When heated, the rubberlike sap could easily be fashioned into a golf ball. The gutty was considerably more durable than the feathery ball and much more affordable. After golfers discovered that bramble patterns and other markings on the gutty enhanced its aerodynamics, this ball swiftly achieved dominance in the marketplace.

After 1900, the Haskell rubber-cored ball quickly replaced the gutta percha as the ball of choice. Invented two years earlier by Cleveland resident Coburn Haskell and manufactured by the B. F. Goodrich Rubber Company of Akron, Ohio, the Haskell ball, which featured a gutty cover and a wound rubber core, traveled farther (up to 20 yards more on average) and delivered greater durability.

It didn't take much time for this new ball to gain acceptance, especially after Alexander "Sandy" Herd defeated renowned Harry Vardon and James Braid in the 1902 British Open at Hoylake, England, using the same Haskell ball for 72 holes. Most golfers today, on the other hand, use six to eight golf balls during a single round of a tour event.

The rest of the 20th century was spent refining the Haskell. In 1905, William Taylor invented the first dimpled ball; the dimple pattern improved flight because it maximized lift and minimized drag. Around the time Taylor was playing with his dimples, Elazer Kempshall of the United States and Frank Mingay of Scotland were independently experimenting with liquid-core balls. In 1920, gutta percha began to fade entirely from use, replaced by a soft rubber called *balata.* It was another 50 years before a popular alternative to the Haskell came along: In 1972, Spalding introduced the first two-piece ball, the Executive.

Today, multilayered balls dominate the market. (A three-piece ball has a thin extra layer between the cover and the core; a four-piece ball has a core within a core. TaylorMade's Penta has a cover, three "mantles" and a core — much like the planet Earth, but without all the lava.) Many pros use three- or four-piece balls whose cover hardness, launch angle, and spin rate are perfectly tuned to their games.

Knowing What Clubs to Put in Your Bag

In the game's early centuries, players could carry as many clubs as they liked. Since 1938, however, 14 clubs has been the limit. Those clubs come in several varieties:

- ✔ **Driver:** The *driver*, the big-headed club with the longest shaft, is what you use to drive the ball off the tee on all but the shortest holes.

- ✔ **Woods:** *Woods* are lofted clubs (*loft* is the angle at which a clubface is angled upward) that got their names because they used to have wooden clubheads. These clubs are numbered, from the 2-wood and 3-wood up to more-lofted 9- and even 11-woods. Today almost all woods have steel or titanium heads.

- ✔ **Irons:** *Irons* are generally more lofted than most woods; you most commonly use them to hit shots from the fairway or rough to the green. These include *wedges* for hitting high shots from fairway, *rough* (long grass), or sand.

- ✔ **Hybrids:** *Hybrids,* sometimes called *utility* or *rescue* clubs, are like a cross between a wood and an iron.

- ✔ **Putter:** You reach for your *putter* to roll the ball into the hole.

Deciding which clubs to put in your golf bag can be as simple or as complicated as you want to make it. You can go to any store that doesn't have a golf pro, pick a set of clubs off the shelf, and then take them to the tee. You can go to garage sales or order clubs online. You can check with the pro at your local municipal course. Any or all of these methods can work. But your chances of choosing a set with the correct loft, lie, size of grip, and all the other stuff involved in club fitting are worse than my chances of winning on *Dancing with the Stars.*

Having said that, I must add that it wasn't so long ago that *unsophisticated* was a fair description of every golf-club buyer. Even local champions may waggle a new driver a few times and "know" that it wasn't for them — hardly the most scientific approach! The following sections show you some options for putting together your set of clubs.

If you're just starting out in golf, keep in mind that you may discover that this game isn't for you. So you should start with rental clubs at a driving range. Most driving ranges rent clubs for a few dollars apiece. Go out and test-wield these weapons to get a feel for what you need. You can always buy your own clubs when the time comes.

Women and juniors should beware of swinging clubs made for men, which may be too long or too heavy for them. That only makes golf more frustrating! Juniors should start out with junior clubs, women with women's clubs.

Find an interim set of clubs

In your first few weeks as a golfer (after you've swung rental clubs for a while), find cheap clubs to use as an interim set during your adjustment period. You're learning the game, so you don't want to make big decisions about what type of clubs to buy yet. If you keep your ears open around the golf course or driving range, you may hear of someone who has a set that he or she is willing to sell. You can also ask whether people have any information on clubs that you can get cheaply. Many garage sales and yard sales offer golf clubs. And, of course, you can check the Internet — the fastest-growing marketplace in golf. (More on that in Chapter 19.) You can become your own private investigator and hunt down the best buy. Buy cheap for now but pay close attention to proper length and weight of the golf club — you've got plenty of time for bigger purchases.

You're in your experimental stage, so try all sorts of clubs — ones with steel shafts, graphite shafts (which are lighter and therefore easier to swing), big-headed clubs, *investment-cast clubs* (made by pouring hot metal into a mold), *forged clubs* (made from a single piece of metal), and *cavity-backed clubs* (ones that are hollowed out in the back of the iron). You have more choices than your neighborhood Baskin-Robbins.

Don't be afraid to ask your friends if you can try their clubs on the range. I do it all the time on the tour when a new product comes out. Try out these clubs and judge for yourself whether they feel good. But if you don't like the club that you just tried, don't tell the person who loaned it to you that the club stinks — that's not good golf etiquette. Simply hand the club back and say thanks.

Try this on for size

Today, club fitting is big business. Tour pros and average amateur golfers have access to the same club fitting technology and information. It's important for all golfers — male and female — to use the right equipment for their body types and physical conditions. For instance, many manufacturers of golf clubs specialize in creating clubs for women that have softer shafts, which are lighter and more flexible.

Here are some factors every golfer should consider:

- **The grip:** Determine how thick the grip on your clubs should be. Grips that are too thin encourage too much hand action in your swing; grips that are too thick restrict your hand action. Generally, the proper-sized grip should allow the middle and ring fingers on your left hand to barely touch the pad of your thumb when you hold the club. If your fingers don't touch your thumb, the grip is too thick; if your fingers dig into the pad, the grip is too thin.

- **The shaft:** Consider your height, build, and strength when you choose a club. If you're really tall, you need longer (and probably stiffer) shafts.

What does your swing sound like? If your swing makes a loud *swish* noise and the shaft is bending like a long cast from a fly-fishing rod at the top of your swing, you need a very strong shaft. If your swing makes no noise and you could hang laundry on your shaft at the top of your swing, you need a regular shaft. Anybody in between needs a medium-stiff to stiff shaft.

✔ **Loft:** Think about your typical ball flight and then how you can enhance it with club loft. If you slice, for example, you can try clubs with less loft — or perhaps offset heads — to help alleviate that common problem. For more information about slicing, see Chapter 11.

✔ **The clubhead:** Consider the size of the clubhead. Today, you can get standard, midsize, and oversize heads on your clubs. The biggest are a relatively mammoth 460 cubic centimeters. I recommend bigger clubheads for your early days of playing golf. They're more forgiving — your mishits go longer and straighter. A big clubhead can help psychologically, too. With some of today's jumbo drivers, your swing thought may well be, "With this thing, how can I miss?"

✔ **The iron:** Advanced players choose irons that are perfectly suited to their swings. Forged, muscle-backed irons are for elite players who hit the ball on the clubface precisely. Cavity-backed irons (also called *perimeter-weighted*) are for players who hit the ball all over the clubface.

The bigger the clubface, the more room for error — hence the bigger-headed metal woods that are popular today for all the wild swingers out there. They're more forgiving on mishits.

Because of all the technology that's available, purchasing golf clubs nowadays is like buying a computer: Whatever you buy may be outdated in six months. So be frugal and shop for your best buy. When you get a set that fits you and you're hitting the ball with consistency, stick with that set. Finding a whole set of clubs that matches the temperament of your golf swing is hard. Find the ones that have your fingerprints on them and stick with 'em.

The DIY way: Building your own clubs

Here's the ultimate in custom fitting: You can literally build your own set of clubs to your own specifications. You just have to do some homework first. A lot of people are building their own clubs, judging by the success of firms like Golfsmith. And DIY clubs are cheaper than the ones you can buy off the shelf.

Although building your clubs requires time and effort, the end result can be rewarding. A hobby to go with your favorite new sport! You can get catalogs from component companies, call their toll-free numbers, or visit their Web sites (see Appendix B). Component companies offer grip tape, solvents, clamps, epoxy, shaft-cutting tools, shaft extensions, grip knives, and every kind of shaft, head, and grip imaginable. You name it, they've got it. If you're not sure, order a club-making video or book first. You never know — you may end up a golfsmith yourself.

Eleven questions to ask before you buy

✔ **Do you have a club fitting program?** If your local PGA professional doesn't have a club fitting program, he can direct you to someone in the area who does. After you've started this game and found you like it enough to continue playing, choosing the right equipment is the biggest decision you have to make. Don't leave your PGA golf pro out of that decision.

✔ **What's the price of club fitting?** Don't be too shy to ask this question. Club fitting can be expensive. You should be the judge of how much you can afford.

✔ **What shaft length do I need for my clubs?** Golfers come in different heights and builds. Some are tall with short arms, and some are short with long arms. People have different postures when they bend over to address the golf ball, and they need different shaft lengths to match those postures. This issue is where PGA golf professionals can really help; they're trained to answer questions like these and can make club fitting very easy.

✔ **How about shaft flex?** Most golfers should use clubs with regular flex, signified by an *R* on the shaft. Don't let your ego spur you to ask for a stiff shaft unless you're strong enough to generate a lot of clubhead speed. Most female players should use a whippier shaft that requires less strength — look for an *L* for "ladies" on the shaft.

✔ **What lie angle do I need on my clubs?** Here's the general rule: The closer you stand to the ball, the more upright your club needs to be. As you get farther from the ball, the lie angle of your clubs should be flatter.

✔ **What grip size do I need?** The bigger your hands are, the bigger grip you need. If you have a tendency to slice the ball, you can try smaller grips that help your hands work faster. If you tend to hook the ball, you can use bigger grips that slow down your hands.

✔ **What material — leather, cord, all-rubber, half-rubber — do you recommend for my grips?** Leather is the most expensive and the hardest to maintain. It's for accomplished players; I recommend that beginners stick to an all-rubber grip and get new grips every year if they play at least once a week. I use a combination of rubber and cord — and it has nothing to do with my name. These grips help me hold on to the club in hot weather. My hands are callused, though, so they don't hurt from the rubbing of the cord.

✔ **What kind of irons should I buy — investment-cast, forged, oversized, or cavity-backed?** The best advice I can give is to look for an investment-cast, cavity-backed, oversized golf club. For beginners, this choice is simply the best. Take my word for it — I haven't got enough paper to explain all the reasons.

✔ **Should I use space-age materials like boron, titanium, or graphite in my shafts? Or should I go with steel?** Steel shafts are the cheapest; all the others are quite a bit more expensive, so keep your budget in mind. Test some of these other shafts to see how they compare with steel, which is still very good and used by most of the players on tour. In general, you want the lightest shaft you can swing effectively. And don't be intimidated if you see that tricky word *kickpoint*. Think of it this way: kickpoint = trajectory. If you want to hit the ball lower, try a shaft with a low kickpoint; to hit the ball higher, get one with a higher kickpoint.

(continued)

(continued)

✔ **What type of putter should I use: center-shafted or end-shafted? Do I want a mallet putter, a belly putter, or a long putter?** The last few years have seen an explosion of putter technology. You can try out the result at the golf course where you play. Just ask the pro whether you can test one of the putters on the rack. If you have a friend or playing partner who has a putter you think you may like, ask to try it.

✔ **If you're buying new clubs, ask the pro whether you can test them for a day.** Most of the time, someone who's trying to make a sale will give you every opportunity to try the clubs. Golf pros are just like car dealers; they let you test-drive before you buy.

Choosing Your Clubs When You Know Your Game

Although you can only have 14 clubs in your bag at a time, no rule tells you *which* 14 clubs to use. You get to match the composition of your set to your strengths and weaknesses.

I'm assuming that you're going to carry a driver, a 3-wood, a putter, and irons 4 through 9. Nearly everyone does. So you have five clubs left to select. The first thing you need to know, of course, is how far you're likely to hit each club. (That's golfspeak for hitting the ball with the club. Don't go smashing your equipment!) After you know that, you can look into plugging the gaps. Those gaps are most important at the short end of your set.

I recommend that you carry three wedges, each with a different loft. I do. I use a 48-degree pitching wedge, a 53-degree sand wedge, and a 58-degree lob wedge. I hit them 125 yards (pitching wedge), 105 yards (sand wedge), and 85 yards (lob wedge). That way, the yardage gap between them isn't significant. If I carried only the 125-yard wedge and the 85-yard wedge, that would leave a gap of 40 yards — too much. If I leave myself with a shot of about 105 yards, right in the middle of my gap, I've got problems. Carrying the 105-yard wedge plugs that gap. If I didn't have it, I'd be forced to manufacture a shot with a less-than-full swing. And that's too hard, especially under pressure. Full swings, please!

Okay, that's 12 clubs taken care of. You have two left. I recommend carrying at least one lofted wood or hybrid club. Make that two. Low-numbered irons are too unforgiving. So give yourself a break. Carry a 5-wood and even a 7-wood. These clubs are designed to make it easy for you to get the ball up in the air. They certainly achieve that more quickly than a 2-iron.

Another option is the hybrid. It's a fairly recent entry — a forgiving club that gets the ball airborne in a hurry and can be wonderful out of the rough. You can even use it for chipping, as Todd Hamilton did on a shot that clinched the 2004 British Open. Hybrid clubs, which come in different lofts, are getting more popular every day. You should swing a few, and consider carrying a hybrid rather than that 7-wood, 5-wood, or maybe even your 4-iron.

Figure 2-1 shows the clubs that I have in my bag. You can see I have 15 clubs! Depending on the course and weather, I leave one out when I play — probably the 3-iron or 5-wood.

Figure 2-1:
From left to right: my putter, lob wedge, sand wedge, pitching wedge, 9-iron, 8-iron, 7-iron, 6-iron, 5-iron, 4-iron, 3-iron, 19-degree Hybrid Rescue, 5-wood, 3-wood, and driver.

Deciding When to Use Each Club

Table 2-1 shows how far the average golfer generally hits with each club when he or she makes solid contact. When you start to play this game, you probably won't attain these yardages, but as you practice, you'll get closer.

You should know your average. The best way to find out is to hit, oh, 50 balls with each club. Eliminate the longest five and the shortest five and then pace off to the middle of the remaining group. That's your average yardage. Use your average yardage to gauge which club to use on each shot.

Table 2-1	Which Club Should You Use?	
Club	*Men's Average Distance*	*Women's Average Distance*
Driver	230 yards	200 yards
3-wood	210 yards	180 yards
2-iron	190 yards	Not recommended; 4-wood or hybrid = 170 yards
3-iron	180 yards	Not recommended; 5-wood or hybrid = 160 yards
4-iron	170 yards	150 yards (Consider a hybrid instead)
5-iron	160 yards	140 yards
6-iron	150 yards	130 yards
7-iron	140 yards	120 yards
8-iron	130 yards	110 yards
9-iron	120 yards	100 yards
Pitching wedge	110 yards	90 yards
Sand wedge	90 yards	80 yards
Lob wedge	65 yards	60 yards

Debating Tradition versus Technology: High-Tech Tweaks

Technology is the guiding light of fundamental change that is inherent to a capitalistic society in search of a more expensive way to hit the #$&*!?*@ ball farther.

—Quote on the bathroom wall of the Wayward Soul
Driving Range in Temecula, California

Is technology threatening the game? Is the ball too hot? Are big-headed titanium drivers giving the golf ball too much rebound? Is Phil Mickelson left-handed? I think that most players would answer these questions in the affirmative. Should golfers take a stance in the battle between tradition and technology? Most would say, "Probably not."

To see where golf is today, you have to examine its past; you can then try to predict the game's future. This section helps you gaze into Gary's crystal golf ball to focus on the future.

Trying more advanced clubs and balls

Many clubs these days are made of titanium and other composite metals. These clubs allegedly act like a spring that segments of the golfing populace believe propels the ball — also enhanced by state-of-the-art materials and designs — distances it was never meant to travel. This phenomenon is called the *trampoline effect,* which some folks may mistake for a post-round activity for reducing stress. In fact, this effect is the product of modern, thin-faced metal clubs.

This phenomenon has fueled a debate pitting the forces of technology (golf's Dr. Frankensteins) against those of tradition (gents in tweed jackets and tam-o-shanters). Equipment that makes the game easier for the masses helps the game grow, the techno-wizards say. Traditionalists fret that classic courses are becoming obsolete, the need for new super-long courses may make the game cost more in both time and money, and golf may become too easy for elite players. Regardless of which side you're on (you may, indeed, back both camps), one fact is undeniable: Golf equipment has been improving ever since the game began.

People have been developing the golf ball and clubs for centuries. In the last 100 years, however, science has played an increasing role in golf-club development, with a strong influence coming from research into new metals, synthetic materials, and composites. Other developments worth noting:

- ✔ The introduction of the casting method of manufacturing clubheads in 1963.
- ✔ The introduction of graphite for use in shafts in 1973.
- ✔ The manufacture of metal woods in 1979 (first undertaken by TaylorMade). This last creation rendered persimmon woods obsolete, although a small number are still crafted.

Titanium clubheads raised the bar in technological development (yet again). Lighter than previous materials yet stronger than steel, titanium allows club makers to create larger clubheads with bigger sweet spots that push the legal limit of 460 cubic centimeters. Such clubs provide high-handicap golfers a huge margin for error — nothing feels quite like having a mishit ball travel 200 yards! But it's golf balls flying in excess of 300 yards that raise suspicions that these new clubs are making the ball too "excitable."

Golf balls have been under scrutiny for much longer, probably because each new generation of ball has had an ever greater impact on the game.

Modern balls tout varied dimple patterns, multiple layers, and other features that attempt to impart a certain trajectory, spin, greater accuracy, and better feel, as well as the ever-popular maximum distance allowed under the Rules of Golf established by the USGA. A recent change in the Rules added more than 20 yards to the old maximum of 296.8 yards. But even way back in 1998, John Daly averaged 299.4 yards on his measured drives on the PGA Tour. By 2004, the leader averaged 314, and in 2010 the best average poke was up two more yards.

Looking to the future

The rest of the 21st century likely won't come close to rivaling the recent era for technological impact or dramatic innovation. Why? For one thing, scientists are running out of new stuff they can use to make clubheads — at least stuff that isn't edible. An expedition to Saturn may yield possibilities. Metallurgists are going to be challenged, although so far they're staying ahead of the game. New entries in the substance category include beta titanium, maraging steel, graphite in clubheads, and liquid metal, all purportedly better than current club materials.

Dick Rugge, Senior Technical Director for the USGA, is one of the prominent folks standing in the way of radical equipment enhancement. His job is to regulate the distance a golf ball should travel, yet he doesn't want to stifle technology altogether. The goal is to give the average golfer an advantage (whether it comes from the equipment itself or the joy of having better equipment) while keeping the game a challenge for the top players. The USGA demonstrated this approach in 2010 when it banned the U-shaped grooves (often called *square grooves*) on clubfaces that helped pros make their approach shots stop and back up on the greens. Those grooves were banned for the pros only — amateurs who like the clubs they've got can keep using them until at least 2024!

Still, manufacturers keep trying to build a better mousetrap. And although everyone thinks about distance and spin, I think the most revolutionary innovations will come in putter designs.

On average, the USGA approves more than one new putter every day, and many of the new ones look like something out of the *Transformers* movies. But no one has yet invented a yip-proof blade. When somebody does, that genius is going to make a fortune.

The ball may also see changes — although, again, dramatic alterations in ball design are unlikely. Customizing may become more commonplace. You may also find more layering of golf-ball materials to help performance. After the Penta, can an octoball be far behind?

Not to be discounted are improvements in turf technology — an overlooked area boasting significant breakthroughs in the last 20 years. For example, in 1977, the average Stimpmeter reading for greens around the country was 6.6. (The *Stimpmeter* measures the speed of a putting surface — or any surface on a course.) This number means that a ball rolled from a set slope traveled 6½ feet. Today, the average is closer to 9 feet.

Weapons of our fore! fathers

The earliest players carved their own clubs and balls from wood. Long-nosed wooden clubs are the oldest-known designed clubs — and the most enduring equipment ever conceived, remaining in use from the 15th century until the late 19th century. Long noses were made from pear, apple, beech, or holly trees and were used to help achieve maximum distance with the feathery golf ball, which dates all the way back to 1618.

Later, other parts of the golf set developed: *play clubs,* which included a range of spoons with varying lofts; *niblicks,* a kin of the modern 9-iron or wedge that was ideal for short shots; and a *putting cleek* — a club that has undergone (and is still undergoing) perhaps the most rigorous experimentation. I know that my putters have undergone severe tests of stamina and stress. You're probably familiar with the I'm-going-to-throw-this-thing-into-orbit-and-let-Zeus-see-whether-he-can-putt-with-it test, as well as the ever-popular break-it-over-my-knee-so-it-can't-harm-anyone-again test. These tests should be conducted only by professionals.

The gutta percha ball, much harder than a feathery, forced club makers to become truly revolutionary. Some tried using leather, among other materials, in their clubs in an attempt to increase compression and, therefore, distance (obviously, a recurring theme throughout the ages). Others implanted metal and bone fragments in the clubface. In 1826, Scottish club makers began using hickory imported from the United States to manufacture shafts, and hickory was quickly adopted as the wood of choice.

It's probably a good thing that the fore! fathers never saw the orange ball Jerry Pate used to win the 1982 Players Championship, or the pink one favored by Paula Creamer, the 2010 U.S. Women's Open champion.

But the biggest breakthroughs of all will probably come from humans. Physiological improvement and psychological refinement may be the surest paths to more distance and lower scoring. So go to the gym, take up Pilates, hit your sports-psychologist's couch, get in touch with your inner self, eat bran and all the protein bars you can stand, drink green tea, and take a stab at self-hypnotism if you have to.

If all that fails to add 10 yards off the tee, you can try a different ball. Ain't innovation grand?

Clothes: How to Dress Like a Pro

The easiest way to date an old picture of a golfer, at least approximately, is by the clothes he or she is wearing. Sartorially, the game has changed enormously since the Scots tottered around the old links wearing jackets, shirts, and ties.

Back at St. Andrews, the restraint of the clothing affected the golf swing. Those jackets were tight! In fact, I believe that was the single biggest influence on the early golf swings. A golfer had to sway off the ball and then let his left arm bend on the backswing to get full motion. Also, he had to let go with the last three fingers of his left hand at the top of the swing. It was the only way to get the shaft behind his head. Put on a tweed jacket that's a little too small and try to swing. You'll see what the early golfers had to go through.

Fabrics have changed from those days of heavy wool and restricted swings. Light cotton is what the splendidly smart golfer wears today — if he or she hasn't switched to one of the new, high-tech fabrics that wick perspiration away from the body. (I always said golf was no sweat.) Styles have changed, too. When I came on tour in the early 1970s, polyester was the fabric of choice. Bell-bottoms and bright plaids filled golf courses with ghastly ridicule. We've evolved to better fabrics — and a softer, more humane existence on the course. Some guys on tour now wear expensive pants with more-expensive belts. And a few, like Rickie Fowler and Ian Poulter, are more colorful than we were back in the '70s! (Though I can't recall seeing any diamond-encrusted skull belt buckles like Rory Sabbatini's back in the day.) But most players wear off-the-rack clothes provided by clothing manufacturers.

Women have undergone an enormous fashion transformation on the course, too. Years ago, they played in full-length skirts, hats, and blouses buttoned up to the neck. All very restricting, I imagine. Now, of course, they're out there in shorts and pants.

For today's golfer, the most important point is to dress within your budget. This game can get expensive enough; you don't need to out-dress your playing partners. My general rule is to aim to dress better than the *starter* at the course (the person in charge of getting everyone off the first tee). The starter's style is usually a reflection of the dress standards at that particular golf course. If you're unsure about the style at a particular course, give the pro shop a call to find out the dress code.

The bottom line is to dress comfortably and look good. If you dress well, you may appear as if you can actually play this game with a certain amount of distinction. People can be fooled. You never know!

Golf shoes are the final aspect of a golfer's ensemble. Shoes can be a fashion statement in alligator or ostrich. They can be comfortable — tennis shoes or sandals with spikes. They can take on the lore of the Wild West in the form of cowboy boots with spikes or, as my mentor Fairway Louie used to highlight his golfing attire, they can even be military combat boots.

What's on the bottom of the shoe is all the rage now. Except for a few top tour pros who swing so hard they need to stay anchored to the ground, everyone plays in *soft spikes.* Soft spikes reduce spike marks and wear and tear on the greens. They're also easier on the feet. If the style of shoes is worthy, you can even go directly from the golf course to the nearest restaurant without changing shoes. The golf world is becoming a simpler place to live.

Accessories: The Goods to Get

When it comes to accessories, you can find a whole subculture out there. By accessories, I mean things such as

- Covers for your irons
- Plastic tubes that you put in your bag to keep your shafts from clanging together
- Tripod tees to use when the ground is hard, or "brush" tees to aid your drive's aerodynamics
- Telescoping ball retrievers to scoop your lost ball from a water hazard
- Rubber suction cups that allow you to lift your ball from the hole without bending down

I've even seen a plastic clip that fits to the side of your bag so that you can "find" your putter quickly. You know the sort of things. Most accessories appear to be good ideas, but then you often use them only once.

The place to find this sort of stuff is in the back of golf magazines. But take my advice: Don't bother. Real golfers — and you want to look and behave like one — don't go in for tchotchkes. Accessories are very uncool. The best golf bags are Spartan affairs and contain only the bare essentials:

- About six balls
- A few wooden tees
- A couple of gloves
- A rain suit
- A pitch-mark repair tool
- A few small coins (preferably foreign) for markers
- Two or three pencils
- A little bag (leather is cool) for your wallet, money clip, loose change, car keys, rings, cellphone (turned off!), and so on.

Your bag should also have a towel (a real, full-size one) hanging from the strap. Use your towel to dry off and clean your clubheads. Keep a spare towel in your bag. If it rains, you can't have too many towels.

However, one accessory I mention earlier that won't get you laughed off the course is headcovers. Keep them only on your woods or metal woods. Golfers have a wide range to choose from. You have your cuddly-animal devotees. Other players like to be identified with a particular golf club, university, or sports team. Some are content merely to advertise the manufacturer of the club they're using.

Bottom line? I recommend that you get headcovers with which you readily identify. Create your own persona. For example, tour veteran Craig "The Walrus" Stadler always liked walrus headcovers. Tiger Woods has — surprise! — a tiger. (The tiger with that plush job even has a name: Frank.) South Africa's Ernie Els uses a lion, Graeme McDowell of Northern Ireland won the 2010 U.S. Open with a fuzzy dragon on his driver, and Australian Steve Elkington uses no headcovers at all.

As for your golf bag, you don't need a large tour-sized monstrosity with your name on the side. I've got one because I play professionally and someone pays me to use their equipment. But you should go the understated route. Especially if you're going to be carrying your bag, go small and get a stand bag — the kind with legs that fold down automatically to support the bag. That way your bag stays on its feet, even on hot August days when you feel like collapsing.

Chapter 3

Taking Golf Lessons (And Other Sources of Help)

In This Chapter

▶ Pinpointing your strengths and weaknesses

▶ Knowing where you can get lessons

▶ Approaching your golf lesson with the right attitude

▶ Using other helpful sources

S ay you just started to play golf. Your friends took you over to the driving range at lunch; you launched a couple of balls into the sunshine and thought you may actually want to learn the game. What next?

✔ **You can get instruction from friends.** Most golfers start out this way, which is why they develop so many swing faults. Friends' intentions are good, but their teaching abilities may not be.

✔ **You can learn by hitting balls.** I learned to play this way. I'd go to the driving range and hit balls day and night. The pure act of swinging a golf club in a certain way made the ball fly in different trajectories and curves. This process is a very slow one because you have to learn by trial and error.

✔ **You can study books.** You can find many books on golf instruction that can lead you through the fundamentals of the game. But you can go only so far by teaching yourself from a book.

✔ **You can take lessons from a PGA professional.** This option is the most expensive and most efficient way to learn the game. Lessons can cost as little as $8 an hour and as much as $300 or more. The expensive guys are the ones you read about in *Golf Digest* and *Golf Magazine* and see on TV. But any golf professional can help you with the basics of the game.

Eleven things your teaching pro should have

Not all teaching pros are created equal. Look for these criteria when choosing an instructor:

- Plenty of golf balls
- Plenty of sunblock
- Plenty of patience
- A sense of humor
- Enthusiasm
- An ability to teach players at all levels

- An ability to explain the same thing in ten different ways
- An upbeat manner
- A teaching method that he or she believes in
- An ability to adapt that method to your needs
- More golf balls

Pre Pro: Keeping Tabs on Your Game before Lessons

Keep a record of how you've played for a few weeks before your first lesson. And I'm not just talking about recording your scores. Keep accurate counts of

- How often you hit your drive into the fairway.
- How often you reach the green *in regulation;* that is, how often you get to the green in two fewer shots than that hole's par (for example, you hit the green of a par-5 in three shots). It won't be many, at least at first.
- How many putts you average.
- How many strokes you usually take to get the ball into the hole from a greenside bunker.

Tracking so many things may seem like overkill, but it's invaluable to your pro because it helps him or her quickly detect tendencies or weaknesses in your game. Then the pro knows how to help you improve. Figure 3-1 shows how to keep track of all those numbers on your scorecard.

Men's Course Rating/Slope
Blue 73.1/137
White 71.0/130

Women's Course Rating/Slope
Red 73.7/128

Blue Tees	White Tees	Par	Hcp	JOHN	HOLE	HIT FAIRWAY	HIT GREEN	NO. PUTTS	Hcp	Par	Red Tees
377	361	4	11	4	1	✓	✓	2	13	4	310
514	467	5	13	8	2	✓	0	3	3	5	428
446	423	4	1	7	3	0	0	2	1	4	389
376	356	4	5	6	4	0	0	2	11	4	325
362	344	4	7	5	5	0	✓	3	7	4	316
376	360	4	9	6	6	✓	0	2	9	4	335
166	130	3	17	4	7	0	✓	3	17	3	108
429	407	4	3	5	8	✓	✓	3	5	4	368
161	145	3	15	5	9	0	0	2	15	3	122
3207	2993	35		50	Out	4	4	22		35	2701
Initial									Initial		
366	348	4	18	5	10	0	0	2	14	4	320
570	537	5	10	7	11	✓	0	3	2	5	504
438	420	4	2	5	12	✓	0	2	6	4	389
197	182	3	12	4	13	0	0	2	16	3	145
507	475	5	14	5	14	✓	✓	2	4	5	425
398	380	4	4	5	15	0	✓	3	8	4	350
380	366	4	6	5	16	✓	0	2	10	4	339
165	151	3	16	4	17	0	0	2	18	3	133
397	375	4	8	5	18	0	0	2	12	4	341
3418	3234	36		45	In	3	2	20		36	2946
6625	6227	71		95	Tot	7	6	42		71	5647
Handicap									Handicap		
Net Score									Net Score		
Adjust									Adjust		

Scorer Attested Date

Figure 3-1: Recording your golf stats.

Deciding Where to Go for Lessons

Golf lessons are available almost anywhere balls are hit and golf is played: driving ranges, public courses, resorts, private clubs, and so on. The price usually increases in that order — driving-range pros usually charge the least. As for quality, if the pro is PGA-qualified — look for the term *PGA professional* posted in the pro shop or on his or her business card — you can be reasonably sure you'll get top-notch instruction. If not, the pro may still know a lot about the game, but proceed with caution.

A qualified PGA teaching professional may charge as little as $25 or as much as $100 (or more) per session, which can range from 30 minutes to an hour. A professional has a good sense of how much to tell you and at what rate of speed; not all lessons require a specific amount of time. The following sections give you the lowdown on some potential lesson options.

When checking out places that offer golf lessons, ask whether they have video-analysis capabilities. When you're able to watch yourself on video, you and your instructor can pinpoint problem areas for improvement. If nothing else, a video record is a great way to track and monitor your progress as you build your fundamental skills.

Golf schools

No matter where you live in the United States, a golf school should be fairly close by. Golf schools serve all levels of players — and many are designed for those just learning the game. (Appendix B contains a list of recommended golf schools.)

Golf schools are great for beginners. You find yourself in a group from 3 to 20 strong, which is perfect for you — the safety in numbers is reassuring. You discover that you're not the only beginner. And you never know: Watching others struggle with their own problems may help you with *your* game.

Most of the better golf schools advertise in golf magazines. Be warned, though. These schools tend to be expensive. They did very well in the '80s and early '90s, when the economy was perceived to be strong and people had more disposable income. Since then, however, golf schools have been less successful. Golf-school lessons are big-ticket items, which makes them among the first things people omit from their yearly budgets.

Many people still attend golf schools, though. Why? Because they work. You get, on average, three days of intensive coaching on all aspects of the game from a good teacher. Because groups are usually small, you get lots of one-on-one attention, too. And you can pick up a lot by listening to what your fellow students are being told.

Even though you're at golf school, don't feel you have to be hitting shots all the time. Take regular breaks — especially if you're not used to hitting a lot of balls — and use the time to learn. Try to analyze other players' swings. Soak up all the information you can. Besides, regular breaks are the best way I know to avoid those blisters you see on the hands of golf-school students!

Driving ranges

I used to work at a driving range in Riverside, California. I spent hours picking up golf balls on the range and hitting those same balls when I was off work. The range was bare dirt, the balls were old, and the floodlights had lost their luminescence. But it was a great spot to learn the game.

Driving ranges have changed a lot since then. Many are very sophisticated, with two or three tiers and balls that pop out of the floor already teed up. Some offer putting greens; some have miniature golf courses attached to them. Quite a few talented (and a few not-so-talented) instructors work at these facilities. Most of them can show you the basics of the swing and get you off on the right foot.

Country clubs

Even if you're not a member, you can usually take a lesson from the local club pro. He or she likely charges more than a driving-range pro, but the facilities are better. Certainly, the golf balls are. And chances are you have access to a putting green and a practice bunker so that you can get short-game help, too.

A playing lesson

A *playing lesson* is just what it sounds like: You hire a professional to play any number of holes with you. This theme has three main variations:

- ✔ **You do all the playing.** The professional walks along, observes your strategy, swing, and style, and makes suggestions as you go. I recommend this approach if you're the type of person who likes one-on-one direction.

- ✔ **You both play.** That way, you get instruction as well as the chance to observe an expert player in action. If you typically learn more by watching and copying what you see, this type of lesson is the way to go. Pay particular attention to the rhythm of the pro's swing, the way he manages his game, and how you can incorporate both into your own game.

✔ **The pro creates on-course situations for you to deal with.** For example, the pro may place your ball behind a tree, point out your options, and then ask you to choose one. Your choice and subsequent advice from the pro help make you a better player. He may give you two escape routes — one easy, one hard. All the easy one involves is a simple chip shot back to the fairway. Trouble is, you may feel like you're wasting a shot. The difficult shot — through a narrow gap in the branches — is tempting because the reward will be much greater. But if you hit the tree, you could take nine or ten shots on the hole. Decisions, decisions! That's what golf is all about.

Gary's favorite teachers

Many famous teachers will teach absolutely anybody who wants to be taught — male or female, young or old. They're expensive — $100 to $400 an hour and up. Some teach at schools, and some (like my CBS colleague Peter Kostis) are multimedia phenomena. Here are some of the best:

✔ **Mike Bender:** Mike Bender Golf Academy in Lake Mary, Florida (phone 407-321-0444; Web site `mikebender.com`

✔ **Sean Foley:** Orange County National Golf Center in Winter Garden, Florida (phone 888-727-3672 or 407-656-2626; Web site `ocngolf.com`)

✔ **Hank Haney:** Hank Haney Golf Academy in McKinney, Texas (phone 972-346-2180; e-mail `sjohnson@hankhaney.com`, Web site `hankhaney.com`)

✔ **Butch Harmon:** Butch Harmon School of Golf in Las Vegas, Nevada (phone 888-867-3226; e-mail `info@butchharmon.com`, Web site `butchharmon.com`)

✔ **Peter Kostis:** CBS Golf, the Golf Channel, Golf.com — just about anywhere good golf thinking goes on

✔ **David Leadbetter:** David Leadbetter Golf Academy in Orlando, Florida (phone 888-633-5323 or 407-787-3330; e-mail `info@davidleadbetter.com`, Web site `davidleadbetter.com`)

✔ **Jim McLean:** Jim McLean Golf Schools in Miami, Florida (phone 800-723-6725; Web site `jimmclean.com`)

✔ **Dave Pelz:** Dave Pelz Scoring Game Schools in Austin, Texas (phone 800-833-7370 or 512-264-6800; Web site `pelzgolf.com`)

✔ **Rick Smith:** Rick Smith Golf Academy at Treetops Resort in Gaylord, Michigan (phone 888-873-3867; Web site `rick smith.com`) and Rick Smith Golf Academy at Tiburón in Naples, Florida (phone 877-464-6531; Web site `rick smith.com`)

✔ **Stan Utley:** Grayhawk Learning Center in Scottsdale, Arizona (phone: 480-502-2656; e-mail `info@stanutley.com`, Web site `stanutley.com`)

Getting the Most from Your Lessons

Much has been written about the relationship between Nick Faldo and his former teacher, David Leadbetter. Under Leadbetter's guidance, Faldo turned himself from a pretty good player into a great one. In the process, Leadbetter — quite rightly — received a lot of praise and attention. More recently, Tiger Woods switched teachers and retooled his game. After Woods won the 2005 Masters and British Open, his teacher Hank Haney got some of the credit. Five years later, he and Haney split as Woods struggled with personal and professional setbacks.

Ultimately, the teacher is only as good as the pupil. Faldo, with his extraordinary dedication and total belief in what he was told, may have been the best pupil in the history of golf. Tiger at his best is nothing less than the best (and most focused) golfer of our time.

Which leads us to the most important question of all: What kind of golf student are you? Are you willing to put your faith in your instructor and do the work required to improve your game, or do you expect the pro to tap you on the head with a magic golf club and miraculously fix your flaws? The following sections give you some pointers on taking full advantage of your golf lessons.

When you take lessons, you need to keep the faith in your instructor. There's no point in sticking with someone you don't believe in. If you find yourself doubting your teacher, you're wasting everybody's time. Change instructors if that happens — that is, if your instructor doesn't tell you where to go first.

Be honest

Okay, now you're on the lesson tee with your pro. The first thing you need to be is completely honest. Tell your instructor your problems (your golf problems, that is), your goals, and the shots you find difficult. Tell him or her what style of learning — visual, auditory, or kinesthetic — you find easiest. For example, do you like to be shown how to do something and then copy it? If so, you're a *visual learner*. Do you prefer to have that same something explained (making you an *auditory learner*)? Or do you prefer to repeat the motion until it feels natural (which makes you a *kinesthetic learner*)?

No matter which learning technique you prefer, the instructor needs to know what it is. How else can he or she be effective in teaching you? You should also be sure to mention any physical limitations you have due to injury, illness, or other causes.

The bottom line is that the pro needs to know anything that helps create an accurate picture of you and your game. Don't be shy or embarrassed. Believe me, you can't say anything that your instructor hasn't heard before!

Listen up

After you've done some talking, let your teacher reciprocate. Listen to what the pro has to say. After the pro has evaluated you and your swing, he or she can give you feedback on where you should go from there. Feedback is part of every good lesson. So keep listening. Take notes if you have to.

Don't rate the success or failure of a session on how many balls you hit. You can hit very few shots and still have a great lesson. The number of shots you hit depends on what you need to work on. An instructor may have you repeat a certain swing in an attempt to develop a *swing thought,* or feel. You'll notice when the suggested change becomes part of your swing.

Too many golfers swing or hit while the pro is talking. Don't do it! Instead, imagine that you're a smart chicken crossing the road: Stop, look, and listen!

Drop your doubts

Take it from me: Five minutes into every lesson, you're going to have doubts. The pro changes something in your swing, grip, or stance, and you feel weird. Well, think about it this way: You *should* feel weird. What you've been doing wrong has become so ingrained that it feels comfortable. Change what's wrong for the better and, of course, it feels strange at first. That's normal. Embrace the change!

Trust your professional more than you trust your friends or even loved ones, at least with your golf game. Countless pros have heard the line, "My husband told me to do it this way," and bitten their lips to keep from asking, "How much does he get paid for teaching golf?"

Don't panic. You'll probably get worse before you get better. You're changing things to improve them, not just for the heck of it. So give what you're told to do a proper chance. Changes rarely work in five short minutes. Give them at least a couple of weeks to take effect. More than two weeks is too long; go back for another lesson.

Meanwhile, practice! If you don't work between lessons on what you've learned, you're wasting the pro's time — not to mention your time and money.

Golf-lesson do's and don'ts

Here are some tips on making the most of your lesson:

✔ **Find a good teacher and stick with that person.**

✔ **Follow a timetable.** Discipline yourself to work on what the instructor tells you.

✔ **Don't let your mind wander.** *Concentrate!*

✔ **Learn from your mistakes.** You'll make them, so you may as well make them work for you.

✔ **Don't tense up.** Relax, and you'll learn and play better.

✔ **Practice the shots you find most difficult.**

✔ **Set goals.** Golf is all about shooting for targets.

✔ **Stay positive.** Golf is hard enough — a bad attitude only hurts you.

✔ **Don't keep practicing if you're tired.** That's when sloppy habits begin. *Quality* practice matters more than quantity.

✔ **Evaluate yourself after each lesson.** Are you making progress? Do you know what you need to practice before your next lesson?

Ask questions

The pro is an expert, and you're paying good money, so take advantage of the pro's knowledge while he or she belongs to you. Don't worry about sounding stupid. Again, your question won't be anything the pro hasn't heard a million times before. Besides, what's the point of spending good money on something you don't get?

The professional is trained to teach, so he or she knows any number of ways to say the same thing. One of those ways is sure to push your particular button. But if you don't share your impressions, the pro doesn't know whether the message is getting through. So speak up!

Keep your cool

Finally, stay calm. Anxious people make lousy pupils. Look on the lesson as the learning experience that it is, and don't get too wrapped up in where the balls are going. Again, the pro is aware of your nervousness. Ask him or her for tips on swinging smoothly. Nervous golfers tend to swing too quickly, so keep your swing smooth. What's important at this stage is that you make the proper moves in the correct sequence. Get those moves right and understand the order, and the good shots will come.

Finding Other Ways to Get Help

The golf swing is the most analyzed move in all of sports. As such, more has been written — and continues to be written — about the swing than just about any other athletic move. Take a look in any bookstore under "Golf," and you can see what I mean. Maybe you have, because you're reading this book. (Nice choice!) And books are just the beginning; in the following sections, I show you some of the outlets you can peruse for golf instruction.

Golf books that are as good as this one (well, almost)

So where should you go for written advice? Some of the golf books out there are quite good. But most, sad to say, are the same old stuff regurgitated over and over. *Remember:* This game was centuries old in the 18th century!

Ten great golf-instruction books

An amazing number of books have been written on golf. Historians have tried to document every hook and slice throughout golf's existence. Many have tracked the footsteps of the great players throughout their careers.

But instruction is the main vein nowadays. You can get books on every method of golf instruction, from using household tools as teaching aids to employing data compiled by aliens on the planet Blothar. (Okay, maybe that's a stretch.)

Anyhow, here are ten great golf-instruction books, listed alphabetically by author. I've tried to help by reducing the list to my ten favorites, but I could include many more. The material is inexhaustible, so take your time and peruse this golf library with an open mind.

✔ *How to Play Your Best Golf All the Time* by Tommy Armour (Simon & Schuster, 1953)

✔ *On Learning Golf* by Percy Boomer (Knopf, 1992)

✔ *Search for the Perfect Swing* by A.J. Cochran and John Stobbs (Triumph, 2005)

✔ *Natural Golf* by John Duncan Dunn (Putnam's, 1931)

✔ *The Mystery of Golf* by Arnold Haultain (Houghton Mifflin Co., 1908; Nabu Press, 2010 — recently reissued in paperback after 102 years!)

✔ *Five Lessons: The Modern Fundamentals of Golf* by Ben Hogan (Barnes, 1957)

✔ *Swing the Clubhead* by Ernest Jones (Dodd, Mead, 1952)

✔ *The Physics of Golf* by Theodore P. Jorgensen (Springer, 1999)

✔ *Golf My Way* by Jack Nicklaus (Simon & Schuster, 1974)

✔ *Harvey Penick's Little Red Book* by Harvey Penick (Simon & Schuster, 1992)

Here's another secret: Don't expect too much from books "written" by the top players. The information they impart isn't inherently flawed, but if you think you're going to get some stunning insight into how your favorite Tour star plays, think again. In all likelihood, the celebrity author has had little to do with the text. Exceptions exist, of course, but the "name" player's input is often minimal. Some of the most famous athletes have actually claimed they've been misquoted *in their own books.* And another thing: The world's greatest golfers aren't necessarily the best teachers. In fact, some of them have no idea how hard the game can be.

Golf magazines

The monthly magazines *Golf Digest, Golf Magazine,* and *Golf Tips* owe most of their popularity to their expertise in the instructional field. Indeed, most people buy these magazines because they think the articles can help them play better. The magazines all do a good job of covering each aspect of the game every month. If you're putting badly, for example, every month you can find a new tip (or two or three) to try. Best of all, these magazines use only the best players and teachers to author their stories. *Golf Digest* has an elite crew it calls "America's 50 Greatest Teachers," while *Golf Magazine* boasts of its "Top 100 Teachers." Either way, the information you receive is second to none.

But is the information in golf magazines the best? Sometimes. The key is to sift through what you read and subsequently take to the course. The great teacher Bob Toski once said, "You cannot learn how to play golf from the pages of a magazine." And he was right. Use these publications as backups to your lessons — nothing more. Be selective. Don't try everything in every issue, or you'll end up hopelessly confused.

Don't get the idea that I don't like these magazines. I've authored a few *Golf Digest* pieces over the years myself. But, by definition, these articles are general in nature. They aren't aimed specifically at *your* game. Of course, some of them may happen to work for you. But most won't. You have to be able to filter out those that don't.

DVDs: Channel the pixels

Instructional DVDs convey movement and rhythm so much better than their print counterparts, so they're perfect for visual learners. Indeed, watching a top teacher or tour professional hitting balls before you leave for the course isn't a bad idea. The smoothness and timing in an expert's swing has a way of rubbing off on you.

You can buy instructional DVDs at thousands of outlets, including video stores and golf shops, and you can order many of them online or from your favorite golf magazines.

Gary's top instructional DVDs

A bountiful supply of golf DVDs ranges from Tim Conway's hilarious *Dorf on Golf* to sophisticated features on the do's and don'ts of your golf swing. Here are some of my favorites:

✔ *Hank Haney's Essentials:* A four-disk set from a modern master.

✔ **David Leadbetter** *Interactive:* Four instructional DVDs plus one with software that can analyze your swing and offer drills.

✔ **David Leadbetter's** *$10,000 Lesson:* And the DVD only costs $19.99!

✔ **Gary McCord's** *Golf For Dummies* DVD: How could I resist? The same solid, fun

instruction as in this book, plus you get to see me move!

✔ *Phil Mickelson: Secrets of the Short Game:* He even shows you how to hit his patented flop shot.

✔ *Harvey Penick's Little Red Video:* Still available only on VHS, at least until someone puts this classic on DVD.

✔ *Women's Golf Instruction, with Donna White and Friends:* Simple, easy to follow.

Apps ahoy: Golf wisdom in the palm of your hand

The latest form of golf instruction may one day be the best — apps for your smartphone or other interactive gizmo. (Note to my fellow graybeards: *App,* of course, is short for *web application,* a bit of software that runs on a personal electronic device.)

Many course guides and instructional programs are already available as apps, and others soon will be. (I discuss some of the best in Chapter 19.) Other apps include fun golf games; advanced scorekeeping systems; and rangefinders, not all of which are legal under current rules. But the field is growing so fast that picking the best ones is hard. You can find some rotten apps in the orchard, as well as tasty ones that still have a few bugs in them, and ten more will pop up by the time you finish reading this sentence.

Instructional gadgets

A look at the back of any golf magazine or the home page of many Web sites proves that instructional doodads aren't in short supply. Most aren't very good. Some are okay. And a few can work wonders. In Table 3-1, I outline my favorites for you. Figure 3-2 shows a picture of one of the more interesting of these gadgets — the Tour Striker.

Figure 3-2:
The Tour Striker keeps your hands ahead of the ball.

Table 3-1	Gary's Favorite Instructional Gadgets	
Gadget	*Function*	*Where to Get It*
A 2-x-4 board	Lies on the ground to aid your alignment.	Hardware store or lumberyard
Alignment sticks	Flexible fiberglass sticks, usually orange or yellow, that you can poke into the ground or lay flat to aid alignment. An improvement on the old 2-x-4.	Hardware store or online
Camcorder	Probably the best instructional gizmo of all. Have a friend record your swing, and then make sure it looks like the photos in this book.	Department store, electronics store, or online
Chalk line	A builder's tool that can help your putting stroke. The line is caked in chalk. You snap it to indicate the line you want to the hole. Many tour pros swear by this technique.	Hardware store or online
Flammer	A harness across your chest with an attachment for a shaft in the middle. When you turn as if to swing, you your arms and body move together as a telescopic rod connects the club to your chest.	A few sites online
The Perfect Swing Trainer	A large, circular ring that helps keep your swing on plane.	theperfectswing trainer.com
Putting Professor	An inclined panel to use on the practice green — it keeps your stroke consistent.	Several sites online
Swing straps	Hook them to your body to keep your arms close to your sides during the swing.	Most golf shops or online
The Tour Striker	A modified club that teaches ordinary golfers to make contact with the shaft leaning forward, like the pros do.	Tourstriker.com

Chapter 4

Getting in Golf Shape

. . . .

. . . .

Both hands on the club, my body tense in anticipation of flush contact. Eyes preoccupied with a distant stare of the uncertainty of the golf ball's destination. I realize that the swing sequence has begun, and I put all available resources into sending the ball on a wanton mission of distance collection. I sense the fluid nature of Fred Couples's swing, the mass chaos of John Daly's hips as they rotate through the hitting area, the silent stare of Daly's gallery as they try to interpret what they just saw. I'm awakened from my trance by the dull thud of contact: It hurts, it's sickly, and I hear voices from nearby, questioning my masculinity. Impact has all the compression of a gnat flying into a wall of warm butter. My body is vibrating like a marked-down, used Ford Escort, and I nearly pass out from the physical exertion.

Once I get back on my feet to review the moment and wait for the laughter to die down, I realize that the instrument swinging this club has been totally neglected and is in a state of sad disrepair. My "exercise regimen" up to this point has been to get in a bathtub filled with lukewarm water, pull the drain cord, and then fight the current. It's time to end this madness. I'm going to exercise!

—Fairway Louie, circa 1987, after hitting his opening tee shot
in the La Fiesta Restaurant's annual Dos Gringos
Alternate (Tequila) Shot Tournament

My expertise in regard to exercise is minimal at best, and the area of physical therapy is beyond my scope of knowledge. So let me introduce you to a friend of mine: Dr. Paul Callaway, a licensed physical therapist with a PhD in golf-specific sports physiology. I met Paul in 1984 when he was the first Director of Physical Therapy for the PGA Tour. The PGA and Champions tours feature large vans that accommodate physical conditioning apparatuses supervised by physical therapists. This program was started for the betterment of physical conditioning on the tour. Paul is a guy I go to frequently when my senior-tour body heads out of bounds.

Paul created Body Balance for Performance, a complete golf health and fitness-training program, and is now the Director of Golf Fitness at the Cantigny Golf Academy in Wheaton, Illinois. Overall, Paul's concepts have helped more than 7,000 amateur and professional golfers reach their performance potential while preventing injuries. In this chapter, Paul has helped us provide you with the building blocks of golf fitness. If you want more information about this subject, have other questions related to golf health and fitness training, or want Dr. Callaway to contact you, visit www.CallawayGolfFitness.com or e-mail Paul@CallawayGolfFitness.com.

The purpose of this chapter is to embarrass you into getting into shape so that you can hit a little white ball around 150 acres of green grass without falling down. How tough can that be? I identify five essential elements of golf performance and elaborate on the physical requirements for playing your best while reducing your risk of getting hurt. The motivation here is to get you out of the chair where you watch the Golf Channel and into a program that helps you feel better, hit the ball farther, and run circles around your kids in front of their friends. Well, the last one may be a stretch, but the rest of my little spiel's the real golf gospel.

Why So Many New Golfers Give Up

More than 28 million Americans are now screwing up their lives by playing this game. And you thought insanity was rare. But then again, you have to rent shoes to go bowling, tennis is too hard if you're more than 17 years old, and I still don't understand squash, so golf seems like the thing to do if I've got the rest of my life in which to do it.

This game is very hard, and if you take it too seriously, especially in the beginning, it frustrates you enough that you start wearing your shoes backward. Believe me, I know. Also, any pain you have while playing hurts your chances of playing well, discourages you, and sends you to the snack bar to pick up an adult beverage more often than you should. A lot of attrition in golf happens for two main reasons, as I see it:

✔ Frustration from lack of improvement

✔ Injury

If you're going to have fun playing this game, you have to get your body ready to play golf for a lifetime. So let's get physical.

Five Essential Elements for Success

Here's a list of five things that are vital to good performance in anything you do (yes, anything!):

- **A customized and sport-specific physical training program:** "Beer curls" aren't considered specific.

- **Professional instruction:** I personally have an *après-ski* instructor for after I'm done on the slopes.

- **Proper mental skills:** Enough said.

- **Training equipment:** Please, no Speedos.

- **Talent to enjoy the sport.**

When those five elements are part of your plan, that's *integrated performance enhancement,* or "You da man!" as I call it.

To play on the highest level, you need some combination of talent, physical conditioning, mental awareness, instruction, and good ol' perseverance. Simply going out and buying new drivers that are touted to hit the ball 50 yards farther isn't going to cut it. ***Remember:*** You need mental as well as physical skills. Promise me you'll use them.

Today's golfers are in far better shape than the roundbellies I grew up with. Gary Player was the first guy on the tour who I saw preaching the benefits of being in good shape. Even as he approached 75 years old, a milestone he reached in November 2010, Gary could do most things the kids on the PGA Tour can do, short of catching some big air on a snowboard.

Tiger Woods and other top pros are into rigorous physical-exercise programs that will keep them strong into the later stages of the Tour schedule, when other players tire from so much wear and tear. Tiger's work ethic in the weight room used to be unusual; now it's the norm for Tour pros under 40. These days you often see more players on the 50-and-over Champions Tour in the gym than in the bar. That's quite a change from the old days when some pros shot par through rain, wind, and raging hangovers.

The Keys to Golf Fitness

After you're familiar with the elements of integrated performance enhancement (You da man!) in the preceding section, take a look at three concepts that are crucial to any good training program: structure, physical training, and customization.

Structure governs function

This heading, simply put, translates to "Your physique affects the way you play this game." If your range of motion is like the Tin Man's, your golf swing doesn't look very athletic and may actually rust. Oil those muscles with physical conditioning. It's that simple, so get off your wallet and act now!

Here are five areas to address:

✔ Balance

✔ Control

✔ Flexibility

✔ Posture

✔ Strength

If you're deficient in any of these areas, you may develop bad habits in your golf swing to compensate. Not only does your golf game suffer, but your body may also break down from bad swing mechanics. Fix it now or fix it later; it's your choice.

Several factors can cause structural imbalances. They include inherited body characteristics and the natural aging process. Imbalance can increase over time due to consistent thumping of the golf ball.

No matter what causes your imbalances, the connective-tissue system in your body, called the *fascial system,* can develop restrictions that compress and/or pull on muscles, tendons, ligaments, nerves, bones, everything. Left uncorrected, these imbalances in your connective tissue leave you in a mangled mess and adversely affect your performance as you start to compensate for them. Avoid these problems by seeing a health and performance expert trained to work with golfers, and cut out the middleman: bad golf.

Physical training improves structure

This point is a must for prospective golfers: Enhance your structure and boost your game! How can you improve your structure to play better, safer golf? Start with a quick physiology lesson:

Earlier, I talk about fascia, your body's connective-tissue, which contributes to your flexibility, mobility, posture, and function. Connective tissue is everywhere; it's the net that holds your body together.

Connective tissue's main job is to retain your body's normal shape, providing resistance to various stresses. In order to change your body structure and improve your ability to play golf, you benefit most by following a specific sequence of physical training, called "Release, Reeducate, and Rebuild," or, "The Story of Gary McCord's Career":

- ✔ **Release:** First, you have to release your connective-tissue restrictions. Specially designed flexibility exercises reduce tension in the inelastic portion of the connective-tissue system that resists lengthening. You have to do these stretching exercises at low intensity but for a prolonged period — many people with tightness need to sustain a single flexibility exercise for a minimum of three to five minutes before the layers of tissue begin to relax. Gentle, sustained stretching is more effective than a quick, intense stretch because it more effectively and permanently lengthens the tough connective tissue of the body.

- ✔ **Reeducate:** As your tissue's restrictions decrease, you need to reeducate your structure with specialized exercises aimed at improving posture, balance, stability, and control. These reeducation exercises help you capitalize on your improved flexibility by teaching you how to feel the positions in which your body moves most efficiently. The goal for each golfer should be to develop a new postural identity: good athletic posture at *address* (the point before you strike the ball), including proper spine angle, plus swing mechanics that are safe, efficient, reproducible, and highly effective.

- ✔ **Rebuild:** Last comes a program of rebuilding exercises designed to solidify and then reinforce your physical structure and dynamic swing motion. These exercises can also improve your swing speed for added distance and improve muscular endurance for better swing control and performance toward the end of a round and/or during longer practice sessions.

Exercise programs must be golf-specific and, ideally, customized

For an exercise program to be most helpful, it must be golf-specific and personalized. Warming up by throwing a javelin doesn't help your golf game. Fitness programs for other sports aren't designed around the specific muscles, movement patterns, and physical-performance factors that support the golf swing.

Customized fitness training is equally important. If you start an exercise program that isn't designed around your own physical weaknesses, tailored to the special demands of golf, and formulated to accomplish your personal performance goals, you're wasting your time.

Find a specialist to work with and ask what sort of initial physical performance he or she uses to design your program. The elements of any evaluation should include at least the following:

✔ Health history, pain problems, injuries related to golf, and so on

✔ Tests to identify postural, structural, or biomechanical imbalances that may interfere with your ability to swing

✔ Balance assessment

✔ Muscle and joint flexibility testing

✔ Muscle strength, endurance, and control testing

✔ Biomechanical video analysis of the golf swing

✔ Golf skills evaluation (measurement of current swing and scoring performance potential, including elements of the swing such as clubhead speed, swing path, impact position, and launch angle as well as driving distance, greens and fairways in regulation, handicap, and so on)

✔ Goals assessment (evaluation of performance goals, reasons for playing golf, and deadlines for reaching goals)

I'm already proud of you! Following these steps helps you and your specific golf muscles perform better, and it beats watching talk shows all day. Your physical abilities and conditioning will merge, and you'll become a force to be reckoned with out on the links. Enjoy your new, improved golf game!

Tests and Exercises to Improve Your Golf Fitness

I'm going to give you a sample test before you tackle the initial performance tests I recommend in the preceding section. These tests tell you how much serious conditioning you need. If you find that the answer to that question is "a lot," never fear — I also provide you with some corrective exercises that relate to each test.

Please remember, if you're unable to perform any portion of these simple tests or exercises easily and comfortably, you're not alone. I seized up during most of them! Go slowly, and if you can't perform one or the other, stop and turn on *The Ellen DeGeneres Show.* Just don't dance along with Ellen until you loosen up.

In all seriousness, consult your physician before trying any of the exercises suggested in this chapter. Though these exercises are generally safe for most people, if you notice *any* discomfort while performing them, stop and consult your physician *immediately* before continuing.

Test 1: Club behind the spine

This test is a helpful evaluation tool because it can identify several areas of physical weakness and/or imbalance. First, you know that having enough rotation flexibility in your spine is vital for a good golf swing. The area of the spine that should rotate the most is the middle section, the *thoracic spine*. To have maximum flexibility to turn during the swing, you need the physical potential to achieve a straighter thoracic spine at address (see Figure 4-1a). A bent thoracic spine at address blocks your ability to turn (as shown in Figure 4-1b). Therefore, one purpose of this test is to determine your ability to achieve and maintain the ideal, straighter angle through chest and middle-spine flexibility.

Figure 4-1:
A straight thoracic spine gives you flexibility; a bent thoracic spine hinders your ability to turn.

In addition, this test measures (to a degree) the muscle strength of your lower abdominals, hips, thighs, middle and upper back, and shoulder blades — all essential to achieving and maintaining proper posture at address. It can also identify tightness in the *hamstring muscles* in the backs of your legs.

To perform the club-behind-the-spine test, follow these steps:

1. **Stand upright while holding a golf club behind your back.**

2. **Hold the head of the club flat against your tailbone with one hand and the grip of the club against the back of your head with the other, as shown in Figure 4-2a.**

3. **Bend your hips and knees slightly (10 to 15 degrees) and contract your lower abdominal muscles enough to press the small of your back into the shaft of the club.**

4. **While keeping your lower back in contact with the clubshaft, straighten the middle and upper portions of your spine and neck.**

   The goal is to make complete contact between the shaft and the entire length of your spine and back of your head. (See Figure 4-2b.)

5. **Try to bend forward from your hips and proportionately from your knees while maintaining club contact with your spine and head.**

   Keep bending until you're able to comfortably see a spot on the ground in front of you where the golf ball would normally be at address. (See Figure 4-3.)

6. **Remove the club from behind your back and grip it with both hands in your normal address position, trying to maintain all the spine, hip, and knee angles that you just created (see Figure 4-4).**

Figure 4-2:
Keep as much of your spine and back of your head in contact with the clubshaft as possible.

Figure 4-3:
Look for
the spot on
the ground
where
the ball
would be at
address.

Figure 4-4:
The ideal
address
position.

If you execute it properly, the club-behind-the-spine test positions you so that you feel comfortably balanced over the ball in an athletic position with the appropriate muscle activity in your lower abdominals, thighs, hips, upper back, and shoulder blades. You achieve a straighter, more efficient thoracic-spine angle and a neutral, more powerful pelvic position with proper degrees of hip and knee bend. In other words, you achieve a posture at address with the most potential for producing a safe, highly effective golf swing.

If you're unable to achieve the positions of this test easily and comfortably, the next three simple exercises may help.

Exercise 1: Recumbent chest-and-spine stretch

The recumbent chest-and-spine stretch can help you with the release part of physical training that I discuss in "Physical training improves structure" earlier in the chapter. This exercise releases the tightness in your chest, the front of your shoulders, and your lower back. After you've mastered the stretch, you should have the flexibility to nail the club-behind-the-spine test and improve your posture at address.

To perform this releasing exercise, follow these steps:

1. **Lie on a firm, flat surface with your hips and knees bent at a 90-degree angle and rest your lower legs on a chair, couch, or bed, as shown in Figure 4-5a.**

   Depending on the degree of tightness in your chest, spine, and shoulders, you may need to begin this exercise on a softer surface (an exercise mat, blankets on the floor, or your bed), and place a small pillow or rolled-up towel under your head and neck to support them in a comfortable, neutral position. You may also need to place a small towel roll under the small of your back.

2. **As shown in Figure 4-5b, bend your elbows to approximately 90 degrees and position your arms 60 to 80 degrees away from the sides of your body so that you begin to feel a comfortable stretch in the front of your chest and shoulders.**

   This arm position looks like a waiter's arms when he carries a tray in each hand.

   If you feel any pinching in your shoulders, try elevating your arms and resting them on a stack of towels or a small pillow so that your elbows are higher than your shoulders.

3. **Relax into this comfortable stretch position for at least three to five minutes or until you experience a complete release of the tightness in your chest, front of your shoulders, and lower back.**

   You're trying to get your back, spine, and shoulders completely flat on the floor.

Repeat this exercise daily for five to ten days until you can do it easily, with no lingering tightness in your body.

You may want to increase the degree of stretch in your body by removing any support or padding from under your body and/or arms — or by adding a small towel roll under the middle portion of your spine (at shoulder-blade level) perpendicular to your spine (see Figure 4-6). Remember *always* to keep the degree of stretch comfortable and to support your head, neck, spine, and arms so that you don't put too much stress on those structures during the stretch.

Exercise 2: Recumbent abdominal-and-shoulder-blade squeeze

The recumbent abdominal-and-shoulder-blade squeeze is designed to help reeducate your golf posture and begin rebuilding two key areas of muscle strength necessary for great posture at address: your lower abs and your shoulder-blade muscles.

Perform this reeducation and rebuilding exercise as follows (and see the earlier "Physical training improves structure" section for more on these aspects of training):

1. **Assume the same starting position as for the recumbent chest and spine stretch (refer to Figure 4-5a).**

Figure 4-6:
Place a small, rolled-up towel under the middle of your spine to increase the stretch.

2. **Contract the muscles of your lower abdominals and middle and lower shoulder-blade regions so that you feel the entire length of your spine, neck, and shoulders flattening firmly to the floor.**

   If you're performing this exercise properly, you should feel a comfortable degree of muscle contraction while you maintain a normal, relaxed breathing pattern (see Figure 4-7).

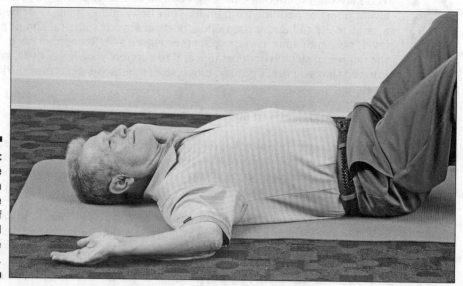

Figure 4-7:
Make sure you feel a comfortable degree of stretch and can breathe normally.

3. **Hold this contraction for three to five breaths, relax, and then repeat the exercise.**

Perform this exercise at least once every other day for two to three weeks, starting with one set of 10 repetitions and building up gradually to one set of 50 repetitions.

Exercise 3: Prone torso lift

You can further challenge your abdominal, spine, and shoulder-blade muscles with the prone torso lift. This exercise provides the same golf-specific benefits as the preceding exercise but to a more advanced degree.

Perform this exercise as follows:

1. **Lie on your stomach with several large pillows under your body and place your arms in the double tray position (from the recumbent chest-and-spine stretch) with your forehead resting on a towel roll, as shown in Figure 4-8.**

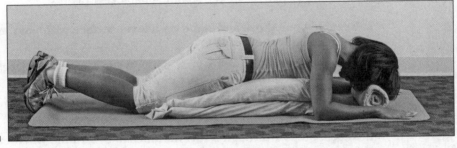

Figure 4-8:
Lie on your stomach with your forehead on a towel roll.

2. **Perform a pelvic tilt by squeezing your lower abdominal muscles and rotate your pelvis forward.**

3. **Keeping your neck long and your chin tucked, lift just your upper torso comfortably off the pillows until your spine is straight (see Figure 4-9).**

   Be sure to keep your neck tucked in and your lower back flat by contracting your lower abdominal muscles. Remember to breathe comfortably.

4. **Hold the lift for three to five breaths and then slowly relax and repeat.**

Do this exercise at least every other day for one to two sets of 8 to 12 repetitions, and for about two to three weeks or until it becomes easy.

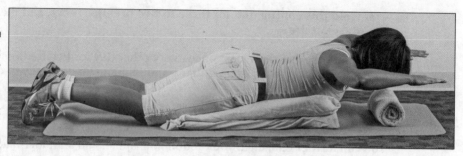

Figure 4-9: Lift your upper torso to achieve a straight spine.

Test 2: Standing balance sway

After posture, the golf swing's next most important physical characteristic is balance. The purpose of the standing balance-sway test is to help you identify muscle and connective-tissue tightness that may be pulling you out of ideal standing posture and balance, which interferes with your posture and balance at address and during your swing.

Follow these steps to tackle the standing balance-sway test:

1. **Remove your shoes and stand on a level surface with your arms hanging relaxed by your sides.**

2. **Close your eyes and relax your body; try to feel which direction your body would tend to drift, tip, or sway if you let it.**

3. **After five to ten seconds, open your eyes and identify the predominant direction of sway.**

4. **Repeat Steps 1 through 3 several times to determine whether you have a consistent direction of sway.**

Much like a tent's center pole leaning toward a support wire that's staked into the ground too tightly, your first and/or strongest direction of sway is probably caused by connective tissue and muscle tightness pulling your body in that direction. If left uncorrected, this tightness pulls you out of posture and balance at address as well as during your swing. Any attempts to correct your swing motion without first reducing the physical causes of your posture and balance dysfunction can lead to inconsistent performance or injury.

Exercise 4: Single-leg balance drill

Many exercises can improve your standing balance as a golfer. Here's a simple balance reeducation drill:

1. **Stand on a firm, flat surface.**

2. **Place a club behind your spine as though you were trying to perform the earlier "Test 1: Club behind the spine" (refer to Figure 4-4).**

3. **With your eyes open, lift your left knee to approximately 90 degrees so that your left thigh is parallel to the floor (see Figure 4-10) and try to maintain your balance in that position for 10 to 15 seconds.**

Figure 4-10:
Try to
balance for
10 to 15
seconds.

4. **Repeat Steps 1 through 3 with your left leg down, lifting your right knee to 90 degrees.**

Perform this exercise 10 to 20 times with each leg at least once each day for two to three weeks or until you do it without losing your balance on one foot for 15 seconds.

To increase the difficulty of this exercise and improve your golf balance even more, try the exercise with your eyes closed! You can imagine how much more balanced you feel at address and throughout your full swing when you can master this exercise with your eyes both open and closed.

Test 3: Seated trunk rotation

This test and the one in the following section can help you evaluate your rotation flexibility in the spine and hips. This flexibility is essential for great (and safe) golf. Without it, you can't make a complete, well-balanced swing, and you're prone to making compensations that force swing flaws such as *reverse pivots* (transferring weight forward during the backswing), *lateral sways* (moving your center of gravity off the ball), and *coming over the top* (an "outside-in" swing that causes slices). These compensations can also stress other body parts that aren't designed to rotate. If left uncorrected, this physical limitation can eventually spell disaster.

To perform this test, follow these steps:

1. **Sit forward in a stiff-backed, non-swiveling chair so that your spine isn't touching the back of the chair.**

2. **Place a golf club across the front of your chest and shoulders (at the collarbone level) and hold the club securely by crossing both hands in front of you as shown in Figure 4-11a.**

3. **Sit as tall as possible in the chair, with your feet flat on the floor and both knees pointing straight ahead, and turn your upper torso as far as comfortably possible to the right (see Figure 4-11b).**

Figure 4-11: Hold a club to your chest and shoulders and turn as far right as you comfortably can.

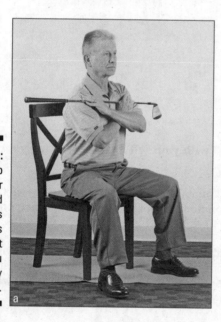

4. **When you've turned completely, look over your right shoulder, mentally mark where the end of the club is pointing, and estimate the number of degrees of rotation that you've turned to the right.**

5. **Slowly return to the neutral starting position and then repeat Steps 3 and 4 to the left.**

Repeat this test in both directions three to five times to get a good estimate of the amount of trunk rotation in each direction — and which direction you can rotate farther or more easily.

Exercise 5: Supine trunk-rotation stretch

The supine trunk rotation stretch can help improve your ability to complete a stress-free backswing and follow-through. If the seated trunk-rotation test in this section identified rotation limitations in one or both directions, this exercise can help you gain flexibility in the proper region of your spine and enable a better turn. Here's how to do it:

1. **Lie on your back with your hips and knees bent so that your feet are flat on the floor and your arms rest comfortably away from your sides in the double tray position from the earlier recumbent chest-and-spine stretch (see Figure 4-12).**

Figure 4-12: Lie on your back with your knees bent and your arms in the double tray position.

2. **Gently squeeze your shoulder blades and flatten your neck to the floor while you slowly and gently rotate your legs to the left.**

3. **Continue to slowly twist, keeping your right shoulder blade and forearm flat to the floor until you begin to feel a comfortable stretch in your spine and possibly your right hip and the front of your right shoulder (see Figure 4-13).**

4. **Hold this position for three to five minutes or until you feel a complete release of the gentle stretch in your body.**

   You can enhance the stretch in this position by bringing your left hand down from the tray position and gently pressing down on your right thigh, as shown in Figure 4-13.

Figure 4-13:
Twist your legs to the left until you feel a comfortable stretch.

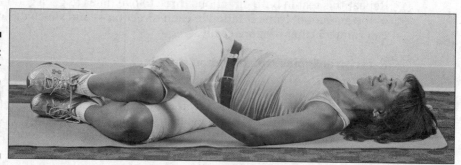

5. **Slowly return to the neutral starting position and then repeat Steps 2 through 4, rotating your legs to the right.**

Practice this exercise at least once a day for two to three weeks until you can stretch equally well in both directions. If your spine was stiffer when turning to your right during the seated trunk-rotation test, spend more time initially rotating your legs to the left, and vice versa. Your goal is balanced rotation in both directions.

Test 4: Seated hip rotation

The seated hip-rotation test is designed to measure the relative degree of rotation flexibility in your hips. It can show whether you have significant tightness in one or both hips that may be interfering with your ability to rotate them during your swing. Poor hip rotation is one of the prime causes of low-back pain for golfers and can cause poor full-swing performance.

To perform the seated hip-rotation test, follow these steps:

1. **Sit forward in a chair so that your spine isn't touching the back of the chair; sit as tall as possible with your spine straight.**

2. **Cross your left leg over your right knee so that the outer part of your left ankle rests on the top of your right knee as shown in Figure 4-14a.**

3. Without losing your sitting posture, take both hands and gently apply downward pressure to the top of your left knee until you can't comfortably push your shin any closer to a position parallel to the floor (see Figure 4-14b).

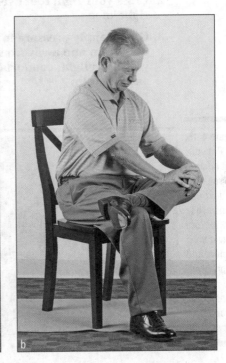

Figure 4-14:
Rest the outer part of your left ankle on your right knee and gently push your left knee toward the floor.

4. When you've reached the limit of stretch for your left hip, observe your relative difficulty in achieving this position, the location and degree of tightness in your body, and the relative angle of your left shin to the floor.

5. Slowly release your left knee and repeat Steps 2 through 4 with your right ankle resting on your left knee.

6. Compare the results of testing both hips and determine whether one or both hips have rotation-flexibility limitations.

Exercise 6: Supine hip-rotation stretch

The supine hip-rotation stretch can help you reduce hip-rotation tightness and therefore improve your ability to make a full turn around your hips during a full golf swing.

To perform this releasing exercise, follow these steps:

1. Lie on your back near a wall; place both feet on the wall so that your hips and knees are bent about 90 degrees (see Figure 4-15a).

2. Cross your right foot over your left knee and rest both hands on your right knee.

3. Gently apply pressure to your right knee with your hands in a direction down and away from your right shoulder (see Figure 4-15b) until you feel a light, comfortable stretch in the outer part of your right hip and/or groin.

Figure 4-15: Put your feet against a wall with your knees bent, cross your foot over your knee, and apply pressure on your knee until you feel a light stretch.

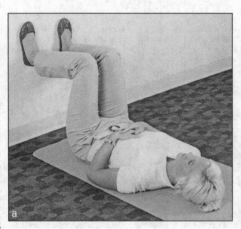

4. Hold this stretch for three to five minutes or until you feel a complete release of the original stretch in your right hip.

5. After the stretch is complete, slowly release the pressure on your right knee and repeat Steps 2 through 4 on your left hip.

Practice this releasing exercise at least once a day for two to three weeks or until you can stretch equally well in both hips. If you find one hip to be tighter than the other during the seated stretch, spend more time stretching the tighter hip. Your ultimate goal is balanced rotation for both hips. Only by achieving complete and balanced hip rotation can you achieve a full back-swing and follow-through with each and every swing.

After you're balanced, you can advance this stretch by moving your body closer to the wall at the start. This change allows your hips and knees to bend at an angle greater than 90 degrees, for more stretch in your hips.

Core Exercises for More Power and Less Pain

The world's top golfers now understand that the large muscles of the torso — the *core* — are the key to increasing power while reducing the risk of lower-back injury. This knowledge is the most important advancement in golf fitness of the past 50 years. As Tiger Woods and every other strong young golfer has proved, a full, powerful rotation of the core muscles is the ultimate key to the power and precision that make great golf possible.

Here are six core exercises that can complement and enhance the other exercises in this chapter, adding core strength and stability to the posture and hip and spine flexibility you've (hopefully) already developed.

Downward belly burners

Downward belly burners can improve your core muscle strength, promote your ability to achieve and maintain an optimal spine angle at address and throughout your full golf swing, and provide significant increases in swing speed that translate into increased power.

Follow these steps to take on this exercise:

1. **Kneel on a padded surface and rest both forearms on an exercise ball (see Figure 4-16a).**

   Keep your back straight enough that a golf club can touch your lower back, upper back, and the back of your head.

2. **Do a neutral pelvic tilt, exhale, and slowly roll the ball forward, extending your hips and shoulders equally, as far as possible, until you feel a strong but comfortable abdominal, chest, and shoulder muscle contraction (see Figure 4-16b).**

3. **Inhale as you slowly roll the ball and pull your body back to the starting position.**

Do one to three sets of 10 to 15 repetitions one to three times per day.

Figure 4-16: Kneel against an exercise ball and then shift forward.

Superman

The superman drill improves your core strength, posture, and balance control, and strengthens your upper back and shoulders. It also improves your ability to maintain a proper spine angle, to stay balanced over the ball, and to make a consistent full swing.

To perform this exercise:

1. **Lie face down over an exercise ball and do a neutral pelvic tilt while holding a club in the tray position (Figure 4-17a).**

   I describe the tray position in "Test 1: Club behind the spine" earlier in the chapter.

2. **Maintain the pelvic tilt and then retract your shoulder blades together and reach your arms over head with your elbows as straight as possible (Figure 4-17b); hold this position for one breath and then bring your arms back to the tray position.**

Do 10 to 30 repetitions of this exercise one to three times a day. When you've mastered it, increase the difficulty by holding hand weights instead of the club.

Figure 4-17: From the tray position, bring your arms up and then back down.

Russian twists

The Russian twist improves your upper and oblique abdominal muscle strength. It also helps you fully turn your shoulders without turning your lower body, which improves your swing speed and power and distance off the tee.

To perform this exercise,

1. **Lie on your back over an exercise ball with a soccer ball, volleyball, or kickball between your knees.**

2. **Hold a weighted medicine ball in your hands with your arms pointed straight up from your chest toward the ceiling.**

3. **As you exhale, slowly rotate your upper torso as far as possible in one direction, keeping your arms in front of your chest as shown in Figure 4-18.**

   Then slowly rotate your upper torso as far as possible in the opposite direction.

Figure 4-18: Rotate as far as possible in one direction.

Do one to three sets of 10 to 15 repetitions one to three times a day. When you're ready to advance, increase the weight of the medicine ball and/or the speed of your upper body rolls.

Seated torso rotations

Seated torso rotations can improve your posture, balance, and core muscle strength. They can help you make a more complete shoulder turn in your full swing, and improve your ability to maintain arm and club connection in front of your body throughout the full swing. Equally important, they can reduce stress and injury potential to your neck, shoulders, arms, and lower back when you play golf. Here's how they work:

1. **Attach fitness tubing with handles around a fixed pole (or in a closed door) and position an exercise ball so that the tubing is at chest height as you sit on the ball, with no slack in the tubing.**

   You want the tubing at an approximately 30- to 45-degree angle to your left. Make sure your exercise ball is inflated so that your hips and knees are bent to 90 degrees when you sit on it.

2. **Hold both handles of the tubing with your arms pulled to the center of your chest as shown in Figure 4-19a.**

3. **Sit tall and perform a neutral pelvic tilt, squeezing your shoulder blades together and, as you exhale, slowly rotating your upper torso as far as possible to the right (see Figure 4-19b).**

 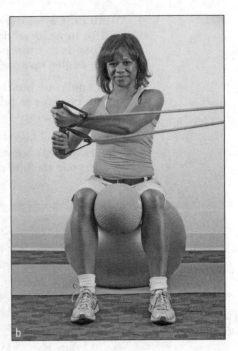

Figure 4-19:
Hold the
tubing in
front of your
chest and
then rotate.

4. **Hold this rotated position for one breath and then inhale as you relax your upper torso back to the starting position.**

Perform one to three sets of 10 to 15 repetitions in both directions one to three times per day. When you're ready to do more, stretch the tubing farther to add stretch resistance to the tubing, or invest in tubing with greater resistance.

As you gain flexibility, you can advance this exercise by extending your arms in front of your chest at the end of your full shoulder turn. You can also perform the exercise while standing.

Bow-and-arrow twister

The bow-and-arrow twister can improve the strength of your core, hips, chest, shoulders, arms, hands, and spine-rotation muscles, as well as your ability to maintain a proper spine angle during your swing. It can also help you make a more powerful shoulder turn during your backswing and follow-through while reducing muscle stress and the risk of injury.

To perform this exercise, follow these steps:

1. Attach fitness tubing with handles in a low position around a fixed pole (or in a closed door) and stand in your golf address position with your hands in front of your body (as shown in Figure 4-20a) so that the tubing angles up approximately 45 to 60 degrees with no slack.

2. Slowly pull one hand toward your body, rotating your spine and shoulders as far as possible while keeping your hips and legs stable (see Figure 4-20b).

   You should feel like you're pulling the string back on a bow to shoot an arrow. Hold this position for one breath and then inhale as you relax back to your starting position.

Figure 4-20: From your address position, pull back and rotate your shoulders.

Do one to three sets of 10 to 15 repetitions in both directions one to three times a day. To add difficulty, stretch the tubing farther, or invest in more-resistant tubing.

Medicine ball twists

Medicine ball twists can improve your core and spinal-rotation strength as well as your posture and balance control. They can also strengthen your arms, shoulders, hips, and legs and improve your ability to maintain a proper spine angle, which creates greater stability over the ball and a more consistent swing path. They can even help you add clubhead speed, for more distance.

To try this exercise, check out the following steps:

1. **Assume your normal posture at address while holding a weighted medicine ball.**

2. **Perform a neutral pelvic tilt and shoulder-blade squeeze and slowly rotate your spine and torso to the right, keeping the medicine ball in front of your chest throughout the full turn as you see in Figure 4-21.**

Figure 4-21:
Rotate while keeping the medicine ball in front of your chest.

3. **Hold this fully rotated position for one breath and then slowly rotate as far as you can to the left.**

Perform 10 to 30 repetitions one to three times per day. When you're ready to do more, gradually increase the weight of the medicine ball. Other ways to advance this exercise are to

✔ Increase the speed of your torso rotations.

✔ Stand on half-foam rolls or any other unstable base — but be sure you maintain a stable lower body.

Chapter 5

Where to Play and How to Fit In

Golfers play in three main settings: at public facilities, private clubs, and on resort courses. In this chapter, I tell you the basics about all three, from the scuzziest driving range to the fanciest country club. I also share tips on how to fit in wherever you play — how to walk, talk, tip, dress, and accessorize like a *real* golfer. I even tell you how to make the best of a round with a jerk. You don't find many jerks in this game — most golfers are great company — but you've gotta be ready for anything.

Exploring Your Golf-Course Options

Start with the basics: Where in the world can you play golf?

Some courses have only 9 holes, while a few resorts offer half a dozen 18-hole courses, or even more. At the famous Pinehurst Resort in North Carolina, you can find eight great 18-hole layouts, including Pinehurst No. 2, one of the finest in the world. (Check out Chapter 22 for more on this and other amazing courses.) China's gigantic Mission Hills Golf Club, the world's largest, features a dozen courses — that's 216 chances to drive yourself nuts!

You can also hit balls at driving ranges, which is how you should start, and gradually work up to a par-3 course, building your confidence level before you play a regulation 18-hole course. If you rush to the nearest course for your first try at golf, tee off, and then spend most of the next few hours missing the ball, you won't be very popular with your fellow golfers. Believe me, they'd rather enjoy a cool beverage in the clubhouse than watch you move large clumps of earth with every swing.

Driving ranges

Driving ranges are basically large fields stretching as far as 400 yards in length. Driving ranges are fun. You can make all the mistakes you want. You can miss the ball, slice it, duff it, top it — do anything. The only people who know are the ones next to you, and they're probably making the same mistakes.

Because driving ranges are often quite long, even Tiger Woods or long-drive king Jamie Sladowski can "let the shaft out" and swing for the fences. But you don't have to hit your driver. Any good driving range has signs marking off 50 yards, 100 yards, 150 yards, and so on. You can practice hitting to these targets with any club.

Many driving ranges lend or rent you clubs, though some expect you to bring your own. As for balls, you purchase bucketfuls for a few dollars — how *many* dollars depends on where you are. In some parts of the United States, you can still hit a bucket of balls for a dollar. But on weekends at Chelsea Piers Golf Club in New York City, it's a lot more: up to 25 times as much. (At least you get a great view of New Jersey. . . .)

Public courses

As you'd expect from their name, public courses are open to anyone who can afford the *green fee,* or the cost to play a round of golf (commonly, but incorrectly, known as the *greens fee*). They tend to be busy, especially on weekends and holidays. At premier public courses like New York's Bethpage Black, the site of the 2009 U.S. Open, some golfers sleep in their cars overnight so they can be first in line for a tee time the next morning. Sleeping in a car may not sound like much fun, but I'm told it's a great bonding experience.

The 21st century is proving to be a great time for public courses. Chambers Bay, a spectacular new facility near Tacoma, Washington, will host the 2015 U.S. Open, joining Bethpage Black and another famous municipal course, San Diego's venerable Torrey Pines, in the Open rotation.

Green fees

As for cost, the price depends on the course and its location. Some humble rural courses charge as little as $10 — and you pay on the honor system, dropping your money into a box! The best public courses can be hard to get on, and they aren't cheap, but most players will tell you they're worth the effort and expense. Upscale public facilities, even those with no hope of ever hosting a U.S. Open, routinely charge $100 and up. Green fees at Chambers Bay, for example, range from $89 to $175. At gorgeous Pebble Beach Golf Links in California, where the green fee way back in the 1950s was a bargain at $5, it's now $495! At least they give you free tees.

Tee-time policies

Each course has its own tee-time rules. Many let you book a time weeks in advance. Others follow a strange rule: You must show up at a designated time midweek to sign up for weekend play. And some courses you can't book at all — you just show up and take your chance (hence, the overnight gang sleeping in their cars). My advice is simple: Phone ahead and find out the policy at the course you want to play.

I'm here! Now what?

You've jumped through whatever hoops are necessary to establish a tee time (see the preceding section) and you know when you're supposed to play. So you pull into the parking lot about an hour before your tee time. That way, you have time to stretch and warm up before you play. What next? Most courses feature a clubhouse. You may want to stop inside to change clothes and maybe buy something to eat or drink.

By all means, make use of the clubhouse, but don't change your shoes in there. If you're already dressed to hit the greens, put on your golf shoes in the parking lot. Then throw your street shoes into the trunk. Don't worry about looking goofy as you lace those spikes with your foot on the car bumper. It's a golf tradition!

The first thing to do at the clubhouse is to find the pro shop. Confirm your time with the pro or *starter* (the person sending groups off from the first tee), and then pay for your round. The pro is sure to be in one of two places: teaching on the practice range or hanging out in the pro shop. If the pro doesn't collect your money, the starter adjacent to the first tee usually does.

After the financial formalities are out of the way, hit some balls on the driving range to warm up those creaky joints of yours.

Your practice sessions may not be as long as mine, but then you're not trying to figure out how to beat Fred Couples on the Champions Tour!

Here's what I do when I'm playing in a pro event: I get to the course one hour before my starting time. I go to the putting green and practice short shots — chip shots and short pitches. (Chapter 8 covers these shots in detail.) Doing so gives me an idea how fast the greens are and loosens me up for full-swing shots.

Make sure that you're allowed to pitch to the practice green on your course — some courses prohibit it.

Then I wander over to the practice tee and loosen up with some of the exercises that I describe in Part II. Start with the wedges and work your way up to the driver.

Next, I hit my 3-wood (some players call this titanium club the *3-metal* — a more accurate term, but it clangs in my ears). Then I proceed to bomb the driver. (If "Boom Boom" Couples is next to me, I quietly wait for him to finish, and *then* I hit my driver.) Immediately after hitting practice drives — ten balls at most — I hit some short sand-wedge shots to slow down my metabolism.

I revisit the putting green next, usually 15 minutes before I tee off. (See Chapter 9 for more about putting.) I start with simple 2- to 3-foot putts straight up a hill, to build my confidence. Then I proceed to very long putts — aiming not for the hole, but for the far fringe of the green. I do that because I don't want to become target-conscious on long putts. Putting the ball to the fringe lets me work on speed. It's the last thing I do before going to the tee. (Well, if it's a big tournament and my knees are shaking, I may make a detour to the restroom.)

Country clubs

In your early days as a golfer, you probably won't play much at country clubs. If you *do* play at a country club — maybe a friend who's a member invites you — it can be intimidating! But don't panic. You're still playing golf; the "goal posts" have just shifted slightly.

To avoid committing any social faux pas, remember a few formalities:

✔ **Before you leave home, make sure you're wearing the right clothes.** Those cool (in your mind, anyway) cutoff jeans or a sweatshirt announcing you as an avid follower of the Chicago Bulls don't work in this environment. Wear a shirt with a collar and, if shorts are allowed, go for the tailored variety that stops just short of your knees. Short shorts are a no-no at most country clubs. In the fall and winter, slacks are acceptable for women. In the summer, shorts cut just above the knees are fine. When in doubt, call the club and ask.

✔ **Get good directions to your destination.** A stressful journey full of wrong turns doesn't do your heart rate or your golf game any good.

✔ **Time your arrival so that you have just an hour to spare before you tee off.** When you drive your car up the road toward the clubhouse, don't make the simple mistake of turning sharply into the parking lot. Go right up to the clubhouse. Look for a sign that reads "Bag Drop." A person is no doubt waiting to greet you. Acknowledge his cheery hello as if you're doing something you do every day. Tell him who you're playing with (the club member who's hosting you). Then get out of your car, pop the trunk, remove your spikes and hand him your keys. Tip him a few bucks (or a $5 bill at a fancy club like Trump International), and stroll into the clubhouse.

Don't worry about your car or your clubs. The car will be parked for you, and the clubs will either be loaded onto a cart or handed to a caddie.

✔ **Don't try to pay for your round.** Most country clubs won't take your money. The club member who's hosting you signs for everything except tips and pro-shop merchandise. Of course, you're free to settle up with him or her on your own — that's between the two of you.

✔ **Once you're inside the clubhouse, head for the locker room.** Drop your street shoes off next to your host's locker and then ask for directions to the bar, or to wherever your host is waiting. Don't offer to buy your host a drink. Your host most likely signs the tab and gets billed at the end of the month. (The one place where your cash or plastic is accepted is the pro shop. The pro will sell you anything, but take my advice: Skip the purchase of that neat-looking shirt with the club logo on it. Every time you wear it, people will assume you're a member there. The questions soon get old.)

✔ **If you have a caddie, remember that he or she is there to help you.** Trust your caddie's advice — he or she knows the course better than you do. Caddie fees at fancy clubs average about $50, which is added to your green fee. You should tip your caddie half the caddie fee at the end of the round, so that's another $25. (Savvy golfers sometimes tip the caddie master before a round — slipping him a $10 bill can get you the best caddie he's got.)

✔ **On the course, be yourself.** And don't worry about shooting the best round of golf you've ever played. Your host doesn't expect that. Even if you happen to play badly, he won't be too bothered as long as you look like you're having fun and keep trying. Just don't complain or make excuses. Nobody likes a whiner.

✔ **After your round, your clubs will probably disappear again, but don't worry: They'll be waiting at the bag drop when you finish your post-round beverage.** Don't forget to tip the bag handlers. Again, a few bucks is usually fine, but be generous if your clubs have been cleaned.

✔ **When you change back into your street shoes, you'll often find them newly polished — that means another few dollars to tip the locker-room attendant.** And when you leave, your golf shoes will have been done, too. Aren't country clubs grand?

✔ **One more tip to go: Give a few bucks to the person who delivers your car back to you and loads your clubs into the trunk.**

Resort courses

You're on vacation, and you're dying to play golf. Where to go? To a resort course, of course. Some of my favorites are Kapalua Resort (Maui, Hawaii), Doral Golf Resort & Spa (Miami, Florida), and Sea Pines Resort (Hilton Head Island, South Carolina).

The great thing about resort courses is that you don't have to be a member or even have one in tow. The only problem arises when you aren't staying in the right place. Some courses are for certain hotel guests only. And again, prices vary, depending on the course and its location. Generally, though, resort courses cost a good deal more than public courses.

Phone ahead of time to find out when you can play.

Resort courses are a lot like public courses, but some have bag handlers and other employees who expect a tip. Tip as you would at a country club (see the preceding section).

You probably have to rent a cart, too. Carts are mandatory at most resort golf courses. So enjoy the ride! You can drive to your drive and then hop back behind the wheel and putt-putt to your putt.

Getting a Deal on Memberships or Green Fees

Back in the go-go 1990s, hardly anyone thought to ask, "Can I get a discount on that country-club membership?" That'd be like asking for a free air-freshener in a new Lamborghini. But times change, and when the economy slows down, the prices of upscale items like club memberships and resort-course green fees sometimes come down, too. That can work to the advantage of you, the smart golfer. In the following sections, I give you some insight into scoring deals on playing golf.

Making the club scene more affordable

The game's most elite clubs never seem to suffer. You don't see members complaining about the cost of belonging to Augusta National, where the pros play the Masters every spring, or Sebonack Golf Club in Southampton, New York, where joining may set you back a cool $1 million. But at other clubs, including some terrific ones, tougher times bring opportunity. Several years ago, the beautiful Newport Beach Country Club in southern California (where yours truly won the 1999 Toshiba Senior Classic) cut its initiation fee from $42,000 to $5,000 for players between 21 and 37 years old. The club wanted to attract younger members who'd keep coming back for decades, and it worked.

Many other clubs reduced their initiation fees from $5,000, $10,000, or even more to nothing. That's right — you could join for free, as long as you paid your monthly dues of a few hundred dollars.

You see, country clubs rely on much more than upfront fees. They need to sell clubs, balls, and shirts in the pro shop, burgers in the grill room, and drinks in the bar. Their caddies need bags to carry.

And this area is one in which golf, which is often seen as the preserve of old white men, may be changing for the better. Many clubs are more eager than ever to welcome younger, minority, and female players.

So if you're thinking of joining a country club, shop around. Don't be afraid to ask whether you can get reduced or waived initiation fees. Tough economic times affect almost everybody — they may just smile and say, "Join the club."

Saving at resorts and public courses

The same belt-tightening that squeezes country clubs hits golf resorts and high-end public courses, too. So when you call to arrange a tee time, don't hesitate to haggle. You may say, "I'm bringing two foursomes. Can you give us a price break?" Or, "I'd love to play there, but your green fees are a little high for me."

Asking (politely) never hurts. Even if the answer is no, you can ask, "Can you steer me to a nice course that's a little more affordable?" You may discover a hidden gem.

Most public facilities and resorts offer *twilight rates*. You tee off in the late afternoon, paying half to two-thirds the usual green fee. Even if you don't finish before dark, you experience a course you may want to play again.

Fitting In on the Course

It all starts at the first tee. I cover the gambling aspect of this initial get-together in Chapter 15, but you should know some other things as well.

If you're playing with friends, you don't need any help from me. You know them, and they know you. You should be able to come up with a game by yourselves. And you can say anything to them, with no risk of offending anyone.

That's not the case if you show up looking for a game. Say you're at a public course and you've asked the starter to squeeze you in (a few bucks in the starter's hand may get you going sooner rather than later). Tell the starter your skill level — and be honest. If you're a beginner, you don't want to be thrown in with three low-handicap players; you'll feel intimidated, probably won't enjoy the round as well, and may even slow up the pace of play. Forget all that talk about how golf's handicap system allows anyone to play with anyone. That propaganda doesn't take human nature into account. (I discuss the handicap system in Chapter 14.)

Golf, like life, has its share of snobs. And some of the worst are single-digit handicappers. Most of them have no interest in playing with a mere beginner. They may say they do, but they're lying. They see 18 holes with someone who can't break 100 as four to five hours of torture. The same is true on the PGA Tour. Some pros genuinely enjoy the Wednesday pro-ams — Mark O'Meara comes to mind — but many would gladly skip them if they could. (They can't, because the tour requires pros to show up for *pro-ams,* tournaments where pros play with amateurs.) That may seem like a rotten attitude, but it's a fact of golfing life. No one will actually *say* anything to you (golf pros are generally much too polite), but the attitude is there. Get used to it.

Maybe I'm being a little harsh, but it's a fact that golfers are more comfortable playing with their "own kind." Watch a few groups play off the first tee, and you soon spot a trend. Almost every foursome consists of four players of relatively equal ability. That happens for a reason. Make that two reasons: No one wants to be the weak link in the chain. And no one wants to play with "hackers who can't keep up." Of course a beginner *can* play as quickly as an expert golfer, but that's not a challenge you need at this stage.

So say the starter groups you with Gary, Jack, and Arnold. Introduce yourself calmly but quickly. Tell them what you normally shoot, if and when they ask, and make it clear that you're a relatively new golfer. This fact is impossible to conceal, so don't try. But don't volunteer any further information. Save that for during the round. Besides, you find that most golfers are selfish — they really don't care about your game. They make polite noises after your shots, but that's the extent of their interest. You'll soon be that way, too. Nothing — *nothing* — is more boring than listening to tales about someone else's round or game. Of course, boring your buddies that way is part of the social order of this game. Golf stories are endless, and most are embellished, but they promote the bonding done over beers in the clubhouse bar, which is also called the *19th hole.*

Beginners sometimes do things that mark them as misfits on the course. Avoid these blunders at all costs:

- ✔ **Don't carry one of those telescoping ball retrievers in your bag.** It suggests that you're planning to hit balls in the water.

- ✔ **Don't wear your golf cap backward.** Ever. No exceptions.

- ✔ **Don't do stretching exercises on the first tee.** Find a place a few yards away, where you don't look like you're auditioning for *The Biggest Loser.*

- ✔ **Don't dawdle — when it's your turn to hit, be ready!**

When You're the Worst in Your Group

Early in your golfing existence, almost everyone is better than you. So you'll probably spend some rounds as the worst player in your foursome. What do you do? This section gives you some survival tips.

Pick it up!

The worst thing you can do is delay your playing partners. After you've hit the ball, oh, nine times on a given hole, pick it up and quit that hole as a courtesy to your playing partners. There's always the next hole.

When you're actually scoring a game, you're required to finish out every hole — that is, you must post a score for each hole. But beginners should feel free to skip that technicality. While you're learning, don't worry about scores.

Find your own ball

This idea comes under the "don't delay" heading. If you happen to hit a shot into the highest spinach patch on the course, don't let your companions help you look for it. Tell them to play on and that you'll catch up after a "quick look." They'll see you as someone who, though having a bad day, would be worth playing with again. (If you don't find the ball within a couple of minutes, declare it lost — put an *X* on your scorecard for that hole.)

Never moan, never analyze

Don't be a pain in the you-know-what. Most golfers gripe and moan when they're playing poorly. That's bad — and boring for the other players, who don't want to hear about your woes. All they care about is the fact that you're slowing things up. So grit your teeth and keep moving.

Analyzing your swing is another common crime: You hit a few bad shots — okay, more than a few. Then you say, "Maybe if I just turn a little more through the ball. . . ." That's the *last* thing your playing partners want to hear. I repeat: *They don't care about your game.* So don't analyze, and don't ask them for swing tips. If one is offered, try it, but keep it quiet.

When You're Not the Worst

How do you behave when another golfer in your group can't get the ball above shin height? Here are some pointers:

- **Zip that lip.** Whatever you do, don't try to encourage your pal as his or her game implodes. After a while, you run out of things to say, and your friend gets annoyed with you.

- **Never give advice or swing tips to the other player.** The other person will only blame you for the next bad shot he or she hits.

- **Talk about other stuff.** The last thing you should discuss is your pal's awful game. Find some common interest and chat about that. Try football, movies, or the stock market. Even politics and religion are safer topics than that 20-yard drive your friend just dribbled off the tee.

Avoiding Playing with a Jerk (And Coping If It Happens Anyway)

Most golfers are princes — tall, smart, and handsome (with or without handlebar mustaches). The game not only tests character but also builds character. I'm willing to bet that you find fewer louts and scoundrels in golf than in any other major sport. But with more than 25 million American golfers out there, you're bound to encounter a few bad apples. Here's how to avoid a rotten matchup and deal with one that comes along despite your best efforts.

Who not to play with

As I mention earlier in the chapter, most foursomes are made up of players of roughly equal ability. That's what you want. In fact, the best scenario is to find three golfers who are just a little bit better than you. By trying to keep up with them, you'll probably improve your usual game.

Those are the sorts of people you should be playing with. The people you shouldn't be playing with are those who play a "different game." That means anyone who shoots more than 20 shots lower than you on an average day. All someone like that does is depress you, and your slower, less-expert play may irritate him or her. Such a situation can bring out the jerk in both of you. So stay away from the best golfers at your course — at least for now. When you get better, playing with them can help you improve.

How to endure

Sometimes you can't help it — you're stuck with a loud, cursing lunkhead who talks during your swing, jabbers on his or her cellphone, and gives everyone unsolicited advice. How to deal?

- ✔ **At first, ignore the jerk.** It's a beautiful day, and you're out on the course playing the best game in the world. Play your game and be glad you're only spending a few hours with Golfzilla. If the jerk's behavior annoys the other members of your group, let them be first to call him or her on it.

- ✔ **If the jerk keeps it up, speak up.** Being firm but polite often works with jerks. Say, "You walked on my putting line — please don't." Or, "You're distracting me by talking on your cellphone."

- ✔ **Treat the jerk as a hazard.** If all else fails, think of Golfzilla the way you think of a strong wind or a lousy lie in a bunker. Golf is all about dealing with adversity. If you can keep your wits and make a good swing despite the jerk, you'll be a tougher, better golfer next time out.

Part II
Getting Into the Swing

"The only thing that will improve Greg's performance around the greens is a prescription for Prozac."

In this part . . .

How can the golf swing, something that takes a little over one second to perform, be so complicated to learn? Do you need to go back to school and study theoretical physics? No. Just enroll here, and I'll make it easy for you.

This part shows you how to swing a golf club the simple, effective way. I show you how to build your swing and then how to do everything from knocking your drive off the opening tee to hitting bunker shots (they're easier than they look) to brushing that three-foot putt into the 18th hole for your par.

Chapter 6

Swing Basics

As the great golf expert Duke Ellington once said, "It don't mean a thing if you ain't got that swing." You can be the most stylish-looking golfer in the world, swinging the most expensive driver at the most exclusive club, but without a sound fundamental swing, you're on the A train to nowhere. This chapter helps you get into the swing of golf.

Understanding Swing Basics

What is a golf swing? That's a very good question, one that has different answers for different people. For most folks, a golf swing means "body parts moving in an undignified manner."

In simple terms, though, a *golf swing* is a (hopefully) coordinated, balanced movement of the whole body around a fixed pivot point. If you do it correctly, this motion swings an implement of destruction (the club) up, around, and down so that it strikes the ball with an accelerating blow on the center of the clubface. I'm starting to feel dizzy. How about you?

Balance is the key to this whole swing thing. You can't play golf with consistency if at any time during your swing, you fall over. In contrast, when your swing consists of a simple pivot around a fixed point, the clubhead strikes the ball on the same downward path and somewhere near the center of the clubface every time. Bingo!

You're probably wondering where this fixed point in your body is. Well, it isn't your head. It's a myth that you must keep your head perfectly still throughout the swing. I don't advise you to try, unless you've got a chiropractor on retainer.

The fixed point in your golf swing should be in the middle of your chest, about three inches below the spot where your collarbones meet, as shown in Figure 6-1. Your swing rotates around that point. If you get that pivot point correct, your head swivels a little bit as you turn back and then through on your shots. If your head moves like Linda Blair's did in *The Exorcist,* you may have a career in the circus, but not in golf.

Your "fixed point" is 3 inches below the middle of your collarbones.

Your head swivels to the right as you swing back . . .

then through . . .

all the way to the finish.

Figure 6-1:
The proper swing pivot point.

Examining Different Strokes

You can swing the club effectively in many ways. For example, there are long swings and short swings. Imagine that you've backed into a giant clock. Your head is just below the center of the clock. If, at the top of your swing, your hands are at 9 o'clock and the clubhead is at 3 o'clock, you're in the standard position. The shaft is parallel to the ground. This is the standard, medium-length swing.

At the top of Jamie Sadlowski's much longer swing, his hands are at 12 o'clock, and the clubhead is approaching 5 o'clock. Other swings have a shorter arc. John Cook succeeded on the PGA Tour with a short swing. His hands only go to 8 o'clock, and the clubhead goes to 1 o'clock. Adam Scott stops short of parallel because he feels that his swing gets *loose* — more erratic — if he goes farther. Physical constraints dictate the fullness and length of your swing; the distance the club travels is unimportant. Any of these swings can work for a particular golfer, depending on his or her training, physique, and even personality.

Golf swings differ in other ways, too.

- Some players swing the club more around their bodies — the way you'd swing a baseball bat.
- Others rely more on their hands and arms to generate clubhead speed.
- Still others place that same emphasis on twisting and untwisting the body.

Physique and flexibility play a major role in how you swing a golf club. If you're short, you have a *flatter* swing — more around your body — because your back is closer to perpendicular at *address* (the motionless position as you stand ready to hit the ball). If you're tall, you either use longer clubs or bend more from the waist at address. Most tall players develop upright swings.

The left arm always swings about 90 degrees to the angle of the spine. Stand straight up and put your left arm straight out in front of you. Now start bending at the waist. See how your arm lowers? It's staying 90 degrees to your back as you bend downward. I wish I'd taken more geometry in school!

Flight School: Getting the Ball in the Air

Although you can swing a golf club in many ways, all good swings have the same goals:

- ✔ You want to hit the ball.
- ✔ You want to get the ball up in the air and moving forward.
- ✔ You want to hit the ball a long way.
- ✔ You want to hit the ball toward your target.
- ✔ You want to hit the ball a long way toward your target while your friends are watching.
- ✔ You become obsessed, just like the rest of us.

Okay, maybe that last one shouldn't exactly be a goal, but if you spend much time at all playing golf, you may find yourself fixating on your ball's flight (or lack thereof). Lucky for you, the following sections give you the lowdown on getting the ball off the ground and moving in the right direction.

Hitting the ball

You'd think hitting the ball would be easy. But golf isn't tennis or baseball, where you can react to a moving ball. In golf, the ball just sits there and waits, beckoning you to make it go somewhere.

Here's your first thought: "I won't turn my body too much; I'll just hit the thing with my hands." That's natural — and wrong. You're worried about losing sight of the ball in your backswing and hitting nothing but air. You're not alone. All golfers have been through this sweat-drenched nightmare of flailing failure. But don't worry. You will evolve! You will make contact!

TIP

More power for women!

I've seen plenty of female golfers with tremendous power — women from Mickey Wright to Laura Davies to Michelle Wie. But for the most part, female golfers struggle to generate power. The average woman simply doesn't have the same upper-body, forearm, and wrist strength as a man. Much to her dismay, she finds it physically impossible to drive the ball 300 yards.

But with a few simple strengthening and conditioning exercises (see Chapter 4), female golfers — or any golfers — can strengthen their upper bodies, wrists, core, and forearms enough to boost the power in their swings.

Here's one simple exercise that improves wrist strength — and you can do it almost anywhere. Take a tennis ball in your hand and squeeze until it hurts. Then switch hands and do the same thing. You don't have to give yourself carpal tunnel syndrome — just repeat this exercise for at least five minutes with each hand. You'll notice gradual improvement in your wrist and forearm strength, which will help you avoid wrist injury and arm fatigue — and add precious yards to your drives.

Getting the ball airborne

Okay, after a few fairly fruitless attempts, you're finally hitting more ball than air. Now you need to understand the aerodynamics of the game. The only time you want the golf ball to be on the ground is when you're close to the hole. To have any kind of fun the rest of the time, you want air under the ball; you need the ball to fly! Then you can stare with horrified fascination at the ridiculous places the ball goes, which is the essence of the game.

One of my *Golf For Dummies* secrets is that the only time you should lift something is when you rearrange your living-room furniture. *Never* try to lift a golf ball with your club. Hit down with every club except the driver and the putter, as shown in Figure 6-2. And when you do hit down, don't duck or lunge at the ball; hit down but keep your head up.

When you use your driver, the ball is set on a tee about an inch above the ground; if you hit down, the ball flies off the top part of the club and the shot is high and short — the dreaded pop-up! With the driver, you want the clubhead moving into the ball on a horizontal path, slightly upward at impact.

When you putt, you don't want the ball airborne. A putter is designed to roll the ball along the ground, so you need a more horizontal hit with that club. (See Chapter 9 for information on putting.)

Figure 6-2:
Hit down to make the ball go up.

Generating power

As soon as the ball is in the air, your ego kicks in. Power with a capital *P* becomes your concern. Power intoxicates your mind. Power makes legends out of mere mortals. Power makes you want to get a tattoo. Power also sends the ball to bad corners of your little green world if you don't harness it.

Some professional golfers can create as much as 4½ horsepower in their swings. That's some kind of giddy-up. The ball leaves their drivers at speeds of more than 150 miles per hour. This power comes from a blending of the body twisting around a slightly moving pivot point with a swinging of the arms and hands up and around on the backswing, and then down and around in the forward swing. All of this occurs in the space of about a second!

To optimize power, try to turn your back to the target on your backswing (see Figure 6-3). This move involves another *Golf For Dummies* must-do: On the backswing, turn your left shoulder under your chin until the shoulder is above your right foot. Make sure to turn your shoulders far enough. Don't just raise your arms. Turning your shoulders ensures that you have power for the forward move. The unwinding of the hips and the shoulders on the downswing creates a power surge.

Figure 6-3:
On the backswing, turn your left shoulder over your right foot.

The same swing principles apply for women. However, to build momentum and swing speed, ladies generally rely less on muscle and more on a longer backswing. A long backswing allows full rotation in the left shoulder, which allows the left arm to extend and cocks the wrist to help release power.

Building Your Swing

To become a golfer, you must master the building blocks of your swing. How do you hold the club so that you can give the ball a good whack? After you have a good grip, how do you align yourself to the target so that the ball goes somewhere near where you aimed? What should your posture look like? How much knee flex should you have, and where in the world should the ball be in your stance? Should you look at the ball or somewhere near the sun? This section has the answers.

For natural left-handers, perfecting the golf swing can be tricky. In the past, not many clubs were designed for lefties, and most course designs put left-handed golfers at a disadvantage. As a result, many lefties learned to play right-handed. Today, however, technology has advanced to the point where left-handers have little trouble finding clubs.

Whether you swing left-handed or right-handed basically all comes down to which side has the stronger, most natural-feeling swing. To find out what works best for you, try swinging the club like a baseball bat from each side (keeping a safe distance from all breakable objects and small children). The muscles used in swinging a bat are similar to those used in a golf swing, so whichever side gives you a more powerful baseball swing is likely your best golf-swing side. Which reminds me of what Sam Snead said when a baseball slugger told him that hitting a baseball was harder than playing golf: "Maybe, but I have to play my foul balls."

This section covers a lot of stuff, and it doesn't even have you take a cut at the ball yet. That's how important these pre-swing routines are. After you get yourself in position to move the club away from the ball, you can forget your address position and concentrate on your swing.

Getting a grip

Although the grip is one of the most important parts of the game, it's also one of the most boring. Few golfers who've played for any length of time pay much attention to hand placement. For one thing, your grip is hard to change after you get used to the way your hands feel on the club. For another, hand placement simply doesn't seem as important as the swing itself. That kind of neglect and laziness is why you see so many bad grips — particularly among bad players.

HAZARD

Get your grip correct and close to orthodox at the beginning of your golfing career. You can fake just about anything, but a bad grip follows you to the grave.

Women tend to have smaller hands than men, so for them, having the right grip size on the club is important. By *grip size,* I mean the width of the rubber (occasionally leather) handle on the club, which is generally smaller for women. Another tip for ladies is to use the closed-face grip position, which can help square the clubface during the swing.

Here's how to sleep well in eternity with the correct grip. Standing upright, let your arms hang naturally by your side. Get someone to place a club in your left hand. All you do now is grab the club and — *voilà!* — you've got your left-hand grip. Well, almost. The grip has three checkpoints:

1. **Place your left thumb and left index finger on the shaft.**

   I like to see a gap of about ¾ of an inch between the thumb and index finger. To get that gap, extend your thumb down the shaft a little. If extending your thumb proves too uncomfortable, pull your thumb in toward your hand. Three-quarters of an inch is only a guide, so you have some leeway. But remember: The farther your thumb extends down the shaft, the longer your swing. And the opposite is also true: Short thumb means short swing. (See Figure 6-4 for a visual of these extensions.)

Long thumb – long swing

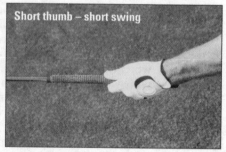
Short thumb – short swing

Figure 6-4:
Long thumb, short thumb.

2. **Make sure the grip crosses the base of your last three fingers and the middle of your index finger, as shown in Figure 6-5.**

   This step is vital. If you grip the club too much in the palm, you hinder your ability to hinge your wrist and use your hands effectively in the swing. More of a finger grip makes cocking the wrist on the backswing, hitting the ball, and then recocking the wrist on the follow-through easy. Just be sure that the *V* formed between your thumb and forefinger points toward your right ear.

Figure 6-5:
Grip more in
the fingers
of the left
hand than in
the palm.

3. **Complete your grip by placing your right hand on the club.**

   You can fit the right hand to the left in one of three ways: the overlapping (or Vardon) grip, the interlocking grip, or the ten-finger grip. I cover each of these grips in the following sections.

Vardon grip

The *Vardon grip* is the most popular grip, certainly among better players. The great British player Harry Vardon, who still holds the record for British Open wins (six) popularized the grip around the turn of the century. Old Harry was the first to place the little finger of his right hand over the gap between the index and next finger of the left as a prelude to completing his grip, as shown in Figure 6-6. Harry was also the first to put his left thumb on top of the shaft. Previously, players kept their left thumbs wrapped around the grip as if they were holding a baseball bat.

Try the Vardon grip. Close your right hand over the front of the shaft so that the *V* formed between your thumb and forefinger points to your right ear. The fleshy pad at the base of your right thumb should fit snugly over your left thumb. The result should be a feeling of togetherness, your hands working as a unit.

This grip is very cool — probably 90 percent of tour players use the Vardon grip.

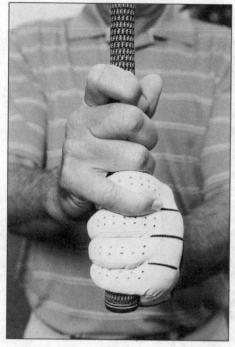

Figure 6-6:
In the
Vardon grip,
the right
pinkie
overlaps the
left index
finger.

Interlocking grip

The *interlocking grip* is really a variation on the Vardon grip (see the preceding section). The difference is that the little finger of your left hand and the index finger of the right actually hook together (see Figure 6-7). Everything else is the same. You may find this grip more comfortable if you have small hands. Jack Nicklaus, possibly the game's greatest player ever, used this grip for that reason. Many top female and junior players use this grip, too.

Ten-finger grip

The *ten-finger grip* is what the name tells you it is. You have all ten fingers on the club, like a baseball player gripping a bat. No overlapping or interlocking occurs; the little finger of the left hand and the index finger of the right barely touch (see Figure 6-8). The ten-finger grip used to be more common, and you still see it occasionally. Bob Estes has used it on the PGA Tour. Dave Barr — one of the best players ever from Canada — also uses this grip. If you have trouble generating enough clubhead speed to hit the ball as far as you want, or if you're fighting a slice, give this grip a try. Keep in mind that controlling the clubhead is more difficult with this grip because more cocking of the hands occurs. This approach can also be particularly helpful for female and junior golfers.

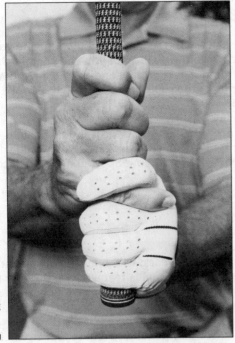

Figure 6-7:
An alternative is to interlock the right pinkie and left index finger.

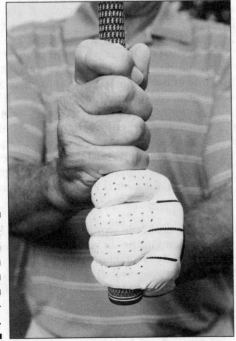

Figure 6-8:
You can place all ten fingers on the club in a baseball-style grip.

Completing the grip

Put your right hand on the club, with the palm directly opposite your left hand. Slide your right hand down the shaft until you can complete whatever grip you prefer. Your right shoulder, right hip, and head lean to the right to accommodate the lowering of the right hand. Your right earlobe moves closer to your right shoulder.

Your grip pressure should never be tight. Your grip should be light — no clenching. You should exert only as much pressure as you would when picking up an egg from a spotted owl. Lightly now! Spotted owls are becoming extinct!

Aiming

I've played pro golf for more than 30 years, which means taking part in a lot of pro-ams. (In a *pro-am,* each professional is teamed with three or four amateurs.) And in every single one of those rounds, I saw someone misaligned at address. Sometimes that someone was me! Aiming properly is that difficult.

Generally speaking, right-handed golfers tend to aim too far right of the target. I don't see many of them aiming left — even slicers, whose shots commonly start left and finish right. Invariably, people tend to aim right and swing over the top on the way down to get the ball started left. (For information on fixing common faults, see Chapter 11.)

What makes aiming so difficult? Human nature is part of it. Getting sloppy with your aim is easy when your mind is on other things. That's why discipline is important. Taking the time and trouble to get comfortable and confident in his alignment is one reason Jack Nicklaus was as great as he was. He worked his way through the same aiming routine before every shot. And I emphasize *routine.* First, he'd look at the target from behind the ball. Then he picked out a spot a few feet ahead of his ball on a line with that target. That spot was his intermediate target. Then he walked to the ball and set the clubface behind it so that he was aiming at the intermediate point. Aligning the club with something 2 feet away is much easier than aiming at something 150 yards away.

How Nicklaus aimed is exactly how you should work on your aim. Think of a railroad track. On one rail is the ball and in the distance, the target. On the other rail are your toes. Thus, your body is aligned parallel with — but left of — the target line. If you take nothing else away from this section on aiming, remember that phrase. Cut out Figure 6-9 and tape it onto the ceiling over your bed. Stare at it before you go to sleep.

Figure 6-9:
Your feet
should be
parallel to
the target
line (left),
not aimed
at the target
(right).

Don't make the mistake that I see countless golfers making: aiming their feet at the target. My buddies all do that, but think about it: If you aim your feet at the target, where is the clubface aligned? To the right of where you want the ball to go! (Refer to the right-hand photo in Figure 6-9.) I'm hammering away on this point because misalignment is one of the most common errors in golf. So save yourself a lot of heartache and get your feet aligned a little to the left of the target line, *parallel* to it. It'll feel like you're aimed to the left — that's a *good* thing!

Nailing down the stance

Okay, you're aimed correctly. But your feet aren't finished yet. Right now you're just standing there. All the books tell you to turn your left toe out about 30 degrees. But what's 30 degrees? If you're like me, you have no clue what 30 degrees looks like or — more important — feels like, so think of it this way:

You know what a clock looks like; if you can read a clock, you can build a stance. You want your left foot pointed to 10 o'clock and your right foot at 1 o'clock. Forget about daylight saving time. Figure 6-10 demonstrates this stance. Keep it simple and always be on time.

Width of stance is easy, too. Keep your heels shoulder-width apart, as shown in Figure 6-11. Not 14 inches or 18 inches. Shoulder width. Let the shape of your body dictate what's right for you.

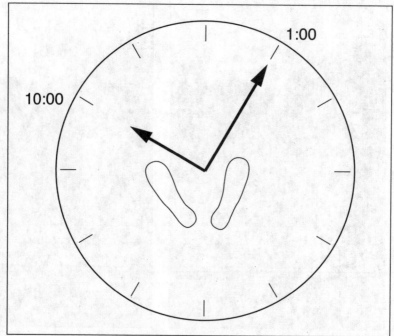

Figure 6-10:
A clock-
based
stance.

With a driver, the gap between your knees
should be shoulder width.
Think "bow-legged."

Figure 6-11:
Your knees
should be as
far apart
as your
shoulders.

Considering knee flex

After you've set your stance (see the preceding section), your next stop is at your knees. Again, you can read all sorts of books that tell you the precise angle at which your knees should flex at address. But that number doesn't do you much good when you're standing on the range without a protractor. What you need is a *feel*.

Think of knee flex as a "ready" position. You've got to set yourself so that movement is easy. So, from an upright start, flex your knees and bend forward until your arms are hanging vertically, as shown in Figure 6-12. That's where you want to be. Just like a quarterback waiting for a snap. Or a soccer goalkeeper facing a shot. Or a shortstop ready for a ground ball. You're ready to move. Left. Right. Back. Forward. Whatever. You're ready. And remember, maintaining balance is the key.

Flex knees and bend forward until arms hang vertically.

Figure 6-12: Flex your knees and bend forward until your arms hang vertically.

Deciding on ball position

Where is the ball positioned between your feet? You want it aligned with your left armpit with a driver. That means the ball is also aligned with your left heel. For other clubs, the ball moves steadily back with each club until you get to the middle of your stance with a wedge (see Figure 6-13).

For a driver, place the ball opposite your left armpit.

Figure 6-13:
Ball
position.

As I mention earlier in the chapter, you want to hit up on the ball with your driver — that's why the ball is forward in your stance (toward the target). You want to hit down with all other clubs, which is why you move the ball back in your stance (away from the target) as the loft of your clubs increases. When the ball is played back in your stance, hitting down is much easier.

Maximizing the bottom of the swing

The bottom of the swing is an important, often-neglected aspect of golf. After all, that's usually where the ball is! The arc of the swing has to have a low point; hopefully, that low point is precisely where your golf ball is as you swing an iron. If you don't know where the bottom of your swing is, how do you know where to put the ball in your stance? You can make the best swing in the world, but if the ball is too far back, you hit the top half of it. Too far forward is just as bad — you hit the ground before the ball.

Fear not; such shots aren't going to be part of your repertoire. Why? Because you're always going to know where the bottom of your swing is: directly below your head.

Think about it. The preceding section discusses how the ball is aligned with your left armpit when you use the driver. That position automatically puts your head behind the ball whenever you swing your driver. In other words, the ball is nearer the target than your head is, which means that you strike the ball a slightly upward blow. The bottom of the swing is behind the ball, so the club-head is moving up as it hits the ball, as shown in Figure 6-14. That's all right because the ball is perched on a tee. The only way to make solid contact (and maximize your distance) is to hit drives "on the up."

Figure 6-14: Tee the ball about an inch high for an upward strike with the driver.

The situation for an iron shot from the fairway differs from that of the driver. Now the ball is sitting on the ground. Plus the club you're using has more loft and is designed to give best results when the ball is struck just before the ground. So now your head should be over the ball at address and impact. In other words, something has to move.

That something is the ball. Start from the middle of your stance, which is where the ball should be when you're hitting a wedge, one of the shortest and most lofted clubs in your bag. Move the ball steadily forward as the club in your hands gets longer. (See Figure 6-15.)

Of course, you're not actually physically moving the ball until you hit it. What's moving in the stance is you — your setup in relation to the ball.

For me, the distance between my left armpit and chin is about 6 inches. With the driver, the ball is aligned with my left armpit, and with the shorter irons, it's opposite my chin (that is, where my head is). In my case, the ball moves about 6 inches. Most golf courses are about 7,000 yards, so 6 inches shouldn't have much significance. Practice this part early in your development, and you'll have more success with the other 7,000 yards.

Figure 6-15: The ball "moves"!

When you use a wedge, place the ball in the middle of your stance.

As the club gets longer, the ball moves targetward.

You may be a little confused by all of that. It may sound weird that the more lofted clubs (which hit the highest shots) are back in your stance so that you can hit down on the ball more. But the explanation is a simple one: The more the clubface is angled back from vertical, the higher the shot flies. Thus, the only way to move a ball from the ground into the air is by exerting downward pressure.

Keeping your eyes on the ball

I see too many players address the ball with their chins on their chests (probably because other golfers have said, "Keep your head down!"). Or, if they've been warned not to do that, they hold their heads so high they can barely see the ball. Neither, of course, is exactly conducive to good play.

So how do you position your head? The answer is in your eyes. Look down at the ball, which is in what optometrists call your *gaze center*. Your gaze center is about the size of a Frisbee. Everything outside your gaze center is in your peripheral vision. Now lift or drop your head slightly. As your head moves, so do your eyes, and so does the ball — into your peripheral vision. Suddenly, you can't see the ball so well. But if you hold your head steady enough to keep the ball inside that Frisbee-shaped circle, you can't go too far wrong (see Figure 6-16).

Keep the ball in the middle of your "gaze center."

That dictates the position of your head.

Figure 6-16:
Stay
focused.

Observing the one-hand-away rule

One last thing about your address position: Let your arms hang so that the *butt* end of the club (the one with the handle) is one hand-width from the inside of your left thigh, as shown in Figure 6-17. You should use this position for every club in the bag except for your putter.

The butt end of the club is a useful guide to check the relationship between your hands and the clubhead. With a wedge, for example, the butt end of the club should be in line with the middle of your left thigh. For a driver, it should be opposite your zipper. Every other club is between those parameters.

The club should be one hand from your body.

Figure 6-17:
Your hands
and the
club.

The shaft of a wedge should point at the
crease in your left pant leg (or the middle of
your thigh).

A driver should point at your zipper.

Unleashing Your Swing

Now it's time to do what you've been wanting to do: Create some turbulence.
Many people think the most effective way to develop a consistent swing is to
stand on the range whacking balls until you get it right. But the best way to

develop a consistent swing is actually to break the swing down into pieces. Only after you have the first piece mastered should you move on to the next one. In the sections that follow, I deal with each of those pieces and a few other swing considerations.

Making miniswings: Hands and arms

I start the swing process with what I call *miniswings*. Position yourself in front of the ball as I describe in "Building Your Swing" earlier in this chapter. Now, without moving anything but your hands, wrists, and forearms, rotate the club back until the shaft is horizontal to the ground and the *toe* of the club (the part of the clubhead farthest from the shaft) is pointing up. The key to this movement is the left hand, which must stay in the space that it's now occupying, in its address position (see Figure 6-18). The left hand is the fulcrum around which the "swing" rotates. The feeling you should have is of the butt of the club staying in about the same position while your hands lift the clubhead.

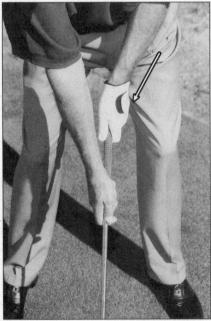 

Figure 6-18: The miniswing.

From address, push down with your left hand as you pull up with your right.

Rotate the club back until the shaft is horizontal, the toe pointing up.

After you get the hang of that little drill, try hitting shots with your miniswing. Let the club travel through 180 degrees, with the shaft parallel to the ground on the backswing and then back to parallel on the through-swing; your follow-through should be a mirror image of the backswing. The ball obviously doesn't go far with this drill, but your hands and arms are doing exactly what you want them to do on a full swing: Cock the wrists, hit the ball, and recock the wrists.

After you have this move down, you can turn on the horsepower and get your body involved.

Testing your rhythm

One of the most effective ways for your brain to master something like the golf swing is to set the motion to music. Music plays a valuable role in the learning process. You learned your ABCs by putting the letters to song. When you start to move the club and your body into the swing, think of a melody. Make the song real music. Rap, with its staccato rhythm, is no good. To me, that suggests too much independent movement. The golf swing should be a smooth motion, so your song should reflect that smoothness. Think Tony Bennett, not Eminem. I've played some of my best golf while humming Hootie and the Blowfish tunes.

To begin adding body movement to your miniswing motion (see the preceding section), stand as if at address, with your arms crossed over your chest so that your right hand is on your left shoulder and your left hand is on your right shoulder. Hold a club against your chest with both hands, as shown in Figure 6-19a.

Now turn as if you're making a backswing (see Figure 6-19b). Turn so that the shaft turns through 90 degrees, to the point where it's perpendicular to a line formed by the tips of your toes. As you do so, let your left knee move inward so that it points to the golf ball. The butt of the club also points at the ball.

The real key here is keeping your right leg flexed as it was at address. Retain that flex, and the only way to get the shaft into position is by turning your body. You can't sway or slide to the right and still create that 90-degree angle.

Your backswing should feel as if you're turning around the inside of your right leg until your back faces the target. That's the perfect top-of-the-backswing position.

Figure 6-19:
Turn your
body.

Unwinding

From the top, you must let your body unwind back to the ball in the proper sequence. (Note that your spine angle must stay the same from address to the top of the backswing.)

Uncoiling starts from the ground up. The first thing to move is your left knee. That knee must shift toward the target until your kneecap is over the middle of your left foot, where it stops. Any more shifting of the knee, and your legs start to slide past the ball. An *alignment stick* (a flexible fiberglass stick used to help with alignment) poked into the ground just outside your left foot is a good check that your knee shift hasn't gone too far. (See the left photo in Figure 6-20.) If your left knee touches the stick, stop and try again.

Next, your left hip slides targetward until it's over your knee and foot. Again, a stick in the ground provides a good test — a deterrent to keep your hip from going too far.

Pay special attention to the clubshaft across your chest in this phase of the swing (work in front of a mirror if you can). The shaft should always parallel the slope of your shoulders as you work your body back to the ball.

Swing through the impact area all the way to the finish. Keep your left leg straight and let your right knee touch your left knee, as shown in the right-hand photo in Figure 6-20. Hold this position until the ball hits the ground — that way, you prove beyond doubt that you've swung in balance.

Figure 6-20: Turn, don't slide.

An alignment stick at address   Bends if you slide forward (wrong)   But not if you turn (nice!)

Getting yourself together

Practice the exercises in the preceding sections. After you put them together, you'll have the basis of a pretty sound golf swing, one that combines hands/arms and body motion.

1. **Practice your miniswing.**

2. **Hum a mellow tune.**

3. **Turn your shoulders so that your back is toward the target.**

4. **Turn, don't slide; sliding automatically takes your head off the ball.**

5. **At the finish, keep your left leg straight, with your right knee touching your left knee.**

Coordinating the parts into a golf swing takes time. The action of the parts soon becomes the whole, and you develop a feel for your swing. But knowledge, in this case, doesn't come from reading a book. Only repetition — hitting enough balls to turn this information into muscle memory — can help you go from novice to real golfer. So get out there and start taking some turf!

Key on the rhythm of your swing. At a certain point in every golfer's life, he or she just has to "let it go." You can work on mechanics as much as you want, but then the moment to actually hit a ball comes. And when that moment comes, you can't be thinking about anything except, perhaps, one simple swing key, or swing thought. That's why top golfers spend most of their time trying to get into a focused, wordless, wonderful place they call the *zone*.

The *zone* is a state of uncluttered thought, where good things happen without any conscious effort from you. You know the feeling: The rolled-up ball of paper you throw at the trash can goes in if you just toss it without thinking. The car rounds the corner perfectly if you're lost in your thoughts. In golfing terms, getting into the zone means clearing your mind so that your body can do its job. The mind is a powerful asset, but it can hurt you, too. Negative thoughts about where your ball may go don't help you make your best swing.

Kevin Costner's rehearsal

When I worked with Kevin Costner on his golf game for the movie *Tin Cup,* one of the first things we talked about was a pre-shot routine. We had to get him to look like a real touring pro, and every pro has a particular routine.

Kevin picked up the pre-shot routine really fast. He'd get about six feet behind the ball and look first at the ball and then at the target (seeing the target line in his mind's eye). He'd then walk up and put his clubface right behind the ball and his feet on a parallel line to his target line, establishing the correct alignment. He'd look at the target once, give the club a little waggle, and then — *whack!* — off the ball went. By the time the golf sequences were shot for the

movie, Kevin had the look of a well-seasoned touring pro. In fact, as we were walking down the second hole together in the Bob Hope Chrysler Classic, I asked Kevin where he got all his mannerisms — tugging on his shirt, always stretching his glove by pulling on it, and pulling his pants by the right-front pocket. He looked at me and said, "I've been watching you for the past three months." I had no idea I was doing all those things in my pre-shot routine! So I'm living proof that your mannerisms become automatic if you do them enough.

By the way, my pre-shot routine looks a lot better when Kevin Costner does it!

Of course, getting into the zone is easier said than done. So how do you get there? Perhaps the best way is to focus on the rhythm of your swing. By *rhythm,* I don't mean speed. We've seen fast swings and slow swings and a lot in between, and all can have good rhythm. For example, three-time major winner Nick Price has a fast swing. Blink and you miss it. In contrast, 1987 Masters champ Larry Mize has an extremely slow motion. Congress works faster. Yet Price and Mize both have perfect rhythm. You can still see it on the Champions Tour. And their rhythm is the key.

The rhythm of your swing should fit your personality. If you're a fairly high-strung, nervous individual, your swing is probably faster than most. If your swing is slower, you may be more laid back and easygoing. But the potential for great rhythm is within every golfer.

Selecting swing triggers: What's a waggle?

Good rhythm doesn't just happen. Only on those days when you're in the zone can you swing on autopilot. The rest of the time, you need to set the tone for your swing with your waggle. A *waggle* is a motion with the wrists in which the hands stay fairly steady over the ball and the clubhead moves back a foot or two, as if starting the swing. (Check one out in Figure 6-21.) In fact, a waggle is a bit like the miniswing drill I describe in the section "Making miniswings: Hands and arms" earlier in this chapter.

Waggling the club serves three main purposes.

- ✔ **It's a rehearsal of the crucial opening segment of the backswing.**

- ✔ **It can set the tone for the pace of the swing.** In other words, if you have a short, fast swing, make short, fast waggles. If your swing is of the long and slow variety, make long, slow waggles. Be true to your species.

- ✔ **It gives your swing some momentum.** In golf, you don't want to start from a static position. You need a running start to keep your swing from getting off to an abrupt, jerky beginning. Waggling the clubhead eases tension and introduces movement into your setup.

Figure 6-21:
Get in
motion with
a waggle.

But the waggle is only the second-to-last thing you do before the backswing begins. The last thing is your *swing trigger,* which frees you up to get the club away from the ball. A swing trigger can be any kind of move. For example, 1989 British Open champion Mark Calcavecchia shuffles his feet. Gary Player, winner of nine major championships, always kicked his right knee in toward the ball. A slight turning of the head to the right was Jack Nicklaus's cue to start his swing. Your swing trigger is up to you. Create the flow!

Visualizing shots

As you practice your swing and hit more and more shots, patterns — good and bad — emerge. The natural shape of your shots becomes apparent. Few people hit the ball dead-straight; they either *fade* most of their shots (the ball flies from left to right, as shown in Figure 6-22) or *draw* them (the ball moves from right to left in the air). If you hit a ball that curves from left to right, aim far enough left to allow the curve of your ball to match the curve of the hole, and vice versa.

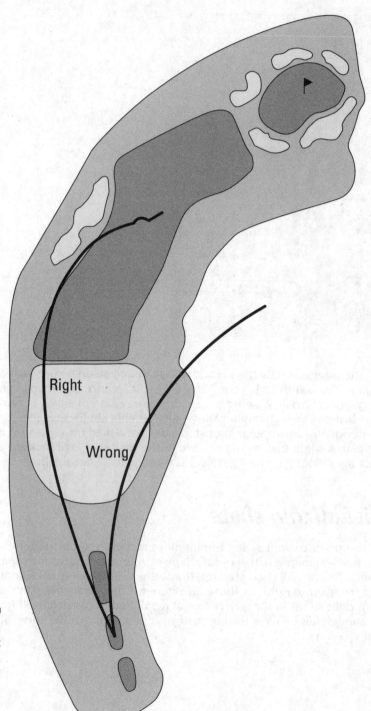

Figure 6-22:
The right
and wrong
paths for
correcting a
fade.

If either tendency gets too severe and develops into a full-blooded slice or hook (a *slice* is a worse fade, and a *hook* is a worse draw), you should stop playing. Go get a lesson. One session with your local pro should get you back on track.

Lessons are important. Faults left to fester and boil soon become ingrained into your method. When that happens, curing them can become a lengthy, expensive process. The old adage comes to mind: "Pay me now, or pay me later." Pay your pro early, when your woes are easier to fix. (Chapter 3 offers valuable information on golf lessons. For a list of golf schools, see Appendix B.)

Anyway, after you've developed a consistent shot shape, you can start to visualize how that shape fits the hole you're playing. Then, of course, you know exactly where to aim whether the hole is a *dogleg right* (turns right), *dogleg left* (turns left), or straightaway. You're a real golfer.

Watching a near-perfect swing: Hey, that's me!

When you put together all the connected parts I discuss in this chapter, they should flow into a swing. The first time you see yourself swinging in a series of photos, a video clip, or a DVD, you'll swear that that person isn't you. What your swing feels like versus what really occurs can be deceiving.

If you can master the basic mechanics described in this book and apply them to your own personality, your swing should bloom into something unique. Work hard to understand your swing and watch how other people swing. The great Ben Hogan told me how he watched other golfers: If he liked something they did, he'd go to the practice tee and incorporate that particular move into his swing to see whether it worked. What finally came out was a mix of many swings blended to his needs and personality. A champion works hard.

My golf swing isn't the one that got me to the PGA Tour. In 1986, at the age of 38, I started working with Mac O'Grady to revamp my entire swing. Mac gave me a model that I blended with my existing swing, shown in the nine photos of Figure 6-23. What came out is a pretty good-looking golf swing, if I do say so myself. Thanks, Mac, for at least making me look good!

Address: The calm before the chaos. All systems are go and flight is imminent.

Monitor your swing speed at this time. Checking to see if my seatbelts are fastened.

Turn and stay balanced over your feet. Feel the sun and breeze on your face.

I've reached the top. I'm in attack mode, my swing is growing teeth.

The start down is a slooooooow accumulation of speed. At this time, I've forgotten the sun and wind on my face.

I've organized my chaos. Liftoff is precise. My soul feels the ball.

Figure 6-23:
Not a bad-looking golf swing!

The hit is relayed up from the shaft to my hands, through my arms into my command center. Post-impact, I feel I've been here forever.

My first glimpse at the sphere that is targetbound. The anxieties of flight and destination consume my brain.

Who cares where it went? I look good enough to be on the top of a golf trophy.

Chapter 7

Improve Your Move: Refining Your Swing

his chapter comes with the golfing equivalent of a health disclaimer: The information on the next few pages isn't for everyone. That's not to say anything you read here is wrong; it isn't. But for many people — especially those at an early stage of development as golfers — it may be a lot to assimilate without little puffs of smoke coming from their ears.

So follow the wise man's advice: Golfer, know thyself. Are you the type who brings a new HDTV home and starts hooking this cable to that port and plugging this into that without looking at the instructions? Do you start punching buttons without taking the manual out of its wrapper? If so, skip this chapter. You already know all you need to know about the golf swing — at least for now.

But if you're the type who goes from page one to the end of the manual as you piece components together, you need to know more about the swing before you can unleash your swing with confidence. If that's you, read on, brave explorer.

What Type of Golfer Are You?

My friend, the renowned teacher Peter Kostis, breaks golfers into four personas. When you know the basics of the game, you can probably recognize yourself as one of them:

- ✔ **Analytics** are organized. You can always spot their desks in the office — they're spotless.

- ✔ **Drivers,** as you'd expect, are driven to get the job done. They don't stop till they've reached their goal.

- ✔ **Amiables** are easy to deal with. They accept any advice you offer without questioning it.

- ✔ **Expressives** go with the flow; rather than rein in their feelings, they adjust to whatever comes their way.

In recent golf history, an analytic is someone like Nick Faldo or Bernhard Langer. Jack Nicklaus, Tom Watson, and Annika Sorenstam are drivers. Tiger Woods is a little of both. Correction — make that *a lot* of both. Nancy Lopez, Fred Couples, Ernie Els, and Ben Crenshaw are amiables. And Phil Mickelson and Lee Trevino are classic expressives.

Drivers and analytics don't play like amiables and expressives. For a driver or analytic to score well, he needs confidence in his mechanics. An amiable or expressive doesn't — if he feels like he's playing okay, his swing must be okay, too.

At this stage of your development, your best bet is to be an amiable or an expressive. As a new golfer, you've got an enormous amount of information to absorb. Anything that limits confusion (such as a playing style where you roll with the punches) is a plus. Amiables and expressives may find more of what they need in Chapter 9; this chapter is more tailored to the analytics and drivers out there.

To better illustrate the difference among the types, suppose four of history's greatest golfers plan to play an exhibition. Lee Trevino, Ben Crenshaw, Jack Nicklaus, and Nick Faldo are scheduled to tee off at Running Rut Golf Course precisely at 11 a.m. Because of a mix-up with the courtesy cars that deliver the players to the golf course (Nicklaus and Faldo don't like the color of their car; Trevino and Crenshaw couldn't care less about it), the players are late getting to Running Rut.

When they arrive with only ten minutes to tee time, the analytic (Faldo) and the driver (Nicklaus) hurry to the driving range. Faldo has to swing to gain confidence, and Nicklaus has to hit balls because he likes to work at his game.

The expressive (Trevino) and the amiable (Crenshaw) don't have to hit balls to get ready. They wake up ready and go from there. They're in the locker room putting on their golf shoes. Trevino is deep in conversation with the locker-room attendant about the virtues of not having to tune up his Cadillac for 100,000 miles due to the technologies of its good old Northstar system.

Crenshaw is puffing a cigarette, telling a club member that he was flabbergasted yesterday when three 40-foot putts _lipped out_ on him (touched the edge of the cup and didn't go in). By the way, the match never happens. Faldo and Nicklaus refuse to come to the tee because Faldo wants to keep hitting balls on the practice tee, and Nicklaus ends up redesigning the practice range. I hear the locker-room attendant buys Trevino's old Cadillac.

Establishing Your Swing Plane

The _swing plane,_ at its most basic, is the path the club's shaft follows when you swing. Many factors affect your swing plane, including your height, your weight, your posture, your flexibility, the thickness of your torso, any physical limitations, and maybe even the magnetic field of your wristwatch. Swing plane can get complicated and for the beginner golfer must be simplified — especially if you want to cover all the possible variations in the plane from _address_ (your stance over the ball) to the end of the follow-through.

The plane of your swing is dictated to a large extent by the shaft's angle at address. The swing you make with a wedge in your hands is naturally more upright — or should be — than the swing you make with a driver. The driver has a longer shaft than the wedge and a flatter _lie_ (the angle at which the shaft emerges from the clubhead), so you have to stand farther away from the ball.

In this book, I'm assuming that you maintain the plane and spine angle you establish at address throughout your swing. This scenario isn't always the case: If a player's favored shot bends a great deal in the air, the swing plane tilts to the right or left to compensate for the ball's flight. But if you're trying to hit straight shots — as most amateurs should — one consistent plane is the way for you. The following sections give you some pointers on getting your swing plane down.

Mastering checkpoints

The simplest way to keep your swing on plane is to use a series of checkpoints, as shown in Figure 7-1. For purposes of illustration, I'm assuming that you're swinging a driver and that you're right-handed. Here are the checkpoints:

Start with the shaft at 45 degrees to the ground.

At the top, the shaft should be parallel with a line along your heels.

Impact should look a lot like address, except that the hips are opening to the target.

Figure 7-1: The swing plane.

✔ **Checkpoint 1:** At address, the shaft starts at a 45-degree angle to the ground.

✔ **Checkpoint 2:** Now swing the club back until your left arm is horizontal. At this point, the club's *butt end* (the end of the grip) points directly along the target line. (The *target line* is the line between the target and the ball that continues forward past the target and behind the ball in the opposite direction. What I'm talking about in this case is one long, straight line.) If the end of the grip points along the target line, you're *on plane*. If the club's butt end points above the target line, your swing is too flat, or *horizontal;* if the butt end is below the target line, your swing is too upright, or *vertical*.

✔ **Checkpoint 3:** At the top of your backswing, the club should be parallel with a line drawn along your heels, while your hands are positioned over your right shoulder. That's on plane. If the club points to the right of that line, you've crossed the line and will probably *hook* the shot from right to left. A club pointing to the left of that line is said to be *laid off*. In that case, expect a *slice* (which curves from left to right).

✔ **Checkpoint 4:** Halfway down, at the point where your left arm is again horizontal, the butt end should again point at the target line. This position and the one described in Checkpoint 2 are, in effect, identical in swing-plane terms.

✔ **Checkpoint 5:** *Impact* is the most important point in the swing. If the clubface is square when it strikes the ball, what you do anywhere else doesn't really matter. But if you want to be consistent, try to visualize impact as being about the same as your address position, except that your hips are aimed more to the left of the target than at address, and your weight is shifting to your left side.

To analyze your swing, use a camcorder, a series of still photos, or a mirror — or have someone watch you.

These checkpoints show a perfect-world situation. Your size, flexibility, and swing shape will probably produce different results. Don't be alarmed if you don't fit this model perfectly; no more than a dozen players on the PGA Tour do. As with anything else, there's room for deviation. Different folks make different strokes.

Taking it from the top

Take a closer look at the top of the backswing. If you can get the club on plane at the top, you'll probably hit a good shot.

Look for four things in your backswing:

- ✔ **Your left arm and your shoulders must be on the same slope.** In other words, your arm and shoulders are parallel to the target line.

- ✔ **The top of your swing is controlled by your right arm, which forms a right angle at the top of the swing (see Figure 7-2).** Your right elbow is about a dollar bill's length (around six inches) away from your rib cage.

- ✔ **Your shoulders are at 90 degrees to the target line.**

- ✔ **The clubface is parallel to your left arm and your shoulders.** Your left wrist controls this position. Ideally, your wrist angle remains unchanged from address to the top, making the clubface square at the top of the swing. That way, the relationship between the clubface and your left arm is constant. If your wrist angle does change, the clubface and your left arm will be on different planes, and that's a problem.

Your right arm should form a right angle at the elbow.

Figure 7-2: The top of the backswing; get this angle right.

Keep swinging, seniors

After 28 winless years as a touring pro, I finally broke through by winning the 1999 Toshiba Senior Classic. So when I address all you members of the Social-Security swing set, I know what I'm talking about!

And as I ponder the pitfalls of my maturing body and mind, I'm determined to enjoy this game right down to the last, desperate 210-yard drive. I'm not moving to Leadville, Colorado (elevation 11,000 feet), where the ball goes screaming for mercy through the alpine air. No, I'm using all my cunning (and lots of technology) to keep up with the kids right here at sea level.

I have brewed in my golf kitchen a recipe to keep my fellow seniors in the championship flight of their clubs' member-member tournament . . . from the back tees! And so, gramps and grannies, my two-stage plan to keep launching the long ball. Part one: the swing:

1. **Narrow your stance so that you can turn your torso without straining.**

   As we get older and less flexible, we tend to swat the ball with our hands instead of turning our bodies. Resist!

2. **Turn your left foot in.**

   This adjustment helps you make a bigger turn with your shoulders and hips.

3. **Turn your left knee behind the ball to ensure a bigger turn on the backswing.**

4. **Don't be afraid to lift your front heel off the ground on the backswing.**

   Jack Nicklaus did it, and he won the Masters at age 46 and played great golf into his 60s.

5. **Get the club parallel to the ground at the top of your backswing — even if you have to bend your left arm.**

   This strategy adds the clubhead speed you need to hit it a senior-citizen mile!

Okay, now that my pacemaker's smoking, here's part two, the easy stuff: high-tech help for great senior moments.

✔ **Get the lightest possible shafts for your clubs.** As we get older, our egos can get in the way of good golf. But there's no shame in playing with the clubs that give you the best results. Manufacturers now make shafts as light as 45 ounces. Get a low *kickpoint* (the spot where the shaft bends the most) to help you get the ball into the air. The lower the kickpoint, the higher the *launch angle* (the angle at which the ball leaves the clubface). That's golf talk!

✔ **Go to the longest shaft on your driver that you can control and add the lightest grip and clubhead you can find.** You'll strike fear in your foes at Sun City with this fast-moving, lightweight beast! I use a 46-inch, 55-ounce driver shaft on the Champions Tour.

✔ **Use irons with stronger lofts.** Instead of starting with a 48-degree wedge and dropping four degrees per iron, some manufacturers start with a 43-degree wedge and go down from there. That's basically the same as using a longer-hitting club without doing anything. Add light shafts and today's superior golf balls and bingo — grandpa's revenge!

If your wrist angle changes, it's either bowed or cupped (check out Figure 7-3). A *bowed* (bent-forward) left wrist at the top makes the clubface "look" skyward in what is called a *closed* position. From that position, a hook is likely. A *cupped* (bent-backward) wrist makes the clubface more visible to someone looking you in the face. A cupped wrist leads to an *open* position, which probably results in a slice.

You *can* play good golf from an open or closed position at the top of the backswing, but it's not easy. To compensate, your swing must feature some kind of repeatable mechanism that squares the clubface at impact. And compensations take a lot of practice. Only if you have the time to hit hundreds of balls a week can you hope to play well with an inherently flawed swing. Even then, that compensated swing is going to be tough to reproduce under pressure. For classic examples, watch Corey Pavin (open) and Lee Trevino (closed).

When your left wrist is "bowed," watch out for a hook.

When your left wrist is "cupped," watch out for a slice.

Figure 7-3:
Bowed- and cupped-wrist swings.

Slow-motion swing sequences tend to show three very different methods. The legendary Sam Snead crossed the line at the top and came over every shot to make the ball go straight. Annika Sorenstam was the opposite: She laid the club off at the top. And 1995 PGA Champion Steve Elkington stayed on plane. Make a swing like Elkington's your model, and you won't go too far wrong.

Boldly Going Where Others Have Gone Before: Mirroring Great Swings

Some of the latest sports science suggests that watching someone perform an action can be almost as helpful as doing it yourself. It activates "mirror neurons" in the brain that can help you imitate the action. When he was a toddler, Tiger Woods spent many hours watching his father hit golf balls — and when Tiger took his first whacks with a cut-down club, he already had a pretty good swing.

Phil Mickelson may be an even better example. A natural right-hander who was 18 months old when he began imitating his father, Phil literally mirrored what he saw — by swinging lefty!

No matter what your skill level, you can improve by observing good players, particularly those with some of the same characteristics that you have. Look for similarities in body size, pace, and shape of swing. You can also learn from the mistakes others make under pressure — just don't mirror those!

Start by identifying your goals. Do you want to emulate the game's big bombers, guys like Davis Love III, Bubba Watson, and Dustin Johnson, who regularly blast drives beyond 300 and even 350 yards? Or do you want to follow the short-game experts, such as all-time great Walter Hagen and tour veteran Brad Faxon? Phil Mickelson is long off the tee and has a great lob wedge. Tiger Woods, at his best, does everything well.

Maybe swing speed is your demon. Are you trying too hard to copy someone you admire, or is the pace you use as natural for you as tour golfers' swings are for them? Down through the years, Ben Crenshaw, Nancy Lopez, and Jay Haas have displayed slow-paced swings. Larry Mize's swing was so slow it looked like slo-mo. Ernie Els has a syrup-smooth motion that builds great power at impact. Jack Nicklaus, Sam Snead, and Annika Sorenstam all won with medium-paced swings. Ben Hogan, Lanny Wadkins, and Tom Watson swung fast. One of the quickest swingers of all is Nick Price. And those players have all had great careers.

Mimicking the moss bosses

If you want to follow some really fine putting, keep your eyes peeled for my Champions Tour colleague Loren Roberts, who putts so well his nickname is "Boss of the Moss." Some of the best putters in the world today are Brad Faxon, Jim Furyk, and Steve Stricker. Nancy Lopez was another great putter in her heyday. (Head to Chapter 9 for more on putting.)

Grip can affect your putting stroke as well as your swing, so you may want to study the grips of various pros. Billy Casper was an all-time great putter who used his wrists to create momentum in the clubhead during his putting stroke. Fred Couples uses the cross-handed grip for putting. Chris DiMarco, who was once such a poor putter he almost quit the tour, made it big with a grip called "the claw."

Maybe you want to keep tabs on golfers who have modified their games to adapt to a situation such as the yips (see Chapter 9), like Bernhard Langer, who invented his own grip, and Sam Snead, who putted sidesaddle. Golfers also adapt to accommodate new tools, such as the long putter Tom Lehman switched to, or Vijay Singh's *belly putter* — longer than a standard model, shorter than a long putter.

Notice how the attitudes of famous players affect not only how they play but also how much they enjoy the game. Arnold Palmer was a master of special shots and a bold golfer. Other daring players include Mickelson and Ireland's Rory McIlroy, who are as fun and expressive as Lee Trevino in his prime. Fred Funk is a Champions Tour fan favorite whose love for the game is infectious. On the other end of the attitude spectrum, you find Hall of Famer Jackie Burke, who created intense drills for himself so that he knew all about pressure: His motivation was to win. Ben Hogan was another steely competitor, a perfectionist who surrendered not to any other player but only to the yips. Other perfectionists include Jack Nicklaus, Tom Watson, Annika Sorenstam, and many of the Asian players doing so well on today's LPGA tour — hard workers like Jiyai Shin and Song-Hee Kim of South Korea, and Japan's Ai Miyazato.

Whomever you choose to emulate, keep in mind that golf is an individualist's game. You can mix and match facets of great players' styles, or develop your own — whatever works for *you*.

Chapter 8

Chipping and Pitching: Short-Game Secrets

Five-time PGA champion Walter Hagen had the right approach. As he stood on the first tee, the great Haig knew that he'd probably hit at least six terrible shots that day. So when he did hit one sideways, he didn't blow his top. Hagen simply relied on his superior *short game* (every shot within 80 yards of the hole) to get out of trouble.

Of course, everything within 80 yards of the hole includes putting (which I discuss in Chapter 9) and sand play (Chapter 10). So what's left for this chapter to cover? Pitching and chipping — two versions of short shots to the green.

Golf's Ups and Downs: Exploring the Short Game

Hang around golfers for a while and you inevitably hear one say something like, "I missed the third green but got up and down for my par." At this stage, you're probably wondering what in the world *up and down* means. Well, the *up* part is the subject of this chapter — *chipping* (hitting a low, short shot) or *pitching* (hitting a higher, more airborne short shot) the ball to the hole.

The *down* half of the equation, of course, is holing the putt after your chip or pitch (see Chapter 9). Thus, a golfer with a good short game is one who gets up and down a high percentage of the time (anywhere above 50 percent).

Now here's the weird thing: Although a good short game can erase your mistakes and keep a good round going, many amateurs tend to look down on golfers blessed with a delicate touch around the greens. They hate to lose to someone who beats them with good chipping and putting. Somehow a strong short game isn't perceived as "macho golf" —not in the same league as smashing drives 300 yards and hitting low, raking, iron shots to greens. Good ball strikers tend to look down on players with better short games. This attitude is more than a snobbery thing — it's also a missing-the-point thing.

In golf, you want to move the ball around the course in the fewest possible strokes. How you get that job done — great drives, expert chipping — is up to you. No rule says that you have to look pretty or hit picturesque drives when you play golf. Your scorecard won't be hung in an art gallery.

You can make up for a lot of bad play with one good short shot. As someone once said, "Three of them and one of those makes four." Remember that saying; even if you need three cruddy shots to get near the green, you can save par with a nice chip or pitch. Short-game master Walter Hagen won his matches without having hit his full shots too solidly. He proved that golf is more than hitting the ball well; it's a game of managing your misses.

You don't hear professionals downplaying the importance of a good short game. We know that the short game is where we make our money. Here's proof: If you put a club champion and a tournament pro on the tee with drivers in their hands, their drives don't look all that different. Sure, you can tell who the better player is, but the amateur at least *looks* competitive.

The gap in quality grows on the approach shots, again on *wedge play* (shorter approaches hit with wedges), and then again in the short game. In fact, the closer the players get to the green, the more obvious the difference in level of play. And the green is where a mediocre score gets turned into a good score, or where a good score gets turned into a great one. (Take a look at the sample scorecard in Figure 8-1, which pays special attention to short-game shots. Keeping that kind of record for yourself once in a while to monitor your short game doesn't hurt.)

Men's Course Rating/Slope Blue 73.1/137 White 71.0/130				JOHN				H O L E	HIT FAIRWAY	HIT GREEN		No. PUTTS	Women's Course Rating/Slope Red 73.7/128		
Blue Tees	White Tees	Par	Hcp										Hcp	Par	Red Tees
377	361	4	11	4				1	✓	✓		2	13	4	310
514	467	5	13	8				2	✓	0		3	3	5	428
446	423	4	1	7				3	0	0		2	1	4	389
376	356	4	5	6				4	0	0		2	11	4	325
362	344	4	7	5				5	0	✓		3	7	4	316
376	360	4	9	6				6	✓	0		2	9	4	335
166	130	3	17	4				7	0	✓		3	17	3	108
429	407	4	3	5				8	✓	✓		3	5	4	368
161	145	3	15	5				9	0	0		2	15	3	122
3207	2993	35		50				Out	4	4		22		35	2701
		Initial											**Initial**		
366	348	4	18	5				10	0	0		2	14	4	320
570	537	5	10	7				11	✓	0		3	2	5	504
438	420	4	2	5				12	✓	0		2	6	4	389
197	182	3	12	4				13	0	0		2	16	3	145
507	475	5	14	5				14	✓	✓		2	4	5	425
398	380	4	4	5				15	0	✓		3	8	4	350
380	366	4	6	5				16	✓	0		2	10	4	339
165	151	3	16	4				17	0	0		2	18	3	133
397	375	4	8	5				18	0	0		2	12	4	341
3418	3234	36		45				In	3	2		20		36	2946
6625	6227	71		95				Tot	7	6		42		71	5647
		Handicap											Handicap		
		Net Score											Net Score		
		Adjust											Adjust		

Scorer   Attested   Date

Figure 8-1: A scorecard can tell you more than just your score.

Making Your Pitch

Pitch shots, which you play with only your wedges and 9-iron, are generally longer than chips and stay mostly in the air. That introduces wrist action into the equation, which introduces the problem of how long your swing should be and how fast. In other words, pitch shots need some serious feel.

Even the best players try to avoid pitch shots. They're in-between shots. You can't just make your normal, everyday, full swing — that would send the ball way too far. You're stuck making a partial swing — which is never easy, especially when you're under pressure.

Anyway, here's how to build your pitching swing.

1. **Set up a narrow stance about 12 inches from heel to heel and open, with your left foot back from the target line.**

   Your shoulders should be open to the target which makes it easier to sense the target and to swing the club back closer to the intended flight line with your hands ahead of the ball, leading the clubhead. Stand so that the ball is about two inches to the left of your right big toe, as shown in Figure 8-2.

2. **Make a miniswing (which I describe in Chapter 6).**

   Without moving the butt end of the club too far in your backswing, hinge your wrists so that the shaft is horizontal. Now swing through the shot.

3. **Watch how far the ball goes and make adjustments.**

   That distance is your point of reference. Do you want to hit the next pitch 10 yards farther? Make your swing a little bit longer (see Figure 8-3). Shorter? Your swing follows suit. That way, your rhythm never changes. You want the clubhead accelerating smoothly through the ball. And you best achieve that acceleration if you build up the momentum gradually from *address* (the point right before you hit the ball).

When you pitch, your shoulders and feet must be aligned to the left of where you want the ball to go.

Figure 8-2:
Set up to pitch.

From address...

swing the club with hands/arms only...

Figure 8-3: Achieving the proper momentum.

accelerate through impact to a relaxed finish.

Poor pitchers of the ball do one of two things: Either they start their swings too slowly and then speed up too much at impact, or they jerk the club away from the ball and have to decelerate later. Both swings lead to what golf columnist Peter Dobereiner christened "sickening knee-high fizzers" — low, thin shots that hurtle uncontrollably over the green — or complete duffs that travel only a few feet. Not a pretty sight. The most common cause of both is tension. So relax!

In golf, you get better by doing, *not* by doing nothing, so improve your pitching by practicing. Here's a game we play at the back of the range at our facility at Grayhawk Golf Club in Scottsdale, Arizona. We get five empty buckets and place them in a straight line at 20, 40, 60, 80, and 100 feet. We then have one hour to hit one ball into each bucket, starting at 20 feet. The winner gets the title to the other guy's car. We're still driving our own cars — we usually get frustrated and quit before the one-hour time limit expires, or we go to lunch. But at least we get some good pitching practice.

Last pitching thought: Although pitch shots fly higher than chips, you still want to get the ball back to the ground ASAP so that it doesn't sail too far. Pick out your landing area somewhere short of your final target and let the ball roll the rest of the way. See the shot in your mind's eye before you hit the ball, and remember your *Golf For Dummies* secret: To make the ball go up, hit down — don't try to lift it. The loft on the club's face is designed to get the ball airborne.

Imagine that you're swinging with a potato chip — the thin, crispy American kind — between your teeth. Focus on *not* biting down on it. That'll keep you relaxed.

Chips Ahoy! Setting Up a Solid Chip

Chip shots are shorter than pitches; they stay mostly on the ground. Chips are also easier than pitches, or at least they should be. With the proper technique, you can chip the ball close enough to the hole to tap the ball in . . . unless, of course, you sink that chip!

Chips are played around the greens with anything from a 5-iron to a wedge. (Head to Chapter 2 for the lowdown on these and other clubs.) The basic idea is to get the ball on the green and rolling as soon as you can. If you get the ball running like a putt, you have an easier time judging how far it will go. The following sections show you some important chipping considerations.

Use the philosophy I outline in these sections as a starting point, not as holy writ that you must follow to the letter. Let your own creativity take over. Go with your instincts when you need to choose the right club or shot. The more you practice this part of your game, the easier it gets.

Pick your spot

Your first point of reference is the spot where you want the ball to land. If at all possible, you want that spot to be on the putting surface. The turf there is generally flatter and better prepared, which makes the all-important first bounce more predictable. You want to avoid landing chips on rough, uneven, or sloping ground.

Pick a spot about two feet onto the green (see Figure 8-4). From that spot, I like to visualize the ball rolling the rest of the way to the hole. Visualization is a big part of chipping. Try to picture the shot before you hit the ball. Then be as exact as you can with your target. Don't aim for an area. Try to hit a blade of grass! You can't be too precise. For a specific practice exercise, see the later section "Chip away!"

Figure 8-4:
Pick a spot
on the
putting
surface.

Choose the right club

Your club choice depends on how much room you have between your landing point and the hole. If you have only 15 feet, you need a more *lofted* club (one with a face that's severely angled back from vertical), such as a sand wedge or even a lob wedge, so that the ball doesn't run too far. If that gap is bigger (say, 60 feet), a straighter-faced club, such as a 7-iron, is more practical. Figure 8-5 illustrates this concept.

From address...

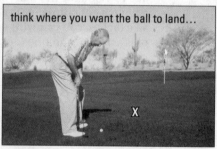
think where you want the ball to land...

then try to hit it...

so that the ball runs to the hole.

Figure 8-5: Get the ball rolling.

If you watch golf on TV, you've probably seen Phil Mickelson or Tiger Woods use a full swing to hit the ball straight up in the air and cover only a short distance on the ground. Phil can do another thing that's really astounding: You stand about six feet away from Phil and turn your back to him. You then cup your hands and hold them straight out from your chest. Phil takes a full swing with his wedge and lofts the ball over your head and into your sweaty, waiting hands — all from only six feet away. Now that's a *lob!* It requires a club with a lot of loft and a golfer with real talent to pull off a lob (a high, short, soft wedge shot) like that.

Practice, and only practice, makes you better. Try all sorts of clubs for these shots. Sooner or later, you develop a feel for the short game. I can't stress this point enough: Use as many clubs as possible when practicing! Observing how different clubs perform in different situations is one of the secrets of a successful short game.

Lies and secrets: Consider your ball placement

Next comes the problem of how your ball is lying on the ground. If it's in longer grass, you need to use a more lofted club and make a longer swing, no matter where the hole is. (**Remember:** Longer grass means a longer swing.) You need to get the ball high enough to escape the longer rough. If the ball is lying *down* (in a depression) and you can't get it out with a straighter-faced club, you have to go to more loft and move the ball back a little in your stance — closer to your right foot — to make the shot work (see Chapter 12 for more on low shots). This part of the game calls for creativity.

Chip away!

Short game guru Phil Rodgers taught me my chipping technique, which is basically the same one I employ for putting. I use a putting stroke with a lofted club — and I want you to do the same. Take your putting grip and stroke, and go hit a few chip shots. Right now — unless you're operating heavy machinery.

One key to chipping is your setup. Creating the right positions at address is essential. Your stance should be similar to the one you use on pitch shots (which I cover earlier in the chapter): narrow, with about 12 inches from heel to heel, and open, with your left foot back from the target line. Your shoulders should be open to the target as well. Now place about 80 percent of your weight on your left side. By moving your hands ahead of the ball, you encourage the downward strike that you need to make solid contact with the ball. The ball should be about 2 inches to the left of your right big toe, as shown in Figure 8-6.

During your stroke, focus on the back of your left wrist. That wrist must stay flat and firm, as in putting (see Figure 8-7). To keep your left wrist flat, tape a pen to the back of that wrist (slipping the pen under your watchband works almost as well). You feel any breakdowns right away. Now go hit some putts and chips.

When I play a tour event, one of the first things I do is go to the putting green, where I hit putts and chips to get an idea of the speed of the greens. I find a flat spot on the green and drop some balls about five feet from the putting surface. Then I put a coin on the green two feet from the *fringe* (the collar of grass around the green — it's longer than the grass on the green but shorter than the grass on the fairway). Then I take an 8-iron, 9-iron, and wedge and chip balls onto the green, trying to bounce each ball off the coin so that it runs to the hole. This strategy gives me a good idea of how fast the greens are that week — and when you miss as many greens as I do, the practice comes in handy.

Narrow your stance...

and keep your left wrist flat...

through impact...

and beyond.

Figure 8-6:
Chip with your weight on your left side and your hands ahead of the ball.

Figure 8-7:
Keep your
wrist flat
and firm
while
chipping.

Put a pen inside your watchband.

That'll firm up your wrist.

Chapter 9

Putting: The Game Within the Game

In This Chapter

▶ Finding your own putting style

▶ Visualizing putts

▶ Choosing the right putter

▶ Hitting good long and short putts

▶ Trying a sidesaddle putting style

▶ Overcoming the yips

*T*he chapters in this book are all my babies — I love 'em each and every one. But this chapter may be the most important, because putting skills are vital in golf.

Statistically, putting is 68 percent of the game of golf, so you may want to take notes. You'd be smart to keep a "reminder book" of putting tips from this chapter, because you can't score well if you can't putt — it's that simple.

If you want proof, look at the top professionals on tour who average about 28 putts per round. In other words, these professionals are one-putting at least 8 of the 18 greens in a round of golf. The average score on tour isn't 8 under par, so even these stars are missing their fair share of greens. And where are they making up for their mistakes? That's right: on the greens.

Golfers often say they're *rolling the rock* on the green rather than *rolling the ball.* Don't ask me why. I suspect it has to do with the difficulty of rolling a hard, irregular object that can hurt you. Or maybe *rock* and *roll* just go together.

No other part of golf induces as much heartache as putting. Many fine strikers of the ball have literally been driven from the sport because they couldn't finish holes as well as they started them. Why? Because putting messes with your internal organs. Every putt has only two possibilities: You either hole it or miss it. Accept that, and you won't have nightmares about the ones that "should" have gone in.

You Gotta Be You: Throwing Mechanics out the Window

Putting is the most individual part of this individual game. You can putt — and putt successfully — in myriad ways. You can break all the rules with a putter in your hands as long as the ball goes in the hole. Believe me, you can get the job done by using any number of methods. You can make long, flowing strokes like Phil Mickelson and Ben Crenshaw. Or shorter, firmer, "pop" strokes like Corey Pavin and Gary Player. You can create the necessary momentum in the clubhead with your wrists — the great Billy Casper proved how well that can work. Or if none of these styles appeals to you, you can switch to a belly putter — tour stars from Stewart Cink and Vijay Singh to U.S. Open champions Jim Furyk and Retief Goosen have tried that — or go to a long putter. Pros including Bernhard Langer and Carl Pettersson have had success with long putters, and Tim Clark won the 2010 Players Championship wielding a long wand. (Head to "It's a lo-o-ng story: Long putters and belly putters" later in this chapter for more on belly and long putters.)

Putting is more about those ghostly intangibles — feel, touch, and nerve — than about mechanics. That's why I think getting too caught up in putting mechanics is a mistake. If you don't have the touch, you can have the most technically perfect stroke in the world and still be like an orangutan kicking a football on the greens.

Even more than the rhythm and tempo of your full swing (refer to Chapter 6), your putting stroke should reflect your own personality. Your hands probably shouldn't be behind the ball at impact, but other than that, your style is up to you.

If any aspect of this often-infuriating game is going to drive you to distraction, it's likely to be putting. Putting may look simple — and sometimes it is — but on some days you just *know* that little ball will never fall into the hole. You know it, your playing partners know it, your shrink knows it — everyone knows it. Putting is mystical; it comes and goes like the tide.

Putting is golf's great equalizer. Players who can't drive the ball out of sight should focus on refining their short-game skills, such as chipping, pitching, and putting. (Check out Chapter 8 for more on chipping and pitching.) *Remember:* A putt counts the same on the score card as a 300-yard drive.

Preparing for Putting's Mind Games

In putting, visualization is everything. You can visualize the hole in two ways: You see it either as a pinpoint or as a crater so big any fool could drop the ball in. The former, of course, is infinitely more hazardous to your mental health. When you picture a small hole, the ball doesn't seem to fit into it. You can keep telling yourself that the ball is 1.68 inches in diameter and the hole 4.25 inches across, but the fact remains that the ball is too big. I know; I've been there. It just won't fit! When I start thinking that way, I usually seek psychiatric care and surround myself with pastel colors.

And on other days, happily, the hole is so big that putting is like stroking a marble into the Grand Canyon. Simply hit the ball, and boom, it goes in. When this sensation happens to you, savor it. Drink in the feeling and bathe in it so that you don't forget it — because you may not take another bath like that for a *long* time.

The crazy thing is that these two scenarios can occur on consecutive days, sometimes even in consecutive rounds. I've even experienced both feelings on consecutive holes! Why? I have no idea. The answer is way beyond my feeble intellect. Try not to think too deeply about putting.

The Most Important Club in the Bag: Examining Putters

Because putting is such a crucial part of golf, your putter is the most important weapon you've got. Club makers seem to have noticed: In recent years, they've brought out a dizzying array of high-tech putters. Some are as sleek as a sports car, while others look more like anvils or spaceships. One new model has been likened to "a fire hydrant on a stick." How can you choose the putter that's best for your game? It's not as tricky as you may think.

Your stroke shape tells which putter you need

Although you have many putters to choose from, you can eliminate most of them by knowing the type of putter you are. In other words, the shape of your stroke is the main factor in choosing a putter. Figure 9-1 shows two types of putters.

Figure 9-1:
Which kind
of putter?

My good friend and noted teaching professional Peter Kostis explains that almost all putting strokes fall into one of two shapes. They either move "straight back and straight through" with the blade staying square, or "inside to inside," the blade doing a mini-version of the rotation in a full swing. Conveniently, most putters are designed to suit one of those stroke shapes. The two main types are

- Face-balanced, center-shafted putters
- Putters that aren't face-balanced, such as heel-shafted blades

If keeping the blade square throughout the putting stroke is your style, get a face-balanced, center-shafted model. You can test to see if a putter is face-balanced by resting the shaft on your finger. If the putterface stays parallel to the ground, it's face-balanced. The inside-to-inside stroke is easier to make on a consistent basis with a heel-shafted putter. It hangs toe-down while resting on your finger. (The *toe* is the end of the putter, the part farthest from the shaft.)

Be warned, though. Some putters hang at an angle of 45 degrees. They're equally good — or bad! — for either stroke.

Picking a putter: From MOI to you

Don't be confused by all the high-tech (and high-priced) new putters on the market, several of which you can see in Figure 9-2. Although they appear as colorful and as different as new cars, most offer only one or two features — features that may seem confusing at first.

Figure 9-2: Wands of wonder: A few new-millennium putters.

One term that puzzles most beginners is *MOI,* which is short for *moment of inertia.* It sounds scientific, and MOI putters do in fact have a lot of science behind them, but don't worry about that. All you need to know is that MOI putters resist twisting on off-center hits. That means your bad putts turn out better than they would otherwise. How much better? That's hard to say, but a study cited in *Golf Digest* suggested that an MOI putter may make a 4-foot difference on a 22-foot putt. That's a massive difference — almost as massive as some of these putters.

Many modern putters also feature alignment aids, like the white circles behind the face of Odyssey's putters. Other manufacturers put bold lines or arrows on their weapons to help golfers start the ball on the target line. (For more on alignment, see "The Art of Aiming" later in this chapter.) Another new wrinkle is adding an insert to the face of the putter — often a panel of *urethane,* the same stuff golf balls are made of — for a softer feel when the putter strikes the ball.

As with other technological fixes, from titanium drivers to graphite shafts to super-comfy golf shoes, such features have their benefits — especially if you *believe* they can help your game. Because, as you know by now (or will soon figure out), this game is as much mental as it is anything.

Still, the best feature of all is sound fundamentals. Without them, all the tech support in the world can't do you much good.

It's a lo-o-ng story: Long putters and belly putters

Some golfers swear by extra-long putters. Others swear *at* them, saying the long putter ought to be illegal. You can even hear talk of banning long putters. But if you're struggling to make putts, you may want give one a try.

The terminology can be confusing: What's the difference between a long putter and a belly putter? It's simple: Both are longer than a standard model, but a *long putter* is really lo-o-onnng. Its handle tucks under the golfer's chin, while the handle of a *belly putter* is anchored to the golfer's midsection. Both are used almost exclusively by players who've struggled to make putts the usual way.

The longer putters are generally a last resort. If you can make putts with a standard-length putter, that's what you should use.

Long putters

The long putter is the final refuge of the neurologically impaired. If you watch any Champions Tour event on TV, you can see more than a few long putters. And now they're making inroads on the PGA Tour.

Long putters range from 46 to 50 inches long and up. They remove all wrist action from your putting stroke because your left hand anchors the club to your chest. Your left hand holds the club at the butt end of the shaft while your fingers wrap around the grip so that the back of your left hand faces the ball. Your right hand is basically along for the ride. In fact, it should barely touch the club. Its only role is to pull the putter back and follow it through on a straight line toward the hole.

Long putters are easy on the nerves, which is why they enjoy such popularity on the Champions Tour. But senior players aren't alone. No fewer than three members of the European Ryder Cup team back in 1995 used long putters. All three won their singles matches on the final afternoon, perhaps the most pressure-packed day in all of golf. So long putters definitely have something going for them. You've got nothing to lose by trying one.

Belly putters

A variation on the long putter is the midlength belly putter. You anchor it to your midsection so that it looks like the club is stabbing you in the navel. Belly putters are 40 to 45 inches long. Like long putters, they're designed to minimize wrist action in the stroke. Vijay Singh, Fred Couples, Jim Furyk, Retief Goosen, and other pros have fought putting woes with these midlength mallets, though many putted better when they went back to a standard model. If you're struggling with jumpy wrists on the greens, you may want to try the belly method. (Keep in mind that it takes practice and patience.)

Building Your Putting Stroke

As I note earlier in the chapter, you can putt well using any number of methods or clubs. But I'm going to ignore that for now. At this stage, you should putt in as orthodox a manner as possible. That way, when something goes wrong — which it will — the fault is easier to fix. The trouble with being unorthodox is that finding order in the chaos is more difficult.

The putting grip

The putting grip isn't like the full-swing grip (which I cover in Chapter 6). The full-swing grip is more in the fingers, which encourages your wrists to hinge and unhinge. Your putting grip's purpose is exactly the opposite.

Grip the putter more in the palm of your hands to reduce the amount of movement your hands make. Although you may putt well with a lot of wrist action in your stroke, I prefer that you take the wrists out of play as much as possible. Unless you have incredible touch, your wrists aren't very reliable when you need to hit the ball short distances. You're far better off relying on the rocking of your shoulders to create momentum in the putterhead.

Not all putting grips are the same — not even those grips where you place your right hand below the left in conventional fashion. But what almost all putting grips have in common is that the palms of both hands face each other so that your hands can work together. The last thing you want is your hands fighting one another. Too much of either hand, and your ball has a bad experience. If your left hand dominates, your right hand sues for nonsupport. Both hands need to work together.

In the conventional grip, your hands can work together in one of two ways, as shown in Figure 9-3. Start by placing the palms of your hands on either side of the club's grip. Slide your right hand down a little so that you can place both hands on the club. You should feel like you're going to adopt the ten-finger grip (refer to Chapter 6). Then do one of the following, depending on which grip you prefer:

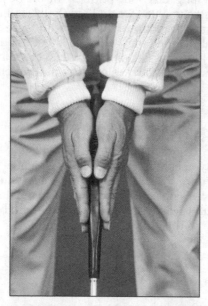

Place your palms on opposing sides of the grip.

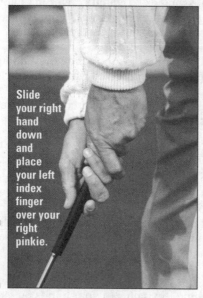

Slide your right hand down and place your left index finger over your right pinkie.

Or extend your left index finger over the fingers of your right hand.

Figure 9-3: A gripping start.

> ✔ **Place your left index finger over the little finger of your right hand.** Known as the *reverse overlap,* this putting grip is probably the most popular option on the PGA and LPGA tours.
>
> ✔ **Extend your left index finger past the fingers of your right hand until the tip touches your right index finger.** I call this grip the *extended reverse overlap.* The left index finger, when extended, provides stability to the putting stroke.

Go with the grip that feels most comfortable. I describe other methods of gripping the putter in the following sections.

Left hand low

This method is commonly referred to as *cross-handed.* The left hand hangs below the right with the putter (or vice versa if you're a lefty). Many players use this method today because it helps keep the lead hand (the left, in this case) from bending at the wrist as you hit the ball. (See Figure 9-4.)

One of the biggest causes of missed putts is the breakdown of the left wrist through impact. When the left wrist bends, the putter blade twists. This twisting causes the ball to wobble off-line, even if you've got an MOI putter. (Check out the earlier section "Picking a putter: From MOI to you" for more on these clubs.) That's why you should maintain the bend of your left wrist from the address position all the way through the stroke.

The cross-handed grip can make maintaining that wrist position easier. PGA Tour stars — including Jim Furyk and Stuart Appleby — have won with this type of grip.

The few times I've tried the cross-handed grip, pulling with the left wrist seemed to be easier. It seems that pulling with the lead hand makes it harder to break down with the wrist.

Another reason you see many of today's pros using a cross-handed grip is that, with the left arm lower on the shaft, you pull the left shoulder more square to your target line. Pulling your left shoulder happens automatically with this grip. I tend to open my shoulders (aim to the left) with my putter. As soon as I tried a cross-handed grip, my left shoulder moved toward the target line, and I was squarer to my line.

I think the left-hand-low method's best asset is that you swing the left arm back and forth during the stroke. The trailing hand (right) goes along for the ride, which is a great way to stroke your golf ball. I suggest that you try putting with your left hand low. You may stick with this method forever.

A left-hand-below-right putting grip helps stop left-wrist breakdown.

Figure 9-4:
Keep that left wrist firm.

The claw

This weird-looking grip got a boost at the 2005 Masters, where claw-gripper Chris DiMarco took eventual winner Tiger Woods into a thrilling playoff. To try the claw, start with a standard putting grip. Turn your right palm toward you and bring it to the putter's handle so that the handle touches the spot between your thumb and index finger. Now bring your index and middle fingers to the shaft, leaving your ring finger and pinkie off, as shown in Figure 9-5.

DiMarco had gone through a spell of such terrible putting that he nearly gave up hope; with this grip, he rejuvenated his career and clawed his way to the top.

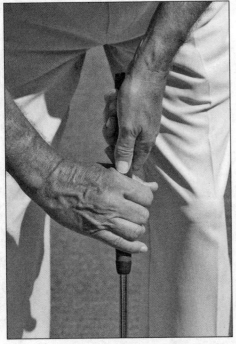

Figure 9-5:
The claw
grip —
another
option.

Putting posture: Stand and deliver

As you crouch over the ball to putt, your knees should flex slightly. If your knees are locked, you're straining your back too much. Don't bend those knees too much, though, or you may start to look like a golf geek!

Bend from your waist so that your arms hang straight down. This position allows your arms to swing back and forth from a fixed point in a pendulum motion. Hold your arms straight out from your body. Bend down with those arms outstretched from the waist until your arms are pointing to the ground. Now flex your knees a little, and you're in the correct putting posture.

You can break a lot of rules in how you stand to hit a putt (see Figure 9-6). Ben Crenshaw, one of the best putters ever, always stood open to the target line, his left foot drawn back. Gary Player did the opposite: He set up closed, his right foot farther from the target line than his left. But that's their style; I keep things simple with a square stance so that I don't need to make many in-stroke adjustments to compensate.

To putt, you can stand open.

Or closed.

Or square.

Figure 9-6:
Putting
stances
vary.

Toeing the line

As in a full swing (see Chapter 6), the line of your toes is the key. Regardless of which stance you choose, your toe line should always be parallel to your target line. Be aware that the target line isn't always a straight line from the ball to the hole — if only putting were that simple! Few greens are flat, so putts *break* or bend from right to left or from left to right. (See "Reading the break" later in this chapter.) So sometimes you aim, say, five inches to the right of the hole, and other times maybe a foot to the left (see Figure 9-7). Whatever you decide, your toe line must be parallel to your target line.

Sometimes your target isn't the hole.

Sometimes you have to allow for the ball to bend on a sloping green.

Figure 9-7: Playing the break.

On breaking putts, aim your feet parallel to the line you've chosen, not toward the hole (see Figure 9-8). In effect, you make every putt straight. Applying a curve to your putts is way too complicated and affects your stroke. Imagine how you'd have to adjust if you aimed at the hole and then tried to push the ball out to the right because of a slope on the green. You'd have no way to be consistent.

Standing just right

Okay, now what about width of stance? Again, you have margin for error, but your heels need to be about shoulder-width apart at address, as shown in Figure 9-9.

You have to bend over to place the putter behind the ball. How far should you bend? Just far enough to get your *eye line* (the direction of your gaze — a much-neglected part of putting) directly over the ball. To find that position, place a ball on your forehead between your eyes, bend over, and let the ball drop, as shown in Figure 9-10. Where does the ball hit the ground? That's where the ball should be in relation to your body. It shouldn't be to the inside, the outside, behind, or in front of that point. It should be right there, dead center. This alignment places your eyes not just over the ball but also over the line that you want the ball to ride.

Figure 9-8:
Feet parallel
to your put-
ting line.

For putting, your heels should be
shoulder-width apart.

Figure 9-9:
Heels and
shoulders
are the
same width.

Drop the ball from a point between your eyes.

Where the ball lands is where it should be positioned in your stance.

Figure 9-10:
Your eyes should be over the ball.

Matching your putt to your full swing

TIP

One basic rule for a beginning golfer is to match the length of your golf swing to your putting stroke. That is, if you have a *short swing* (your left arm, if you're right-handed, doesn't get too far up in the air on your backswing), make sure that your putting stroke is a short one, too. If your full swing is *long,* make your putting stroke long. This way, you're not contradicting yourself.

Look at two of the greatest putters in history: Ben Crenshaw and Phil Mickelson. Both have long, slow swings, and their putting strokes are — you guessed it — long and slow. On the other hand, major champions Nick Price and Lanny Wadkins have quick swings and quick putting strokes.

Your swing tells a lot about your personality. If your golf swing is long and slow, you're probably an easygoing person. If your swing is short and fast, you're probably the type who walks around with his hair on fire.

GARY SAYS

I believe that a putting stroke that contradicts your full swing leads to problems. Sam Snead had a great long putting stroke that went with his beautiful swing, but as the years came on the golf course, the swing stayed long and the stroke got shorter. The yips took over (see "Shh! Nobody Mentions the Yips," later in this chapter). Johnny Miller had a big swing with his golf clubs and a putting stroke that was so fast you could hardly see it. He had a contradiction, and he had to go to the TV tower because he couldn't roll 'em in anymore. The change wasn't all bad; Johnny brings great insight to the game from his seat in the announcing booth.

Getting up to speed

In my decades in pro golf, I've seen players of all shapes and sizes with a lot of different putting methods. Some putted in what could be termed mysterious ways, and others were totally conventional. So analyzing different putting methods is no help. The best way to look at putting is to break it down to its simplest level. The hole. The ball. The ball fits into the hole. Now get the ball into the hole in the fewest possible strokes.

You want to get the ball rolling at the right speed. That means hitting a putt so that if the ball misses the cup, it finishes 14 to 18 inches past the hole, as shown in Figure 9-11. This distance is true no matter the length of the putt. Two feet or 40 feet, your aim must be to hit the ball at a pace that has it finish 14 to 18 inches beyond the hole. If it doesn't go in, that is.

A putt can't possibly go in if you don't get it to the hole.

You're probably wondering why your ball needs the right speed. Well, the right speed gives the ball the greatest chance of going into the hole. Think about it: If the ball rolls toward the middle of the cup, you don't want it moving so fast that it rolls right over the hole. If it touches either side of the cup, it may drop in. Your goal is to give the ball every chance to drop in, from any angle — front, back, or side. I don't know about you, but I want that hole to seem as big as possible.

The only putts that *never* drop are the ones you leave short of the hole. If you've played golf for any length of time, you've heard the phrase "never up, never in." The cliché is annoying but true. As the Irish say, "Ninety-nine percent of all putts that come up short don't go in, and the other 1 percent never get there." Remember that saying! Also remember that you should try to sink every putt from 10 feet or closer. I *hope* to make every putt from 10 to 20 feet, and I try to get every putt close from 20 feet and beyond.

Figure 9-11:
Just past:
Here's how
hard to hit
your putts.

Reading the break

After you have the distance control that a consistent pace brings, you can
work on the second half of the putting equation: reading the break. The
break is the amount a putt moves from right to left, or left to right. Slope, the
grain of the grass, topographical features such as water and mountains, and,
perhaps most important, how hard you hit the ball dictate the break. For
example, if I'm an aggressive player who routinely hits putts five feet past the
cup, I'm not going to play as much break as you do. (***Remember:*** You should
hit your putts only 14 to 18 inches past the cup.)

TIP

The firmer you hit a putt, the less the ball breaks on even the steepest gradi-
ent. So don't be fooled into thinking that you can hole a putt one way only. On,
say, a 20-footer, you probably have about five possibilities. How hard you hit
the ball is one factor.

The key, of course, is consistency. Being a bold putter isn't a bad thing (if you're willing to put up with the occasional 5-footer coming back if you miss), as long as you putt that way all the time — and are still in your teens. Otherwise, you want to leave your misses within tap-in distance, 14 to 18 inches past the hole.

The first thing I do when I arrive at a golf course is to find the natural slope of the terrain. If the course is near mountains, finding the natural slope is easy. Say the mountains are off to the right on the first hole. Any slope on that hole runs from right to left. In fact, the slope on every green is going to be "from" the mountain (unless, of course, a particularly humorless architect has decided to bank some holes toward the mountain). So I take that into account on every putt I hit.

If the course is relatively flat, go find the pro or course superintendent. Ask about nearby reservoirs or, failing that, the area's lowest point. This point can be 5 miles away or 20 — it doesn't matter. Find out where that point is and take advantage of gravity. Gravity is a wonderful concept. Every putt breaks down a hill — high point to low point — unless you're in a zero-gravity environment. But that's another book.

After you know the lowest point, look at each green in detail. If you're on an older course, the greens probably slope from back to front to aid drainage. Greens nowadays have more humps and undulations than ever and are surrounded by more bunkers. And the sand tells a tale: Most courses are designed so that water runs past a bunker and not into it. Take that insight into account when you line up a putt. And don't forget the barometric pressure and dew point — just kidding!

Reading the grain

Golf is played on different grasses (ideally, not on the same course). Climate usually dictates the kind of grass you find on a course. When dealing with grasses, architects try to use the thinnest possible blade, given the climate, and then try to get that grass to grow straight up to eliminate grain. Grasses in hot, tropical areas have to be more resilient, so they typically have thick blades. *Bermuda grass* is the most common. Its blades tend to follow the sun from morning to afternoon — in other words, from east to west. Because the blade is so strong, Bermuda grass can carry a golf ball according to the direction in which it lies. Putts *downgrain* (with the grain) go faster than putts *into* (against) the grain. All that, of course, has an effect on your putt.

Look at the cup to find out which way the Bermuda grass is growing. Especially in the afternoon, you may see a ragged half and a smooth, or sharp, half on the lip of the cup — that shows the direction in which the grass is growing. The ragged look is caused by the grass's tendency to grow and fray. If you can't tell either way, go to the *fringe* (the edge of the green). The grass on the fringe is longer, so you can usually see the direction of the grain right away. The grain of the fringe is the same as on the green.

Another common type of grass is *bent grass*. You see this strain mostly in the northern and northeastern United States. Bent grass has a thinner blade than Bermuda grass, but it doesn't stand up to excessive heat as well.

Bent grass is used by many golf-course builders because it allows them to make the greens fast, and the recent trend for greens is to combine slope with speed. Try getting on the roof of your car, putting a ball down to the hood ornament, and making it stop. That's how slippery greens with bent grass can feel.

I don't concern myself much with grain on bent greens. Bent is better than Bermuda when it comes to growing straight, so grain is rarely a factor on bent greens. I just worry about the slope and the 47 things on my checklist before I putt. Putting could be so much fun if I didn't have a brain.

If you get the chance to play golf in Japan, you'll play on grass called *korai*. This wiry grass can be a menace on the greens because it's stronger than AstroTurf and can really affect the way the ball rolls on the green. If the blades are growing toward you, you have to hit the ball with a violent pop. Isao Aoki, a great Japanese player, developed a unique putting stroke in which he kept the toe of the putter way off the ground and then gave the ball a pop with his wrist to get it going — an effective way of dealing with the korai grass he grew up on.

Long Putts: Lags

Long putts are a test of your feel for pace. Nothing more. The last thing I want you thinking about over, say, a 40-foot putt is how far back to take the putter or what path the putter will follow. Instead, focus on smoothness, rhythm, and timing — all the factors that foster control over the distance a ball travels. Or as Chevy Chase said in the cult golf movie *Caddyshack,* "Be the ball."

Here's how I practice my long putting: First, I don't aim for a hole. I'm thinking distance, not direction. I figure that hitting a putt 10 feet short is a lot more likely than hitting it 10 feet wide, so distance is the key. I throw a bunch of balls down on the practice green and putt to the far fringe (see Figure 9-12). I want to see how close I can get to the edge without going over. I don't care about where I hit the putt, just how far. If you practice with this technique, you'll be amazed at how adept you become.

To get a feel for distance, putt a few balls to the far side of the practice putting green.

Figure 9-12: Think pace, not direction.

Another exercise to foster your feel for distance is what I call the *ladder drill.* Place a ball on the green about 10 feet from the green's edge. From at least 30 feet away, try to putt another ball between the first ball and the fringe. Then try to get a third ball between the second ball and the fringe and so on. See how many balls you can putt before you run out of room or putting gets too difficult. Obviously, the closer you get each ball to the preceding one, the more successful you are.

Short Putts: Knee-Knockers

Story time: Every day, Jackie went to the practice putting green with 100 balls. He stuck his putterhead in the cup and let the club fall to the green. Where the butt end of the putter hit the ground, he put a ball. Then he went over to the caddie shed and grabbed a caddie. Jackie handed the guy a $100 bill and told him to sit behind the cup. Jackie then putted 100 balls from the distance he'd established. If he made all 100 putts, Jackie kept the money. If he missed even one, the caddie pocketed the cash.

Jackie followed this routine every day. All of a sudden, every short putt he hit meant something. All short putts counted. And when he got to the golf course and was faced with a short putt, he knew that he had already made 100 of them under a lot of pressure. (A $100 bill in those days was backed by real gold.)

Pressure is the key word in Jackie's story. To avoid taking short putts for granted, you must create a situation in which missing hurts. It doesn't have to hurt you financially. Any kind of suffering is fine. But you have to care about the result of every putt. If all you have to do after missing is pull another ball over and try again, you're never going to get better. You don't care enough.

So put yourself under pressure, even if you only make yourself stay on the green until you can make 25 putts in a row. You may be amazed at how difficult the last putt is after you've made 24 in a row. It's the same putt in physical terms. But you're feeling nervous, knowing that missing means that you've wasted your time over the previous 24 shots. In other words, you've created tournament conditions on the practice green. And trust me, you'll improve.

Here's some instruction to get you started: Because you don't want the ball to travel far, the stroke should be equally short, which doesn't give the putterhead much of an arc to swing on. But the lack of arc is okay. On a short putt, you don't want the putterhead to move inside or outside the target line (at least on the way back). So think "straight back, straight through." If you can keep the putterface directly toward the hole throughout the stroke and you're set up squarely, you're sure to make more knee-knockers than you miss.

To make sure you're keeping steady over the ball, don't look up to watch your short putts go in. *Listen* for them to hit the bottom of the cup.

My instructions sound easy, but as with everything else in golf, knowing how short putting feels helps. Place a two-by-four on the ground. Put the toe of your putter against the board. Hit putts while keeping the toe against the board until after impact, as shown in Figure 9-13. Keep the putterhead at 90 degrees to the board so that the putter moves on the straight-back-and-straight-through path that you want. Practice this drill until you can repeat the sensation on real putts. And remember one of my *Golf For Dummies* secrets: Never allow the wrist on your lead hand to bend when putting. If you do bend, you'll end up in putting hell.

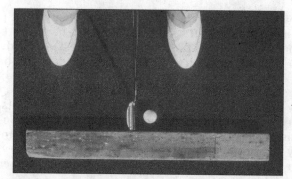

Keep the toe of your putter touching the board...

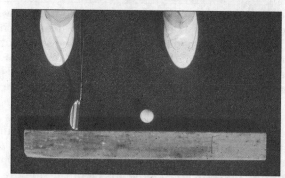

when you move the putter back...

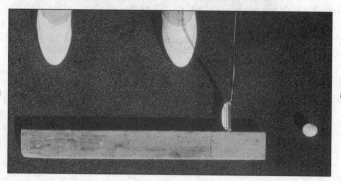

and through.

Figure 9-13: Wood that it could be this easy.

Shh! Nobody Mentions the Yips

"I've got the yips!" may be the most feared phrase in golf. Any professional golfer with the yips may as well be setting fire to $100 bills. Simply put, the *yips* are a nervous condition that prevents the afflicted from making a smooth putting stroke. Instead, the yipper makes jerky little snatches at the ball, the putterhead seemingly possessing a mind all its own.

Some of the best players in history have had their careers — at least at the top level — cut short by the yips. Ben Hogan, perhaps the steeliest competitor ever, was one victim. (He was the one who famously called putting "the game within the game.") Hogan's great rival Sam Snead was another golf immortal who suffered from the yips. Arnold Palmer has a mild case. Bobby Jones, winner of the Grand Slam in 1930, had them, too. So did Tommy Armour, a brave soldier who lost an eye fighting in the trenches during World War I. He later won a British Open and a PGA Championship, but his inability to hole short putts finished his playing career. Peter Alliss, a commentator on ABC, found that he couldn't even move the putter away from the ball toward the end of his career.

Two-time Masters winner Bernhard Langer has had the yips not once, not twice, but three times. To Langer's eternal credit, he has overcome them each time. First he came up with a rather unique, homemade style where he seemed to be taking his own pulse while over a putt. Later, he resorted to using a long putter and was the Champions Tour's Player of the Year in 2008 and again in 2009.

Langer is the exception rather than the rule. As Henry Longhurst, the late, great writer and commentator, said about the yips, "Once you've had 'em, you've got 'em."

Longhurst, himself a yipper, once wrote a highly entertaining column on the yips that opened with the following sentence: "There can be no more ludicrous sight than that of a grown man, a captain of industry, perhaps, and a pillar of his own community, convulsively jerking a piece of ironmongery to and fro in his efforts to hole a 3-foot putt." Longhurst is right, too. Pray that you don't get the yips.

So what causes the yips? Mostly, I think it's fear: fear of missing, fear of embarrassment, fear of who knows what. Point is, it starts in the head. It can't be physical. After all, you're only talking about hitting the ball a short distance. What could be easier?

The yips spread insidiously through your body, like a virus. When the yips reach your hands and arms, you're doomed. Your only recourse is a complete revamping of your method. Sam Snead started putting sidesaddle, facing the hole, holding his putter with a sort of split-handed grip, the ball to the right of his feet. (I describe a variation of Sam's method later in this chapter in "Sidesaddling Up: Face-On Putting") Other players have tried placing the left-hand-low putting style, the claw grip, and/or switching putters every time they blink. (Check out "The putting grip" and "The Most Important Club in the Bag: Examining Putters" earlier in the chapter for more on grips and putters, respectively.)

When Mac O'Grady did a study on the yips, he mailed 1,500 questionnaires to golfers everywhere. When doctors at UCLA's Department of Neurology looked over the results, they decided that the only way to fool the yips is to stay ahead of them.

When you do something long enough, like bending over to putt a certain way, your body is in what the doctors call a *length tension curve*. The brain recognizes this posture, and after you've missed putts for a long period of time, the subconscious takes over and starts directing muscles to help get the ball into the hole. Your conscious and subconscious are fighting. Now your right hand twitches, or your left forearm has spasms trying to help you get the ball into the hole. You're in full *focal dystonia* (involuntary spasms), and that's no fun.

The remedy the scientists suggested was changing the length tension curve, or simply changing the way a yipper stands over a putt. The long putter surely makes you stand up to the ball differently, and maybe that's why golfers almost always putt better immediately after trying a long putter.

So if you get the yips, which usually come with age, simply change something drastic in the way you set up the ball, try a different grip, or take a break and go bowling. Sometimes the yips go away by themselves.

The real secret, however, is getting over the notion that using any of those methods identifies you as a yipper, someone who is psychologically impaired. Don't be afraid to look different. The best golfers all share one trait: They do whatever works.

Sidesaddling Up: Face-on Putting

Here's another alternative that's starting to surface in the wonderful world of golf. It's called *face-on* or *sidesaddle putting*. If you've been struggling with your putter, this stroke may be the cure.

It starts with common sense. Now, that may not be the first quality people associate with me — I'm hoping charm and virility are up there, too — but it comes into play when I ask golfers to putt without a putter.

"How?" they ask.

I toss them a golf ball. "Just roll it to the hole."

At this point everyone, from Ben Crenshaw to the greenest golf novice, faces the hole and rolls the ball underhand. *Nobody* turns sideways first. Why? Because it's more natural to face your target. Impractical for full swings, but perfectly practical for putting, if you know how to do it.

If you adopt the face-on method shown in Figure 9-14, you need a putter designed for it. (They're becoming more common, but can still be hard to find. For information on ordering putters and other equipment from Web sites, see Chapter 19.) You can get a feel for it with a regular long putter, but remember: To do it right, you need a face-on putter.

Here's how to try face-on putting:

1. **Use the same posture as if you were rolling a ball by hand: Face the target, knees flexed, with the ball slightly to your right, just ahead of your right foot.**

2. **Place your left hand at the top of your putter's grip; keep the face of your putter square to the line of your putt.**

   The left hand acts as the fulcrum for your putting stroke.

3. **With your eyes on the ball, bring the putter straight back with your right hand, and then straight through along your putting line.**

4. **Let your head come up naturally as you follow the ball on its merry way into the hole.**

For more on face-on putting, check out `Puttmagic.com`.

Figure 9-14: Face-on putting.

The Art of Aiming

The golf swing is an assortment of trajectories flung around in time and space. Manifestations of your binocular acuity are the key to your pilgrimage. Are you in alignment with the parallel universe of focal obedience?

—Gary McCord, circa 1998, just after eating a lungfish tart

Golf requires an assortment of physical skills and techniques. It also requires you to use your mind, which makes the final decisions and tells your motor system where and when things will happen, hopefully in some sort of harmony. For putting, all of that starts with alignment.

Some golfers aim at a spot a few feet in front of the ball. When they place their putters behind the ball, they aim the face of the putter or the lines on the putter at that spot. Aligning to a spot a foot or so in front of the ball is easier than aligning to the hole, which may be much farther away.

Bowlers use this same kind of alignment strategy. If you've ever bowled, you know about the spots a few feet in front of you on the lane. You look at the spots and then pick a line to roll the ball over. After I discovered this technique in my bowling league, the Gutter Dwellers, my average rocketed to 87.

You can also use other strategies to help with alignment. One is to take the logo of the golf ball and set it along the line that you want the putt to follow. This method can help you get a better visual reference to the line. Some players, such as Tiger Woods, use a permanent marker to make a line about an inch in length on the ball (see Figure 9-15) for the same reason: to achieve a better visual reference for directing the ball down the intended path. When you stand over the putt, the ball is already aimed.

The eyes like lines

Players say they putt better when they "see the line" of the putt. Some days when I play, the line seems so visible that I can't miss. Unfortunately, that happens about as often as Halley's Comet comes around. Most of the time, I have to concentrate to see the line.

Another set of lines that can help your optics are the lines of your feet, knees, and shoulders. By keeping them *square* (at a right angle) to the target line, you help your eyes appreciate what is straight — and keep your stroke on line.

Or make a line on the ball with a Sharpie pen.

Figure 9-15: Aim the logo of the ball or a drawn line toward the target.

To help you keep the clubface square to your target line, use tape or a yard-stick on the floor. Aim the tape at a distant target, like a baby grand piano at the far end of your ballroom. Now set up at the end of the tape as if you were going to hit an imaginary ball straight down the tape line. You're practicing visual alignment (which is easier than practicing a 3-wood out of a fairway bunker with a large lip for three hours in a hailstorm). Give this drill a chance — it can really help your perception of straight lines.

When I'm having alignment problems, I take some of the gum that I've been chewing for the last three days and attach a tee to the putter with the fat end flush to the face, as shown in Figure 9-16. Then I aim that tee at the hole from about three feet away. (It's amazing how strong gum is after a three-day chew; in fact, I used it as mortar on my new brick mobile home.)

Instant pre-play

I remember one telecast when I commented on a putt we caught on camera: "That putt must have taken 11 seconds." It was a long one that went over a hill and then down a severe slope to the hole. The player had to visualize the ball's path in order to hit it with the proper speed; he had to visually rehearse the roll of the ball over all that terrain until it looked like an instant replay of the putt he was about to make.

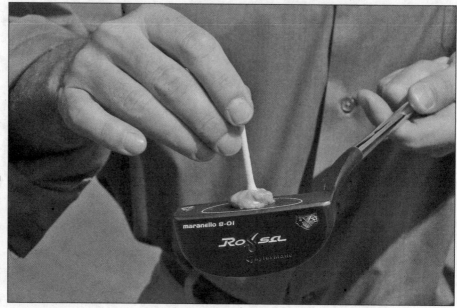

Figure 9-16:
Stick a tee to the face of your putter to help align with your target.

This drill trains your eyes to square the clubface. You can use this exercise to visually process what a square clubface looks like as you look down the attached tee to the hole. Spend a couple of minutes appreciating this perspective. If it looks okay to you on your first try, you're in line for your Bachelor of Alignment degree. If not, repeat the drill daily until it looks okay the first time you place the club down.

The need for speed

One of the best ways to develop a touch for the speed at which putts should roll is to imagine things happening before they really do.

You must optically preview the putt's roll from its stationary point to a resting place near the hole — a tap-in is really nice. This optical preview activates the motor system to respond with the right amount of energy to hit the putt. You'd do the same thing if I told you to throw a ball over a bush and make it land no more than five feet beyond the bush. You'd decide at what arc and speed to toss the ball, and your mind's eye would relay this information to your muscles.

View a putt from a point off to the side of the target line, midway between the ball and the hole, as shown in Figure 9-17. This technique can give you a better feel for the distance. Some professionals swear they can visualize the proper speed of a putt twice as well from the side.

Figure 9-17: Viewing a putt from the side can help you judge distance and speed.

A good rule of thumb: Don't change your mind while you're over a putt. For one thing, putts look different from above than from the side! For another, the ground you stand on may not be sloped the same as it is near the hole. And unless the putt is all downhill, the ball does most of its curving during the last third of the putt. (That's another reason to stand to the side of the putt — assessing the last third of the putt is easier from there.)

Some quick tips you may want to scrawl in your reminder book:

- ✔ **Fast greens break more, so don't hit the ball too hard.** But keep in mind that hitting the ball softly means that the slope affects it more.

- ✔ **Downhill putts act like fast greens because the slope affects the roll of the ball for more than the last few feet.**

- ✔ **Slow greens break less, so you have to hit the ball harder.** That initial burst of speed keeps the ball from breaking as much.

- ✔ **Uphill putts act like putts on slow greens.** Your challenge is to figure out how much uphill slope you're dealing with, and adjust your putt accordingly — the steeper the slope, the more power it takes. Try imagining that the hole is farther away than it really is.

Points of the roll

I give you information on some complicated stuff, so here are some key points:

- **Keep your alignment parallel to the target line.** All the following parts of you stay parallel to that line:
  - Feet
  - Knees
  - Shoulders
  - Eye line
- **Know what your putter blade looks like when it's square to the line.**
- **Use the ball's logo or a line marked on the ball to help you align putts.**
- **Follow the line of your intended putt with your eyes at the speed that you think the ball will roll.**
- **Stare at the line of your putt longer than you look at the golf ball.**

Good putting takes practice. And then more practice. The boys at the club practice their putting less than anything else, and then wonder why they lose bets!

More than half the strokes you make in this silly game may be putts. Create games on the putting green to make putting practice more fun. Your scorecard will thank you.

Chapter 10

Bunker Play: It's Easy (Really!)

I've read countless articles and books on sand play, and they all say the same thing: Because you don't even have to hit the ball, playing from the sand is the easiest part of golf. Well, I say that's bull trap! If sand play were so easy, all those articles and books would never be written in the first place. Everyone would be blasting the ball onto the putting surface with nary a care in the world. And take it from me, that's certainly not the case.

In this chapter, I explain the equipment and techniques you need to get out of the sand. I tell how and why your sand wedge is different from any other club in your bag. At the end of the chapter, I even tell how to hit a successful bunker shot from a terrible lie. Do *that* your next time out and your friends will be amazed.

Don't Call 'Em Traps! Avoiding Trouble in Bunkers

Bunkers, or sand traps (as I'm told *not* to call them on TV), provoke an extraordinary amount of "sand angst" among golfers. But sometimes, *aiming* for a bunker actually makes sense — on a long, difficult approach shot, for example. The pros know that the *up and down* (getting onto the green and then into the hole) from sand can actually be easier than from the surrounding (usually gnarly) grass.

Bunkers began as dips in the ground on the windswept Scottish linksland. Because such areas were sheltered from cold breezes, sheep would take refuge in them. Thus, the dips expanded and got deeper. When the land came to be used for golf, the locals took advantage of what God and the sheep left behind and fashioned sand-filled bunkers. (No word on what the sheep thought of all this.) On these old courses, the greens were positioned so as to maximize the bunkers' threat to golfers' shots, which is why they came to be named *hazards* in the rules of golf. Later, course architects placed these insidious "traps" so as to penalize wayward shots. That's why you generally don't see bunkers in the middle of fairways — they're mostly to the sides.

I don't know too many amateurs who have ever aimed at a bunker. Mired in sand is the last place they want to be. The saga the late Tip O'Neill endured years ago during the Bob Hope Chrysler Classic, a pro-am tournament (see Chapter 15), is a great example of how amateur golfers look at bunkers. The former Speaker of the House, admittedly not the strongest golfer (even among celebrities), found himself in a very deep bunker. He then spent the next few hours (okay, it just *seemed* that long) trying to extricate first the ball, and then his hefty, honorable self, from the trap — all on national television. You could almost hear millions of viewers muttering, "Been there, done that."

Why do bunkers scare most amateurs to death? Just what is it about sand play that they find so tough? Well, after much research, some of it in a laboratory, I've come to the conclusion that the answer is simple. (If it weren't simple, I'd never have discovered it.) It all comes down to lack of technique and/or a lack of understanding.

Bunker mentality

Escaping the sand can be easy after you get a feel for it. I knew at an early age that my scoring depended on getting up and down out of bunkers with a certain regularity, so I practiced bunker shots with a vengeance. As a result, I can get a ball out of a bunker with everything from a sand wedge to a putter.

One day I was playing in the Kemper Open in Charlotte, North Carolina, when I saw another pro, a notoriously bad bunker player, practicing hard on his sand play. After a few moments of idle conversation and general harassing, a bet transpired: He'd hit ten balls with his sand wedge; I'd hit five with a putter. If I got my ball closer than his ball to the hole, he'd have to go in the locker room and announce to everyone that I beat him with a putter out of a bunker. If he won, I'd take him to dinner and then not bother him for the rest of the year.

Ten minutes later, laughter from the locker room echoed throughout the clubhouse, and his reputation as the worst bunker player on tour was safe. I can't divulge his name because he's playing the Champions Tour now (and doing well!). He got much better at getting out of the sand after some much-needed practice — about 20 years' worth.

Welcome to the best game that'll ever drive you nuts. You're next on the tee.

My personal weapons — but I have to take one out to get down to the 14-club limit (see Chapter 2).

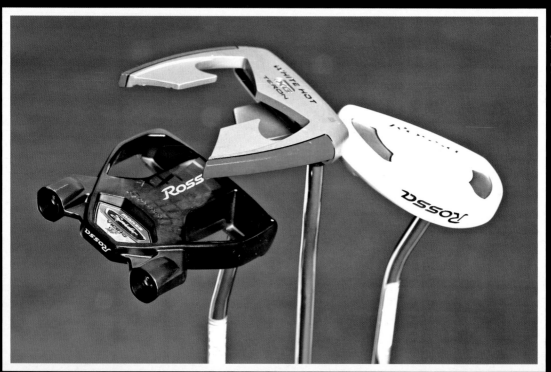

Today's putters look like something from a sci-fi movie.

The perfect practice swing starts with a solid foundation and flows smoothly to a balanced finish.

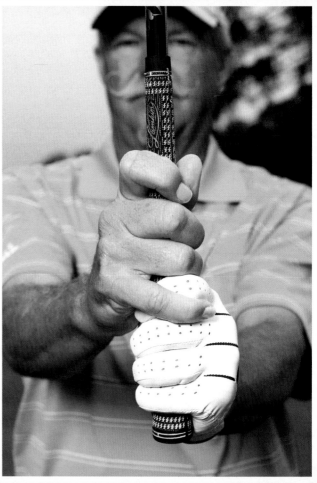

The Vardon grip (shown here from two angles) is golf's most popular grip.

© Erick W. Rasco

Bunker shots (Chapter 10) are easy! At least, they are when you set up properly (shown top)
with your stance and clubface open (shown left). Strike the sand first, and let it carry the

Faced with a bunker shot, many golfers are beaten before they start. You can tell by their constipated looks, sweaty foreheads, and hesitant body language. Their reactions when they fail are also interesting. After a couple of shots finish up back in the bunker, most players don't focus on technique. They merely try to hit the shot harder, making more and more violent swings. Wrong! Swinging harder only makes them angrier, and then the ball sure isn't going to come out. They wind up digging a nice big trench, perfect for burying a small animal but not much good for anything else.

Part of the reason for this all-too-human reaction is that long stretches of failure resign you to your fate. In your mind, you've tried everything, and you *still* can't get the damn thing out. So you trudge into the bunker expecting the worst, and that's what you usually get.

The Trouble with Sand

Golf, and especially bunker play, is mainly the creation of the proper angle that the clubhead must take into the ball. Most golfers address the ball in a way that makes creating the correct angles in their golf swings all but impossible. Ball position is the root of many duffs, hacks, slashes, and other misbegotten shots. If you have the ball positioned way back toward your right foot, as so many people seem to do, you'll never get it out of the trap. You can't hit the ball high enough, for one thing. For another, the clubhead enters the sand at too steep an angle. In other words, the clubhead digs into the sand instead of sliding through it. When that happens, the ball usually stays in the bunker, sucking sand.

Poor bunker players suffer from a lack of understanding. They get into the sand and start "digging" as if they're after buried treasure. Sometimes I feel like throwing poor bunker players a metal detector. Then at least they may turn up an old doubloon or two.

Gotta Bounce: Exploring How a Club's Bounce Affects Sand Shots

To be a competent sand player, you must take advantage of the way your sand wedge is designed. The bottom of the club is wider than the top (see Figure 10-1). The *bounce* is the part of a wedge that hangs below the *leading edge*, the front part of the *sole*. (The sole, like the bottom of a shoe, is the bottom of the clubhead.) Believe me, if you can make the best use of the bounce, you can take bunker play off your list of phobias.

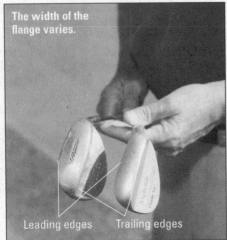

The width of the flange varies.

Leading edges   Trailing edges

Figure 10-1:
Sand
wedges
are differ-
ent from
other clubs
because
wedges
have
bounce.

REMEMBER

The bounce is the part of the clubhead that should contact the sand first. This approach encourages the sliding motion that's so crucial to good bunker play. Think about it: The sand is going to slow the club as you swing down and through, which is okay. But you want to keep the slowdown to a minimum. If the club digs in too much, the ball probably won't leave the bunker. So *slide* the clubhead; don't use it to dig.

Take note, however, that not every sand wedge has the same amount of bounce. The width of the sole and the amount that it hangs below the leading edge varies. The lower the *trailing edge* (the rear part of the sole) hangs below the leading edge, the more bounce your sand wedge has. This, of course, begs another question: How do you know how much bounce your sand wedge needs? The determining factor is the type of sand you play from. The bigger the bounce or the wider the sole on your sand wedge, the less the wedge digs into the sand.

If the sand at your home course is typically pretty firm underfoot, you need a sand wedge with very little bounce. A club with a lot of bounce does just that — bounce. Hard (or wet) sand only accentuates that tendency, so using that club leaves you hitting a lot of shots *thin,* as the clubhead skids off the sand and strikes the ball's equator. Thin shots fly too low. Either you hit the ball into the face of the bunker and don't get out at all, or the ball misses the face and zooms over the green. Neither result is socially acceptable. The first is hazardous to your mental health, the second to your playing partners.

At the other end of the scale is soft, deep sand. For that sort of stuff, you need plenty of bounce. In fact, because the clubhead digs so easily when the sand is soft, you can't have enough bounce.

GARY SAYS

Hoe, Hoe, Hoe!

In 1995, I received an urgent phone call from movie director Ron Shelton, who was shooting the movie *Tin Cup*. He said, "Gary, we forgot to ask you this, but how do you hit a gardening hoe out of a bunker?"

"Gee, Ron," I said, "I haven't done that in a while; let me think."

What I was thinking was, *"Are you nuts? What do you mean, how do you hit a gardening hoe out of a bunker?!!"*

Ron told me that he had to shoot a scene the next day with Kevin Costner hitting a ball out of a bunker with a hoe, and that the ball had to land no more than three feet from the hole. Sure. Right.

I went to the practice green at Singletree Golf Course in Vail, Colorado, with my shag bag full of balls and a hoe. It was pouring down rain. It took me 40 minutes to get a single ball out of the bunker, and I *bladed* (hit the center of the ball with the leading edge) that one to get it out. I finally decided that the bottom edge of the hoe was too sharp and that I needed some bounce to make it perform better in the sand. So I bent the hoe on the bottom and immediately started to get the ball up and out.

I called the movie set and gave directions on how to bend the hoe. They shot the scene, and Kevin Costner hit the first ball out of the bunker two feet from the hole with the hoe. That's a take; wrap it up, as they say.

So if the bounce can work with a garden hoe, imagine what you can do with your sand wedge.

Throwing Sand: Hitting Effective Bunker Shots

Okay, you're in a greenside bunker. You want to get the ball onto the putting surface. Here's what to do:

1. **Open your stance by pulling your left foot back until you start to feel vaguely ridiculous.**

   Your left foot's position must feel funny to you. If it doesn't, pull your foot back even more!

2. **Open (turn to the right) your sand wedge until the face points almost straight up at the sky, as shown in Figure 10-2.**

   Make sure you position the ball forward in your stance toward your left heel. (The ball should be even farther forward if you're unlucky enough to be very close to the face of the bunker.) You should feel like the club will slide right under the ball when you swing at it — and this position should feel just as weird as your wide-open stance. Again, if it doesn't, open the face of your sand wedge even more.

Figure 10-2:
Open your
stance and
wedge face
until they
feel
ridiculous.

Most amateurs I play with don't do either of those things. They stand too square and don't open the clubface nearly enough. In effect, they don't take advantage of their sand wedges. This club works best when the face is wide open (turned clockwise). Sand wedges are designed that way: The open face sends the ball up when you slide it into the sand.

3. Aim about a credit-card length (about 3¼ inches) behind the ball and swing at about 80 percent of full speed.

Think of it as a sliding motion. Don't hit down. Let the clubhead throw a "scoop" of sand onto the green, as shown in Figure 10-3.

Focusing on a full, uninhibited follow-through helps (see Figure 10-4). Forget the ball — all you're trying to do is throw sand out of the bunker. If you can throw sand, the ball gets carried along for the ride. And that's why better players say that bunker play is easy — the clubhead never actually contacts the ball. (**Remember:** The more sand you throw, the shorter the shot is. So if you need to hit the shot a fair distance, hit maybe only two inches behind the ball.)

Remember that your club must not touch the sand before you hit the ball. That's *grounding* the club — illegal in a hazard.

Figure 10-3:
No digging
allowed.

Form a firm, balanced
foundation...

slide the clubhead under the
ball...

throwing some sand and the
ball onto the green.

Figure 10-4:
Keep going!

GARY SAYS When I go home to play, I notice that nobody practices bunker shots, not even my pal Sand Wedge Sam. (He got his nickname after demonstrating uncommon prowess in the much underestimated and neglected art of sand-wedge tossing.) Don't fall into that trap! (I love bad puns.) Instead, get into a bunker and *practice*.

Buried Alive! Extracting a Plugged Ball

Unfortunately, not every *lie* (where the ball is sitting) in a bunker is perfect. Sometimes the ball *plugs,* or embeds itself in the sand so that only part of it is visible. Some golfers call this lie a *fried egg,* but don't reach for a spatula. Instead, after you're through cursing your bad luck, try a different technique.

To exhume your ball from a buried lie, follow these steps:

1. **Set up your stance and clubface.**

   You need to open your stance as you do for any sand shot (see the preceding section). But this time, don't open the clubface. Keep it a little *hooded.* In other words, align the clubface to the left of your target. Shift nearly all your weight to your left side, which puts you ahead of the shot (see Figure 10-5), and play the ball back in your stance. This situation is the one time you *want* the leading edge of the club to dig. The ball, after all, is below the surface of the sand.

2. **Swing the club up and down.**

   And I mean *up* and *down* like you're chopping wood with a dull ax. Hit straight down on the sand a couple of inches behind the ball as shown in Figure 10-6. A follow-through isn't necessary. Just hit down. Hard. The ball should pop up and then run to the hole. With little or no backspin, that sneaky little escapee runs like it just stole something. So allow for extra roll.

   Just how hard you should hit down is difficult for me to say — it depends on the texture and depth of the sand and on how deep the ball is buried. That old standby, practice, tells you what you need to know.

Second-to-last point: Practice with clubs of various lofts, and then use whatever works for you. I often use my pitching wedge (which has less bounce and a sharper leading edge than a sand wedge, and therefore digs more) for buried-lie escapes. (See the earlier section "Gotta Bounce: Exploring How Club Bounce Affects Sand Shots" for more on bounce.)

Put the ball back in your stance...

but don't change your posture.

Close the clubface at address.

Figure 10-5:
A buried
lie in a
bunker: Can
you dig it?

Last point: Always smooth out your footprints when leaving a bunker — that's golf etiquette. If no rake is nearby, use your feet. Or if you're like my buddy Steamroller Ron, just roll around in the bunker until it's real smooth. Golfers used to gather to watch Ron smooth out the sand. We had very few rakes at the municipal course we played, and the Steamroller was the next-best thing. I miss Steamroller; he sold his gravel business and moved to Saudi Arabia.

"Bury" the club in the sand...

which shortens your follow-through.

Figure 10-6:
Hit down
hard!

Part III

Common Faults
and Easy Fixes

The 5th Wave   By Rich Tennant

"Don't laugh — it's added 30 yards to his drive."

In this part . . .

This part is about the many maladies that can afflict your golf game and how to cure them. Have you ever had one of those days when nothing goes right? You hit one ball fat, the next one thin, and when you *do* hit the thing solidly, it slices into the parking lot!

I've got remedies for what ails you. Call it GaryCare. You didn't know you could get health care for golf, did you?

In this part, I also tell you how to play in all sorts of weather, and how to deal with the bad breaks you're sure to encounter. I even give you tips on playing through the winter, in case you're not teeing it up in Honolulu or Palm Springs.

Chapter 11

Did I Do That? Solving Common Problems

In This Chapter

▶ Understanding everyday swing flaws

▶ Taming your errant tee shots

▶ Focusing on direction and ball contact

▶ Dealing with the scary shank

The old saying is true in golf, as in life: Nobody's perfect. In golf, nobody's even close. Even the best players have some little hitches in their methods that bedevil them, especially under pressure. Greg Norman once had a tendency to hit the ball well to the right of the target on the closing holes of big tournaments. Phil Mickelson and Tiger Woods have gone through periods when they drove the ball crookedly at the worst possible times. Watch your playing companions when they get a little nervous; you can see all sorts of unfortunate events. They leave putts short and take longer to play even simple shots. Conversation all but stops. Any flaws in their swings are cruelly exposed.

No matter how far you progress in this game, you're going to develop faults of your own. They're a given. The trick is catching your faults before they get worse. Faults left unattended often turn into major problems and ruin your game. In this chapter, I show you how to head off (pun intended) many faults by controlling your head position. Then I discuss the most common faults you're likely to develop, with cures for each one. After you figure out what you tend to do wrong, you can refer to this chapter regularly to get help.

For Better Golf, Use Your Head

The root cause of most faults is your head position. Your noggin's position relative to the ball as you strike it dictates where the bottom of your swing is. If you don't believe me, try this: Shift your weight and your head toward the target onto your left side while leaving the ball in its regular position. Now make your normal swing with, say, a 6-iron. The divot the club makes is more in front of the ball. The bottom of your swing moves toward the target along with your head. The opposite is also true. Shift your weight and head to the right, and the bottom of your swing moves that way.

The bottom line: If your head moves too much during the swing, you have little chance to correct things before impact, and the result is usually poor contact — and a poor shot.

But don't get the idea that excessive head movement is responsible for absolutely every bad shot. Other poor plays can stem from improper use of your hands, arms, or body. But try to keep your head as steady as possible.

Considering Common Swing Faults

Most bad shots result from a handful of common errors. Fortunately, they're fixable. Here's how to beat back the gremlins that can creep into your game.

Slicing and hooking

Most golfers *slice* the ball, which means that it starts moving toward the left of the target and finishes well to the right. Slices don't go very far. They're horrible, weak shots that affect your DNA for generations to come.

In general, slicers use too much body action, especially upper body, and not enough hand action in their swings. I think slicing stems from the fact that most players tend to aim to the right of their target. When they do so, their swings have to compensate so that the resulting shots can finish close to the target. In most cases, that compensation starts when your brain realizes that if you swing along your aim, the ball will fly way to the right. The resulting flurry of arms and legs isn't pretty — and invariably, neither is the shot. Soon this weak, left-to-right ball flight makes your life a slicing hell.

If you're a slicer, you need to get your hands working in the swing. Here's how:

1. **Address a ball as you normally do.**

   Address is the position of your body just before you begin to swing.

2. **Turn your whole body until your butt is toward the target and your feet are perpendicular to the target line.**

3. **Twist your upper body to the left so that you can again place the clubhead behind the ball.**

   Don't move your feet, however. From this position, you have in effect made turning your body to your left on the through-swing impossible (see Figure 11-1).

   Try it. Should I call a chiropractor yet? The only way you can swing the club through the ball is by using your hands and arms.

If you slice, try this drill: Stand with your back to the target. Then turn your whole body until your butt is to the target and twist your upper body to address the ball.

Swing back...

and then swing your hands and arms through...

to finish. The ball should fly from right to left.

Figure 11-1: Extra hand action cures the slice.

4. Hit a few balls.

Focus on letting the toe of the clubhead pass your heel through impact. Quite a change in your ball flight, eh? Because your hands and arms are doing so much of the rotating work in your new swing, the clubhead is doing the same. The clubhead is now closing as it swings through the impact area. The spin imparted on the ball now causes a slight right-to-left flight — something I bet you thought you'd never see.

After you've hit about 20 shots by using this drill, switch to your normal stance and try to reproduce the feel you had standing in that strange but correct way. You'll soon be hitting hard, raking *draws* (slight hooks) far up the fairway.

Golfers prone to *hooks* (shots that start right and finish left) have the opposite problem of slicers — too much hand action and not enough body. Here's a variation on the earlier drill if you tend to hook the ball:

1. Adopt your regular stance.

2. Turn your whole body until you're looking directly at the target.

3. Twist your upper body to the right — don't move your feet — until you can set the clubhead behind the ball (see Figure 11-2).

4. Hit some shots.

Solid contact is easiest to achieve when you turn your body hard to the left, which prevents your hands from becoming overactive. Your ball flight will soon be a gentle *fade* (slight slice).

After about 20 shots, hit some balls from your normal stance, practicing the technique in the exercise. Reproduce the feel of this drill, and you're that much closer to a successful swing.

Hitting from the top

When you start cocking the wrist in your golf swing, the thumb of your right hand (if you're a right-handed golfer) points at your right shoulder on the backswing. That's good! When you start the downswing, try to keep that thumb pointing at your right shoulder for as long as you can, thus *maintaining the angle*. That's golfspeak for keeping the shaft of the club as close to the left arm on the downswing as possible. If your right thumb starts pointing away from your right shoulder on the downswing, not good! That's known as *hitting from the top*. In essence, you're uncocking the wrist on the downswing.

If you hit hooks, try this drill: Stand with both feet facing the target. Then turn your upper body until you are facing the target.

Swing back...

and then turn your body in concert with the club...

to finish. The ball should fly from left to right.

Figure 11-2: Extra body action straightens your hook.

To stop hitting from the top, reduce your grip pressure. Too much tension in your hands makes you throw the clubhead toward the ball, causing you to hit from the top. After you've relaxed your grip pressure, place an alignment stick (or an old two-by-four) on the side of the ball away from you, parallel to the target line. The ball should be about two inches from the stick. If you keep pointing your right thumb at your right shoulder on the downswing, you don't hit the stick with your club. If you point your thumb away from your shoulder on the downswing, you may just chop that stick in half. (See Figure 11-3 for a visual of this stroke.)

On the downswing, try to point your right thumb at your right shoulder (if you're right-handed).

Keep trying!

So this is how the big bombers do it!

Figure 11-3:
Don't hit from the top!

The reverse pivot

TIP

A *reverse pivot* occurs when you put all your weight on your left foot on the backswing (shown in Figure 11-4) and all your weight on your right foot during the downswing. That's the opposite of what you want to do! Picture a baseball pitcher. Pitchers have all their weight on the right foot at the top of the windup, the left foot is in the air (for a right-hander), and on the follow-through, all the weight goes to the left foot. (The right foot is now in the air.) That's the weight transfer you need. Here's how you can achieve it:

Figure 11-4:
The dreaded
reverse
pivot.

1. **Start your backswing; at the top of your swing, lift your left foot off the ground.**

   Now you can't put any weight on that foot! You'll feel your whole body resist placing your weight over your right foot.

2. **Take your time and let your weight transfer to your right foot.**

3. **Start the downswing by placing your left foot back where it was and then transfer all your weight over during the swing.**

4. **When you've made contact with the ball (hopefully), put all your weight on your left foot and lift your right foot off the ground.**

5. **Stand there for a short time, feeling the balance.**

This rocking-chair transfer drill lets you feel the proper weight shift in the golf swing. Take it easy at first. Practice short shots until you get the feel, and then work your way up to your driver.

Swaying off the ball

In a *sway,* your hips and shoulders don't turn on the backswing, but simply slide back in a straight line, which moves your head away from the ball, as shown in Figure 11-5. Here's a good drill to help you stop swaying:

Figure 11-5:
The sway ain't the way.

1. **Find a bare wall.**

2. **Place a 5-iron on the ground with the clubhead touching the wall and the shaft extending straight into the room.**

3. **Place your right foot against the end of the shaft with the little toe of your right shoe hitting the end of the club.**

   Now you're standing exactly one club length from the wall.

4. **Put your left foot in the normal address position for the 5-iron and, without moving your feet, bend over and pick up the club.**

5. **Take a backswing.**

   If you sway with your hips one inch to the right on your backswing, you hit the wall immediately with the club.

Practice this setup until you can do it without hitting the wall. I put so many marks and holes in a motel room doing this drill, I could watch the TV in the next room!

I suggest practicing this drill in your garage at first to save the walls at home. You may want to use an old club, too.

The belly-button twist

Another common fault is doing the *belly-button twist:* sliding your hips too far toward the target at the start of the downswing. How far should your hips slide before they start turning left? They must slide until your left hip and left knee are over your left foot. Then those hips turn left in a hurry!

Here's how to improve your hip position at the downswing:

1. **Get a broken club that has just a shaft and a grip on it.**

   You can find broken clubs in lost-and-found barrels, or just ask somebody at a driving range. Your golf pro can also help you find one. You can also use a broom handle or alignment stick — any stick you can plant in the ground.

2. **Stick the broken club into the ground just outside your left foot; the top of the grip should be no higher than your hip.**

3. **Now hit a few shots.**

   When you swing, your left hip should not hit the club stuck in the ground. It should turn to the left of the shaft. The key here is to straighten the left leg in your follow-through. To help you stay balanced, try to "hold" your finish at the end of the follow-through.

A swing that's too short

In most cases, a short swing comes from too little shoulder turn. Turn your left shoulder over your right foot at the top of your backswing. If you can't, lift your left heel off the ground until you can. Many players I see with short swings also keep their right elbows against their rib cages at the top of the swing. The right elbow should be six inches away from the rib cage to allow some freedom in the swing and give the needed length to your swing arc.

A swing that's too long

If your swing is too long and sloppy (going beyond parallel to the ground at the top of the swing), here are two positions to work on:

- ✔ The right arm in the backswing (for a right-handed golfer) must not bend more than 90 degrees. It must stay at a right angle (see Figure 11-6).
- ✔ The right elbow must not get more than six inches away from your rib cage at the top of the backswing.

If you can maintain these two simple positions at the top of your swing, you don't overswing.

Your right arm should form a right angle at the elbow.

Figure 11-6: Do the right (angle) thing in your backswing.

Tackling Trouble off the Tee

What's worse than starting a hole with a pitiful bloop or a screamer into uncharted lands? That's trouble with a capital tee! To get well off the tee, you need to avoid the common blunders in the following sections.

Popping up your tee shots

One of the most common sights I see on the first tee of a pro-am or member-guest tournament is the *skied* tee shot — the ball goes higher than it goes forward. The golfer usually hits the ball on the top part of the driver, causing an ugly mark to appear, which is one reason a tour player never lets an amateur use his driver. If the amateur hits such a *fountain ball* (as my wife likes to call it because she says a skied tee shot has the same trajectory as one of those fountains in Italy) with another player's driver, he has a lot of apologizing to do.

At the municipal course where I nurtured my game, we had few special rules. One was that if you could catch your drive off the tee, you could play it over again with no penalty. We had so many guys wearing tennis shoes for speed that it looked like a track meet.

If you're hitting the ball on the top side of your driver, you're swinging the club on too much of a downward arc. What's that mean, you ask? It means that your head is too far in front of the ball (toward the target side of the ball) and your left shoulder is too low at impact.

Here's what to do:

1. **Go find an upslope.**

2. **Stand so that your left foot (if you're right-handed) is higher than your right.**

3. **Tee the ball up and hit drivers or 3-woods until you get the feeling of staying back and under the shot.**

   The uphill lie promotes this feeling.

Here's a secret: People who hit down on their drivers want to kill the stupid ball in front of their buddies. These golfers have a tremendous shift of weight to the left side on the downswing. If you hit balls from an upslope, you can't get your weight to the left side as quickly. Consequently, you keep your head behind the ball, and your left shoulder goes up at impact. Practice on an upslope until you get a feel and then proceed to level ground. You'll turn your pop-ups into line drives.

Suffering from a power outage

Every golfer in the world wants more distance. Tiger Woods and Michelle Wie want more distance. I want more distance, and I'm sure you do, too. For that, you need more power. Here's how to make it happen:

✔ **Turn your shoulders on the backswing.** The more you turn your shoulders on the backswing, the better chance you have to hit the ball longer. So really stretch that torso on the backswing — try to put your left shoulder over your right foot at the top of your swing. Thinking that you're turning your back to the target may help.

If you're having difficulty moving your shoulders enough on the backswing, try turning your left knee clockwise until it's pointing behind the ball during your backswing. This setup frees up your hips to turn, and subsequently your shoulders. A big turn starts from the ground up.

✔ **Get the tension out of your grip.** Hold the club loosely; you should grip it with the pressure of holding a spotted owl's egg. If you have too much tension in your hands, your forearms and chest tighten up, and you lose that valuable flexibility that helps with the speed of your arms and hands.

Turning your hips to the left on the downswing and extending your right arm on the through-swing are trademarks of the longer hitters. Here's a drill to help you accomplish this feat of daring:

1. **Tee up your driver in the normal position.**

2. **Place the ball off your left heel and/or opposite your left armpit.**

3. **Now reach down, not moving your stance, and move the ball toward the target the length of the grip.**

4. **Tee up the ball there; it should be about a foot closer to the hole.**

5. **Address the ball where the normal position was and swing at the ball that's now teed up.**

   To hit that ball, you have to move your hips to the left so your arms can reach the ball, thereby causing you to extend your right arm.

Practice this drill 20 times. Then put the ball back in the normal position. You should feel faster with the hips and feel a tremendous extension of your right arm.

Direction, Please: Hitting the Ball toward the Target

Why doesn't the ball go where you aim it? Maybe it *wants* to, but you're giving it bad directions like a busted GPS. Here are three common directional maladies, with remedies.

Pushing

The *push* is a shot that starts right of the target and just keeps going. It's not like a slice, which curves to the right (see "Slicing and hooking" earlier in the chapter); the push just goes right. This shot happens when the body doesn't rotate through to the left on the downswing and the arms hopelessly swing to the right, pushing the ball in that direction.

Hitting a push is like standing at home plate, aiming at the pitcher, and then swinging your arms at the first baseman. If this scenario sounds like you, here's how to hit one up the middle: Place an *alignment stick* (flexible fiberglass stick used to aid alignment) or a wooden two-by-four parallel to the target line and about two inches beyond the golf ball. If your arms go off to the right now, splinters are going to fly. Naturally, you don't want to hit the stick, so you — I hope! — swing your hips left on the downswing, which pulls your arms left and cures the push.

Pulling

The *pull* is a shot that starts left and stays left, unlike a hook, which curves to the left. (Check out the earlier section "Slicing and hooking" for more on fixing hooks.) The pull is caused when the club comes from outside the target line on the downswing and you pull across your body.

Hitting a pull is like standing at home plate and aiming at the pitcher but swinging the club toward the third baseman, which is where the ball would go. This swing malady is a little more complicated than a push, and picking out one exercise to cure it is more difficult, so bear with me.

Pulls happen when your shoulders open too fast in the downswing. For the proper sequence, your shoulders should remain as close to parallel to the target line as possible at impact. Here's a checklist that can help you cure your pull:

- ✔ **Check your alignment.** If you're aimed too far to the right, your body slows down on the downswing and allows your shoulders to open at impact to bring the club back to the target.

- ✔ **Check your weight shift.** If you don't shift your weight to your left side on the downswing, you spin your hips out of the way too quickly, causing your shoulders to open up too quickly and hit a putrid pull. So shift those hips toward the target on the downswing until your weight is on your left side after impact.

- ✔ **Check your grip pressure.** Too tight a grip on the club causes you to tense up on the downswing and come over the top for a pull.

- ✔ **Check your distance from the ball.** If you're too close, you instinctively pull inward on your forward swing — which means pulling to the left.

Spraying the ball

If your shots *spray* (take off in more directions than the compass has to offer), check your alignment and ball position. Choose the direction you're going and then put your feet, knees, and shoulders on a line parallel to the target line. Be very specific with your alignment.

Ball position can play a major part in spraying shots. If the ball is too far forward, you can easily push it to the right. If the ball is too far back in your stance, you can easily hit pushes and pulls. The driver is played opposite your left armpit. (Flip to Chapter 6 for more on ball placement.)

Here's a check-up for your ball position: Get into your stance — with the driver, for example — and then undo your shoelaces. Step out of your shoes, leaving them right where they were at address. Now take a look: Is the ball where it's supposed to be in your stance? Two suggestions: If it's a wet day, don't try this exercise. And if your socks have holes in them, make sure nobody is watching.

Do Yourself a Solid: Getting Proper Ball Contact

Less-than-solid contact is the payoff you get for a bad day's work on fundamentals. It happens to everyone. The cure is to review — and apply — a few reliable swing basics.

Topping the ball

Topping isn't much fun. Plus, it's a lot of effort for very little return. *Topping* is when you make a full-blooded, nostrils-flaring swipe at the ball only to tick the top and send the ball a few feeble yards. Topping occurs because your head is moving up and down during your swing. A rising head during your downswing pulls your shoulders, arms, hands, and the clubhead up with it. Whoops!

To whip topping, you must keep your head from lifting. The best way to do that is to establish a reference for your eyes before you start the club back. Stick an umbrella in the ground just beyond the golf ball, as shown in Figure 11-7. Focus your eyes on the umbrella throughout your swing. As long as you stay focused on the umbrella, your head and upper torso can't lift, which ends topped shots.

Avoiding the worm burner

Do worms fear your dreaded worm-burner drives? Does your drive look like a scared cat skittering along the ground? If you're having this problem with your driver, make sure your head stays behind the ball at address and at impact. Moving your head back and forth along with your driver can cause too low a shot.

Drivers come in different lofts. If you're hitting the ball too low, try a driver that has 11 to 12 degrees of loft.

If you're having a problem with low iron shots, you're probably trying to lift those golf balls into the air instead of hitting down, as I cover in Chapter 6.

Focus on the umbrella while you swing.

Figure 11-7:
The umbrella drill can help you avoid topped shots.

Duffing and thinning chip shots

Duffing and thinning are exact opposites, yet, like the slice and the hook I describe earlier in the chapter, they have their roots in a single swing flaw (see Figure 11-8).

When you *duff* a chip (also called a *chili-dip*), your swing is bottoming out behind the ball. You're hitting too much ground and not enough ball (also called *hitting it fat*), which means that the shot falls painfully short of the target and your playing partners laugh outrageously. Duffing a chip is the one shot in golf that can get you so mad that you can't spell your mother's name.

If you continually hit duffs, jam an alignment stick or old club shaft into the ground. Get your nose to the left of the stick, which moves the bottom of your swing forward. Doing so allows you to hit down on the ball from the right position. Make sure that your head stays forward in this shot. Most people who hit an occasional duff move their heads backward as they start their downswings, which means that they hit behind the ball.

Thinned chips (*skulls,* as they call it on tour, or *Vin Scullys,* as I call them, after the famous Dodgers baseball announcer) are the opposite of duffs. You aren't hitting enough ground. In fact, you don't hit the ground at all. The club strikes the ball above the equator, sending the shot speeding on its merry way, past the hole into all sorts of evil places. You need to hit the ground slightly so that the ball hits the clubface and not the front end of the club.

Neutral position, head over the ball.

If you tend to hit it thin, place your head behind the ball.

If you tend to hit it fat, place your head ahead of the ball.

Figure 11-8:
The cure for chipping nightmares.

Double the chip, double the trouble

One shot you rarely witness is the *double chip,* where you hit the chip fat, causing the clubhead to hit the ball twice — once while it's in the air. You could never do that if you tried, but sometime, somewhere, you'll see it performed and will stand in amazement.

I was playing a tournament when one of the amateurs, standing near the condos surrounding the course, hit a chip shot. He had to loft the ball gently over a bunker and then have it land on the green like a Nerf ball on a mattress. He hit the shot a little fat, the ball went up in the air slowly, and his club accelerated and hit the ball again about eye level. The ball went over his head, out of bounds, and into the swimming pool. The rule says that you may have only four penalty strokes per swing maximum, but I think he beat that by a bunch with that double-hit chip shot. When I saw him last, he was still trying to retrieve his ball with the homeowner's pool net.

If you're prone to hit an occasional Vin Scully, set up with your nose behind or to the right of the ball, which moves the bottom of your swing back. When you find the right spot, you hit the ball and the ground at the same time, which is good. I've found that most people who hit their shots thin have a tendency to raise their entire bodies up immediately before impact. Concentrate on keeping your upper torso bent the same way throughout the swing. Then the next time you hear "Scully," it'll be during a baseball game.

Worrying about backspin

How can you back up the ball like the pros on the tour? People ask me this question all the time. The answer: The more steeply you hit down on the ball and the faster you swing, the more spin you generate. People who play golf for a living hit short irons with a very steep angle of descent into the ball, which creates a lot of spin. Our swings get the clubhead moving quickly, creating force that adds more spin. We also tend to play three-piece golf balls with relatively soft covers — balls that spin more than the two-piece ball most people play. (Chapter 2 explains the different types of golf balls.)

We also play on grass that's manicured and very short so that we can get a clean hit with the club off these fairways. All these considerations help when you're trying to spin the ball.

The good news: You don't *need* to spin the ball like the pros. Spin is simply our way of controlling the distance a ball goes. All you need is a consistent swing that hits the ball predictable distances. Whether the ball backs up or rolls forward to get to the target doesn't matter.

So there: Do you like how I made that swing fault disappear?

Avoiding Shanks and Point-Blank Misses

They're two of the most-feared mishaps in the game: the short putt and the shank. Shanks can strike when you least expect, sending the ball squirting sideways while you shake your fist at the golf gods. Short, point-blank putts that somehow miss the hole can be just as aggravating — or more aggravating, if you just lost a match by missing one.

But don't despair! The following sections offer simple fixes to these vexing visitations.

Shanking

Bet the man who has the shanks, and your plate will be full.

—Gary McCord

Flash back a few centuries: Alone with his sheep in a quiet moment of reflection, a shepherd swings his carved crook at a rather round rock toward a distant half-dead, low-growing vine. The rock peels off the old crook, and instead of lurching forward toward the vine, it careens off at an angle 90 degrees to the right of the target. "Zounds! What was that?!" cries the shocked shepherd. "That was a shaaank, you idiot!" cries a sheep. "Now release the toe of that stick, or this game will never get off the ground!"

This story has been fabricated to help with the tension of a despicable disease: the shanks. A *shank* (also called a *pitchout*, a *Chinese hook, El Hosel*, a *scud,* or a *snake killer*) occurs when the ball strikes the hosel of the club and goes 90 degrees to right of your intended target. (The *hosel* is the neck of the club, where the shaft attaches to the clubhead.) The shanks are a virus that attacks the very soul of a golfer. They come unannounced and invade the decorum of a well-played round. They leave with equal haste and lurk in the mind of the golfer, dwelling until the brain reaches critical mass. Then you have meltdown. The shanks sound like one of those diseases Hollywood folks make movies about. And to a golfer, no other word strikes terror and dread like *shank.*

Can you cure the shanks? Yes!

Shankers almost always set up too close to the ball, with their weight back on their heels. As they shift forward during the swing, their weight comes off their heels, moving the club even closer to the ball, so that the hosel hits the ball.

When you shank, the *heel* of your club (the closest part of the clubhead to you) continues toward the target and ends up right of the target. To eliminate shanks, you need the toe of the club to go toward the target and end up left of the target.

Here's an easy exercise (shown in Figure 11-9) that helps cure the shanks:

1. **Get a two-by-four and align it along your target line.**

   You can also use a cardboard box.

2. **Put the ball two inches from the near edge of the board and try to hit the ball.**

   If you shank the shot, your club wants to hit the board. If you swing properly, the club comes from the inside and hits the ball. Then the toe of the club goes left of the target, the ball goes straight, and your woes are over (the shanking ones, at least).

As a junior golfer, I was visiting the Tournament of Champions in 1970 when a bunch of the guys were watching the tournament winners hit balls on the driving range. I was completely mesmerized by Frank Beard as he hit shank after shank on the practice tee. My buddies went to watch Nicklaus, but being something of a masochist, I told them that I'd follow Frank the Shank around and meet them afterward. I witnessed one of the greatest rounds I've ever seen. He shot 64 and never missed a shot. How could a man who was so severely stricken by this disease on the practice tee rally and unleash a round of golf like he played? That's the mystery of this affliction.

Release the toe and don't hit the board.

Figure 11-9:
Just
say, "No
shanks!"

Missing too many short putts

Some people argue that putting is more mental than physical. But before you resort to séances with your local psychic, check your alignment. You can often trace missed putts to poor aim.

You can work on alignment in many ways, but my colleague Peter Kostis invented a device called The Putting Professor to help straighten out troubled putters. It's similar to an old, tried-and-true putting aid, the string between two rods, which helped golfers keep the putter going straight back and straight through impact toward the hole. Straight as a string, get it?

But Peter had a better idea. The Putting Professor features a plexiglass panel and a metal bar that attaches to your putter (see Figure 11-10). Keep the bar in contact with the plexiglass as you practice, and you groove a smooth stroke that keeps the face of your putter square to the target. This stroke is particularly important on those knee-knocking short putts.

Of course, you can't use such a device during a round of golf. But after you develop the right stroke on the practice green, you can repeat it on the course — and watch those putts roll straight and true.

An important lesson you can learn with devices like The Putting Professor is the crucial relationship between the putter's face and the target line. Putting takes an imagination: If you can picture the line and keep the face of your putter square to it, stroking the ball along that line to the hole is easy.

Figure 11-10: The Putting Professor keeps a putter's face square to the target.

Chapter 12

Beating Bad Breaks and Bad Weather

*I*f you break golf down into its primal form, it's simple. All you have to do is hit a ball from a flat piece of ground (you even get to tee the ball up) to, say, a 40-yard-wide fairway. You find the ball and hit it onto a carefully prepared putting surface. Then the golf gods allow you to hit not one, but two putts. And even after all that stuff, you still get to call your score par.

However — you knew there had to be a catch, didn't you? — golf often isn't so straightforward. For one thing, you're going to make mistakes. Everyone does. Usually the same ones over and over. (That doesn't change, by the way. Even the best players in the world have glitches in their swings that give them fits.) Everyone has a bad shot that he or she tends to hit when things go wrong. You may not hit that fairway with your drive or that green with your approach shot, or you may miss both. You may take three putts to get the ball into the hole now and again.

And golf doesn't often take place on a level playing field. Very seldom is the ball lying enticingly on a perfectly flat carpet of grass. (Unless you're the guy at our course that we call The Foot. He never has a bad lie.) Sometimes you play three or four holes into the teeth of a howling gale and reach a hole going the other way — just in time for the wind to change direction. And then it starts to rain.

This chapter's all about how to deal when the golfing gets tough.

Understanding the Mental Game

A wise man once said, "Golf is the art of forgetting your last lousy shot." Okay, maybe it wasn't such a wise man. It was me. But it's true: So many things can go wrong in this game that it's easy to start thinking negatively:

- ✔ "How will I mess up this *next* shot?"
- ✔ "This is embarrassing!"
- ✔ "This course is unfair."
- ✔ "I'll just hit it and hope for the best."

Believe me, I've been there, bogeyed that. After 40 years as a golf pro, I still sometimes feel like the great sportswriter George Plimpton, who took so many lessons he began picturing himself as a giant robot with a control room in his head, where an admiral barked orders to his limbs. A crazy, drunken admiral. No wonder George hit so many balls sideways.

But all golfers have had that feeling. Even the world's best players have days when the club feels like "an instrument ill-suited to the purpose," to quote a real wise man named Winston Churchill. Fortunately, more than 500 years of golf history have provided some tried-and-true ways to cope, and I discuss those in the following sections.

Fear can be your friend

Many golfers feel fear on the course. But you can make fear work for you by turning it into something less scary: caution.

You often hear risk-taking golfers described as fearless. Arnold Palmer played that way, and my favorite fictional golfer, Roy McAvoy of the movie *Tin Cup* did, too. And so did Phil Mickelson — especially early in his career. But Mickelson didn't win so much early in his career, when he often tried to pull off low-percentage miracle shots. He was bold, he was dashing. He was also famous as the "best player never to have won a major championship." Because fearlessness can get you in as much trouble as playing scared.

But Phil changed. He was still bold, still willing to go for a miracle when that was the only way to win, but as he got a little older he took fewer foolish chances. Mickelson finally bagged his first major, the 2004 Masters, at the age of 33. Now he's got four majors, and he's not finished yet.

Phil didn't suddenly start playing scared. He started playing smarter. Rather than go for broke, he sometimes *laid up* — hit his ball short of trouble, in good position for the next shot.

If you're facing a scary shot, such as the one in Figure 12-1, stop and think: Can I more safely get to the green? Even if it takes an extra shot, that's better than wasting two or three strokes on failed miracles.

If you get into trouble on the course, you'll often be faced with a choice of escape routes.

Figure 12-1:
What nut designed *this* hole?

And if you've got no choice but to go for broke, channel Arnie and Roy and fire away! There's no shame in hitting a bad shot if you give it your all.

Proving yourself to yourself

Self-doubt can turn the best golf swing into a mess of flying knees and elbows. How can you beat it? Practice.

That may sound obvious, but too many golfers rely on hope to keep them out of trouble. They say, "I hope this works," and flail away, trying to hook a shot between trees, over a lake to a postage-stamp green. But if you've never hooked a ball on purpose before, what hope have you got?

Your chances are far better if you can say these magic words: "I've hit this shot before." That means working on the techniques I show you in this chapter — not just a couple of times but until they feel familiar. That way, you're not guessing and hoping when it counts there. You're trying to repeat past successes.

Positivity

Before every swing, picture a great result. This practice is more than optimism; it's science! Sports psychologists teach visualization for one simple reason: It works. Just as negative thoughts can derail your swing, positive thoughts — and images — can and do help you hit the ball better.

So make picturing a great shot part of your pre-swing routine. Then you have less trouble with the trouble shots I describe throughout this chapter.

Getting Out of a Rough Spot

Well, Mom, if you knew that I was going to end up playing the PGA Tour and Champions Tour with a crooked driver, you probably wouldn't have told me, "Eat your roughage!" Since then, I've chewed up a lot of rough going from tee to green, but I think it's made me a better person.

Rough is the grass on the golf course that looks like it should be mowed. It's usually two to three inches high and lurks everywhere but the tees, fairways, and greens. I grew up on a municipal golf course where the grass was short everywhere because the only thing they watered down was the whiskey.

When you try to hit a ball out of long grass, the grass gets between the clubface and the ball. The ball then has no backspin and flies off like a bat out of heck, and direction can be a concern. But the real problem is that, with no backspin, the ball can take a longer voyage than you expected. The lack of backspin means less drag occurs while the ball is in the air. When that happens, you've hit a *flyer*. That's never been a problem with the driver off the tee, but it's a concern when you're trying to hit the ball a certain distance.

My philosophy is that if the lie is bad enough, just get the ball back into the fairway. If you can hit the ball, the technique for this shot is much the same as the shot out of a divot: Play the ball back in your stance and put your hands forward. A chopping-down motion allows the club to come up in the backswing and avoid the long grass; that way you can hit down on the ball. Swing hard, because if you don't, the grass will wrap around the club and twist it, giving the ball an unpredictable trajectory.

The more you play this game, the more you hit these shots and understand how to play them. Keep your sense of humor and a firm grip on the club, and enjoy your roughage — Mom was right!

Tackling Tree Trouble

A walk in the woods can be a serene, soul-enhancing, mystical journey, blending one's spirit and body into nature and all her beauty. But when I'm walking into the trees to find my golf ball, I feel like I'm in a house of mirrors with branches and leaves. The trees seem to be laughing at my predicament, and I end up talking to them in less-than-flattering dialogue. You've got the picture by now.

The trees are playing games with me. And so, to extract my ball from this boundless maze of bark, I play a game with the trees. Usually, one lone tree is in my way as I try to exit this forest. All I do is take dead aim at that tree and try to knock it over with the ball. The key here is to not be too close to the tree in case you score a direct hit. You don't want to wear that Titleist 3 as a permanent smile.

My reasoning is that I got into these trees with something less than a straight shot. So if I now try to hit something that's 30 yards away from me and only 12 inches in diameter, what's the chance that I'll hit it? If I do hit it, what a great shot it was! I can congratulate myself for that, turning a negative into a positive. I'm still in the trees, but now I'm proud of my accuracy.

Now you probably know why I'm on TV and not on the regular tour anymore.

Making Special Shots

Because golf is a game of mistake management, you're going to get into trouble at least a few times in every round. How you cope with those moments and shots determines your score for the day and, ultimately, your ability to play well. Never forget that even the greatest rounds have moments of crisis. Stay calm when your heart tries to eject through the top of your head.

Trouble lurks everywhere on a golf course. You have to know how to hit shots from the rough, and others that go around, between, or over trees. Long shots, short shots, and, perhaps most important, in-between shots. You may be faced with a shot from 200 yards where a clump of trees blocks your path to the hole. Or you may be only 50 yards from the hole and have to keep the ball under branches and yet still get it over a bunker. Whatever the situation, the key is applying the magic word (drumroll): *imagination*.

Visualization strikes again: If you can picture the way a shot has to curve in the air in order to land safely, you're halfway to success. All you have to do is hit the ball. And the best way to accomplish both things is through practice — practice on the course, that is. You can't re-create on the range most shots that you encounter out on the course. The range is flat; the course isn't. The wind constantly blows the same way on the range. On the course, the only constant about the wind is that it changes direction. That's golf — a wheel of bad fortune.

The best way to practice these weird and wonderful shots is to challenge yourself. See how low you can hit a shot. Or how high. Practice hitting from bad lies and see how the ball reacts. Play from slopes, long grass, and all the rest. Or play games with your friends. The first player to hit over that tree, for example, gets $5. The trick is to make practice competitive and fun — and also beat your friends out of five bucks.

Wait a minute, though. Hang on. I'm getting a little ahead of myself. I have to tell you that many of the trouble shots hit by the pros are not only very low-percentage plays but also way, way out of most people's reach. Even the pros miss the tough shots now and again. And when they do miss, the result can be a *triple bogey* (a score of three over par for one hole — for example, a 7 on a par-4) or worse. So admire the pros who go for broke like the old, even bolder Phil Mickelson. But never, ever try to copy them — if you've got a choice.

The good news is that at this stage of your development, all you really need is a couple of basic shots. Leave the fancy stuff for another time, another book. All you need to know to score well is how to hit the ball low or high back onto the fairway. That's enough to cover 99 percent of the situations that you encounter. Better to give up one shot than risk three more on a shot that you couldn't pull off more than once in 20 tries.

Altitude adjustment

Because golf isn't played in a bubble, you're going to come across situations where a higher or lower shot is required. For example, when you have a strong wind in your face, a lower shot is going to go farther and hold its line better. The great thing is that you make all your adjustments before you begin. Then after you start your backswing, you can make your regular swing. You don't have to worry about adding anything else. Figure 12-2 illustrates the shots in the following sections.

Hitting the ball lower

Hitting the ball low is easy. All you have to do is subtract from the effective loft of the club. The best way to do that is to adjust your address position. Play the ball back in your stance, toward your right foot. Move your hands toward the target, ahead of the golf ball, until they're over your left leg.

For a lower shot, move the ball back in your stance, with hands forward.

Then return your hands, at impact, to your address position. Hands ahead of ball at impact.

Figure 12-2:
The downs and ups of golf.

For a higher shot, move the ball forward in your stance.

Your head should be behind the clubhead when the ball is struck.

Now take your usual swing, focusing on re-creating the positional relationship between your hands and the clubface as the ball is struck. In other words, your hands should be "ahead" of the clubface at impact, thus ensuring that the ball flies lower than normal.

Golfers commonly employ this sort of technique when playing in Florida, Texas, and Hawaii, where golfers often have to deal with strong winds. When you play the ball back in your stance with your hands ahead, you come down into the ground with a more abrupt angle that takes more turf.

I remember one good story about a low shot. It happened years ago during the Bing Crosby tournament on the 7th hole at Pebble Beach (a downhill par-3 of 110 yards). From an elevated tee, you can just about throw the ball to the green. On this particular day, the wind was howling from the coast (the green sits on the ocean), and the 7th hole was impossible. Water was erupting from the rocks; wind was blowing water everywhere; seals were hiding; and seagulls were walking. Definitely a bad day for windblown golf balls.

Billy Casper arrived on the tee and surveyed the situation. Many players were using *long irons* (irons that go 200 yards) because the wind was so fierce. Billy went to his bag and got his *putter!* He putted the ball down a cart path into the front bunker. From there he got the ball in the hole in two for his par-3. Now that's keeping it low into the wind and using your imagination!

Hitting the ball higher

As you'd expect, hitting the ball higher than normal involves making the opposite adjustments at address. Adjust your stance so that the ball is forward, toward your left foot. Then move your hands back, away from the target. Again, hitting the ball is that simple. All you have to do is reproduce that look at impact, and the ball takes off on a steeper trajectory.

Uneven lies

No golf course is totally flat. So every now and again, you need to hit a shot off a slope. The ball may be below or above your feet. Both positions are *side-hill lies.* Or you may be halfway up or down a slope.

When you're faced with these situations, you need to make an adjustment. And as I note in the preceding section, if you can make most of your changes before starting your swing, the shot gets easier. The common factor in all these shots is the relationship between your shoulders and the slope. On a flat lie, you're bent over the ball in a certain posture. You should stand about 90 degrees to the ground.

But if the ball is above your feet, you have to lean a little into the hill to keep your balance. If you stand at your normal posture to the upslope of the hill, you may fall backward. You're close to the ball because of the lean, and you need to *choke up* on the club (hold it farther down the handle on the grip).

The reverse is also true. With the ball below your feet, lean back more to retain your balance on the downslope. Because you're leaning back, you're a little farther away from the ball; grip the club all the way at the end and use the whole length of the shaft.

The main idea for sidehill lies is to stay balanced. I don't want you falling down any hills.

For uphill and downhill lies, the setup is a little different. Imagine that your ball is halfway up a staircase, and you have to hit the next shot to the top. Because your left leg is higher than your right, your weight naturally shifts to your right leg. On a downslope, your weight shifts in the opposite direction, onto your left leg. Let that weight shift happen so that your shoulders stay parallel to the banister. Keep your shoulders and the imaginary banister parallel, as shown in Figure 12-3.

On an upslope, leave your weight on your right side.

On a downslope, shift your weight to your left side.

Figure 12-3:
Keep shoulders and slope parallel.

Finally, follow these three rules:

- ✔ **Adjust your aim when you're on a slope.** Off a downslope or when the ball is below your feet, aim to the left of where you want the ball to finish. Off an upslope or when the ball is above your feet, aim right.

- ✔ **Play the ball back toward the middle of your stance if you're on a downhill lie, or forward off your left big toe from an uphill lie.**

- ✔ Take *more club* (a club with less loft) if you're on an uphill lie because the ball tends to fly higher, and use *less club* (a club with more loft) from a downhill lie because the ball has a lower trajectory in this situation. For example, if the shot calls for a 7-iron, take your 8-iron instead. *Remember:* From these lies, swing about 75 percent of your normal swing speed to keep your balance. Practice with different clubs from different lies to get a feel for these shots.

Digging out of divots

Unfortunately for your blood pressure, your ball occasionally finishes in a hole made by someone who previously hit a shot from the same spot and forgot to replace the grass. These holes are known as *divots*. Don't panic. To get the ball out, first set up with the ball farther back in your stance to encourage a steeper attack at impact. Push your hands forward a little. You need to feel as if you're really hitting down on this shot. A quicker cocking of the wrists on the backswing helps, too. I like to swing a little more upright on the backswing with the club (take the arms away from the body going back). This method allows a steeper path down to the ball. (See Figure 12-4.)

Depending on the severity and depth of the divot, take a club with more loft than you'd normally use. Extra loft counteracts the ball's being below ground level. Don't worry — the ball comes out lower because your hands are ahead of it. That makes up for the distance lost by using less club.

Remember that a shot from a divot comes out a lot lower and runs along the ground more than a normal shot. Aim accordingly.

You have little or no follow-through on the downswing of your shot from a divot. Because the ball is back in your stance and your hands are forward, your blow should be a descending blow that chops the ball toward the green.

The best swing thought for this situation is *Don't swing too hard.* If you swing hard your head tends to move — you don't hit the ball squarely. And when the ball is lying below the ground, you *must* hit it squarely. So take a smooth, downward swing.

When ball is in a divot hole, move your hands forward.

Cock your wrists more than usual...

and then hit down and through.

Figure 12-4:
Escaping a divot.

Hang Onto Your Hat: Handling High Winds

When conditions are rough because of wind or rain, scores go up. Adjust your goals. Don't panic if you start off badly or have a couple of poor holes. Be patient and realize that sometimes conditions make golf even harder. And remember that bad weather is equally tough on all the other players.

I've played professional golf for 40 years, and I've played in some bad conditions. Because I'm not a patient person, my scores in bad weather have been high. If I got a few strokes over par early in my round, I'd take too many chances trying to make birdies. I'd then boil as I watched my score rise with my blood pressure. A calm head and good management skills are just as important as hitting the ball solidly when you're trying to get through tough days in the wind and rain.

I remember playing the TPC Championship at Sawgrass in the late 1980s on one of the windiest days we'd ever seen. J. C. Snead hit a beautiful downwind approach to an elevated green. Somehow the ball stopped on the green with the wind blowing upwards of 50 miles per hour. J. C. was walking toward the green when his Panama hat blew off. He chased it, only to watch the hat blow onto the green and hit his golf ball! That's a two-shot penalty, and rotten luck.

If the wind is blowing hard, try these tips:

- **Widen your stance to lower your center of gravity.** This change automatically makes your swing shorter (for control) because turning your body is more difficult when your feet are set wider apart. (Figure 12-5 illustrates this stance.)

- **Swing easier.** I always take a less-lofted club than normal and swing easier. This way, I have a better chance of hitting the ball squarely. By hitting the ball squarely, I minimize the wind's effects.

- **Use the wind — don't fight it.** Let the ball go where the wind wants it to go. If the wind is blowing left-to-right at 30 miles per hour, aim left and let the wind bring your ball back. Don't aim right and try to hook it back into the wind. Leave that to the airline pilots and the guys on the PGA Tour!

- **Choke down on the club.** You don't have to keep your left hand (for right-handed golfers) all the way at the top end of the grip. Move it down an inch. This grip gives you more control. Keeping my left hand about one inch from the top of the grip gives me more control over the club and the direction of the shot it hits. But more control comes with a cost: The ball doesn't go as far as it would if I used the full length of the shaft.

A wide stance helps you keep your balance in a breeze.

Figure 12-5: Windy means wider.

✔ **Allow for more run downwind and shorter flight against the wind.**
You have to experience this part of the game to understand it. The more you play in windy conditions, the more comfortable you become.

Swingin' in the Rain

I'm from Southern California. I never saw much rain, let alone played in it all the time. The rain that would make us Californians stay inside and play Yahtzee would be nothing for my buddies from the Pacific Northwest, who knew how to swing in the rain. The following sections give you some pointers on playing in wet conditions.

Packing the right equipment: Smooth sailing or choppy seas

The best advice I can give you for playing in the rain is to make like a Boy Scout and *be prepared*. For starters, pack the right all-weather gear:

- **An umbrella:** Pack one of those big golf umbrellas. And never open it downwind; you end up like Mary Poppins, and the umbrella ends up looking like modern art.

- **Rain gear:** That means jackets, pants, and headwear designed to be worn in the rain. If you play in wet weather all the time, get yourself some good stuff that lasts a long time, not a garbage bag with holes cut out for your head and arms. Good rain gear can cost between $100 and $700, but if you're on a budget, you can get decent gear for less — see Chapter 19 for tips on that.

- **Dry gloves:** If you wear gloves, keep a few in plastic bags in your golf bag. They stay dry even if the rain comes pouring in.

- **Towels:** Keep several dry towels in your bag because the one you have outside will get wet sooner or later. On the Champions Tour, I keep one dry towel hanging from the rib on the underside of my umbrella and another inside my side pocket. When it gets really wet, I wipe my club off on the closest caddie.

- **Dry grips:** Having dry grips is one of the most important components of wet-weather golf. I once had a club slip out of my hands on the driving range and fly through a snack-shop window. I blamed it on an alien spacecraft.

- **Waterproof shoes:** Keep an extra pair of dry socks in your bag, too, in case the advertiser lied about those "waterproof" shoes.

Wet course conditions

A golf course changes significantly in the rain. You need to adjust your game accordingly:

- On a rainy day, the greens are slow. Hit your putts harder and remember that the ball doesn't curve as much. You can also be more aggressive on approach shots to the greens.

- If you hit a ball into a bunker, remember that wet sand is firmer than dry sand. You don't have to swing as hard to get the ball out.

✔ A wet golf course plays longer because it's soft — a 400-yard hole seems more like 450. The good news here is that the fairways and greens become, in effect, wider and bigger, because your shots don't bounce into trouble as much as they would on a dry day. That means you can afford to take more club — and more chances.

✔ Try not to let the conditions affect your normal routines. The best rain players always take their time and stay patient.

✔ Playing in the rain is one thing; playing in lightning is another altogether. Here's my tip on playing in lightning: *Don't*. When lightning strikes, your metallic golf club (along with the fact that you tend to be the highest point on the golf course, unless a tree is nearby) can make you a target. So when you see lightning, don't take chances — take cover.

A Game for All Seasons: Weathering the Elements

If you live in Florida, California, or Arizona, you only notice the change of seasons when 40 bazillion golfers from colder climes flood the area trying to get the seven tee times that are still available. If you live in an all-season climate and prefer to enjoy the changing weather without giving up your golf game, this section offers some tips.

Swinging into spring

Golfers anticipate spring like no other season. You've been indoors for most of the winter and read every book pertaining to your golf game. You've watched endless hours of golf on TV and ingested everything announcers like me have told you not to do. It's spring — time to bloom!

One of the first things you need to do is decide your goals for the upcoming year. Is your goal to be a better putter? Become a longer driver? Simply want to get the ball off the ground with more regularity? Establish what you want to do with your game and then set out to accomplish that feat.

More springtime advice:

✔ **See your local golf professional for a tune-up lesson.** All golfers pick up bad swing habits during the off-season. Get off to the right start!

✔ **Practice all phases of your game.** Don't neglect weak areas of your game, but stay on top of your strengths, too. Spring is a time of blossoming — let your game do the same.

✔ **Map out an exercise program.** Did you avoid exercise during the winter? Spring is a good time to map out a game plan for your physical needs. Are you strong enough in your legs? Does your rotator cuff need strengthening? Does your cardiovascular system short out later in a round? Chapter 4 tells you how to develop a golf-specific fitness program.

✔ **Dress for the weather.** Spring is the cruelest time of year to figure out what to wear. It can be hot. It can be cold. It can rain. It can be blowing 40 miles per hour. It can be doing all these things in the first three holes. If you're carrying your bag, it can get heavy with all the extra gear in it, but you don't want to get caught without something you need. Take along your rain gear, a light jacket, hand warmers (I discuss these amazing creations in "Winterize your game" later in the chapter), your umbrella, and an extra towel. And take along some antihistamines — it's spring, and the pollen is everywhere.

✔ **Learn about yourself and your golf game.** Remember, spring is the time of year to be enlightened. In the words of Spanish philosopher Jose Ortega y Gasset, "To be surprised, to wonder, is to begin to understand."

Heading into hot summer swings

I hope you've been practicing hard on your game, working toward those goals you set forth in the spring (see the preceding section). But practicing and playing are two very different animals. The more you practice, the easier you should find it to play the game well. Summer is the time to find out whether your game has improved.

These tips help you make the most of your days in the sun:

✔ **Work on course management.** How can you best play this particular golf course? Sometimes, for one reason or another, you can't play a certain hole. Figure out a plan to avoid the trouble you're having on that hole. Do you have the discipline to carry out your plan? That's why summer is great for playing the game and understanding yourself. You can regularly go out after work and play 18 holes before it gets dark.

✔ **Tailor your equipment for the conditions.** During the summer, I get new grips on my clubs. The grips are called *half cord* because they have some cord blended into the underside of the grip. New grips give me a better hold on the club during sweaty summers. I also use a driver with a little more loft to take advantage of summer's drier air (which makes the ball fly farther).

✔ **Practice competing by playing in organized leagues.** You play a different game when your score counts and is published in the local paper.

✔ **Dress for fun in the sun.** Take along sunblock of at least SPF 15, and put it on twice a day. Not everyone wants to look like Snooki from *Jersey Shore.* And wear a hat that covers your ears. Mine burn off in the summer.

✔ **Play in the morning.** Afternoons are often too darned hot.

✔ **Drink plenty of fluids during those hot days.** You don't want to dehydrate and shrivel up like a prune, so keep your liquid intake constant. I try to drink water on every tee during the heat of summer. One hint: Alcoholic beverages can knock you on your rear end if you drink them outdoors on a hot day. Stick with water and save the adult beverages for the 19th hole.

Having a ball in the fall

Without a doubt, fall is the best time of year to play golf: The golf courses are in good shape, the leaves are turning in much of the country, and the scenery is amazing. The weather is delightful, and all sorts of sports are on TV. Both you and your game should be raring to go.

If you have the time and the money, make travel plans to the Northeast and play golf there. The colors are astounding. I live in Vail, Colorado, which is also breathtaking in the fall. Some vacation planners specialize in golf trips. Get a bunch of friends you enjoy and start planning one now. But you can't stay in my house — it's way too small.

Here are four fall golf tips:

✔ **Dress for the fall much like you do for the spring.** Take a lot of stuff with you because the weather can change faster than you can swing. (Flip to the earlier section "Swing into spring" for more on packing for spring golf.)

✔ **Keep a close eye on your shots.** Especially if you live where trees lose their leaves in the fall — you can easily lose your ball in the leaves.

✔ **Assess everything you did with your game this year.** Did your techniques work? If not, were your goals unrealistic? Was your teacher helpful? Take a long, hard look and start to devise a game plan for next spring.

✔ **Look at new equipment as your game progresses.** Fall is a great time to buy equipment, because all the new stuff comes out in the spring. By fall, prices are lower for last year's clubs. I love a good buy, though I haven't had to buy clubs since I bought a putter eight years ago in San Diego.

Winterizing your game

Get out there and work on your game — you don't have to mow the grass until April!

Preparing for brisk weather

If you're brave enough to venture onto golf's frozen tundra, I have three musts for you:

- **Take a jumbo thermos with something warm to drink.** You may think that bourbon chasers make the day much more fun, but alcohol makes you feel colder. Coffee or hot chocolate works better.

- **Dress warmly.** I've used silk long johns on cold days, and they work well. Women's seamless long johns work best, but if you're a guy, the salesperson looks at you funny when you ask for a women's size 14. That kind of request may lead to the wrong conclusions.

    - **Wear waterproof golf shoes and thick socks.** Some hunting socks have little heaters in them. I also wear wool pants over my silk long johns and then use my rain pants as the top layer when it's really cold. A turtleneck with a light, tightly knit sweater works wonders under a rain or wind jacket made of Gore-Tex or one of those other miracle-fiber, space-age fabrics like Under Armour. A knit ski cap tops off this cozy ensemble.

    - **Get some hand warmers.** Among the great inventions of all time are those little hand warmers that come in plastic pouches. You shake them, and they stay warm for eight hours. I put them *everywhere* on cold days. Let your imagination run wild. Hand warmers can keep you toasty on a cold winter's day when you're three strokes down to your worst enemy.

    - **Keep your hands warm by using *cart gloves*.** These oversized fingerless gloves have a soft, warm lining and fit right over your hand, even if you're already wearing a glove. I put a hand warmer in each one.

- **Walk the course if you can.** Walking isn't just good exercise; it keeps you warmer than taking a cart. Besides, you really feel cold when your fresh face collides with an arctic blast of winter. If you must take a cart, make sure that it has a windshield. Some courses have enclosed carts with heaters in them.

Adjusting your swing for a cold day

When you swing a club with all these clothes on, you probably won't have as long a swing as normal. The clothes restrict your motion. I usually take my jacket off to swing the club and then put it right back on. Because of the restriction of winter clothes, I make my swing a little slower than normal, which puts it in a slow rhythm on a cold day. Join me — and while you're at it, take more club to offset your slower swing than you'd normally use. If you usually hit an 8-iron for the 140-yard shot you're facing, take a 7-iron instead.

Here are a couple of other points to keep in mind when you're playing winter golf:

✔ **Lower your expectations.** When you're dressed for the Iditarod, don't think that you can pull off the same shots that you normally do. Good *short-game* skills (chipping, pitching, putting, and sand play) and game management are the most important aspects of winter golf. (Chapters 8 through 10 give you the lowdown on the short game.)

✔ **If you usually play in extreme conditions — colder than 40 degrees Fahrenheit — seek professional help.** Golf may be too much of a priority in your life. You may be crazy — or you may be the perfect host for a new reality show on Golf Channel.

Indoor golf: Practicing at home

Winter is a great time to become one with your swing (say what) and fix all those faults you accumulated during the preceding year. Here's how:

1. **Place a large mirror behind you.**

2. **Pretend you're hitting away from the mirror, and check your swing when your shaft is parallel to the ground in your backswing.**

   Is your shaft on a line that's parallel to the line made by your toes? If it is, that's good. If not, that's something to work on during your offseason.

3. **Continue to swing and go to the top.**

   Is your shaft on a line that's parallel to the line made by your heels? If it is, that's good. If it isn't, put that on your list of things to improve.

These two positions are crucial to the golf swing. Repeat this exercise until you can do it in your sleep.

Have someone videotape your golf swing. Play the tape over and over until you have a really good picture of what it looks like. *Feel* your own swing. Then work on those areas that you need to improve — an instructor can help (see Chapter 3 for more on working with a teaching pro).

Next, make your changes and make another tape of your swing. Not only should you be able to see the changes, but you should also feel them. Visualization strikes yet again: Seeing your swing can help you understand your movements and get your body and brain on the same page — ready to turn to the next page.

Part IV
Taking Your Game Public

The 5th Wave   By Rich Tennant

"Remember, it's not proper etiquette to immediately talk business on a golf outing. Wait until at least the 6th hole to bring up the pool toy account."

In this part . . .

You've got a handle on the basics of the game. In this part, I show you how to warm up, how to play "smart golf," and how to impress your new friends. In case the idea of betting strikes your fancy, Chapter 15 gives you the skinny. Plus, Chapter 16 tells you how to step your game up from the beginner's level to something even better.

Chapter 13

Step Right Up and Play!

You know the basics of the game. You've got the right equipment, you know your way around different sorts of courses, and you've developed a swing that suits your body and soul. At this point, you could probably hit a terrific bunker shot from a bad lie during a tornado!

Well, maybe during a blustery day. I'll save tornado play for a future edition of this book. The point is, you're ready to get out there and put all your skills to the test. This chapter shows you how.

Loosening Up

After you prepare a few handy excuses (see the nearby sidebar), you're ready to warm up your body. Warm-ups are important. A few simple exercises not only loosen your muscles and help your swing but also help you psychologically. I like to step onto the first tee knowing that I'm as ready as I can be.

Besides, golfers, along with just about everyone else, are a lot more aware of physical fitness and diet today than in days gone by. Lee Trevino, a two-time U.S. Open, British Open, and PGA champion and later one of the top players on the senior tour, started calling the PGA Tour players "flat-bellies." Which they are, compared to some of the more rotund "round-bellies" on the senior tour. I think that's called progress!

Johnny Bench, the great Cincinnati Reds catcher, showed me the following stretches. He used them when he played baseball, and he's in the Hall of Fame — so who am I to argue?

GARY SAYS

The power of positive excuse-making

Even if you aren't a pro, no matter what goes wrong on the course, it's never — I repeat, *never* — your fault. You must always find someone or something else to blame for any misfortune. For example, I once fired my caddie after I played to the wrong green as I was trying to qualify for the U.S. Open (even though I knew the course like the back of my hand). Sometimes, though, you have to be creative in the excuse department.

Golfers have come up with some great excuses over the years. My favorite came from Greg Norman. He once blamed a miscued shot on a worm popping up out of the ground next to his ball as he swung. Poor Greg was so distracted that he couldn't hit the shot properly! Then you have Jack Nicklaus's gem at the 1995 British Open at St. Andrews. In the first round, Jack hit his second shot on the 14th hole, a long par-5, into what is known as Hell Bunker. It's well named, being basically a bottomless sand-filled crater. Anyway, seeing his ball down there came as a bit of a surprise to Jack. He apparently felt that his shot should have flown comfortably over said bunker and chalked the problem up to having his ball deflected by seed heads!

These two examples are extreme, of course, but you should apply the same principle to your game. You can often tell a good player from his reaction to misfortune. He blames his equipment, the wind, whatever. On the other hand, less-secure golfers take all responsibility for bad shots. Whatever they do is awful. In fact, they really stink at this stupid game. That's what they tell themselves — usually to the point that it ruins their next shot. And the next. And the next. Whatever they perceive themselves to be, they become.

So be sure that you err in the former way rather than the latter. To play this game well, you gotta believe — in yourself!

Holding a club by the head, place the grip end in your armpit so that the shaft runs the length of your arm (use a club that's the same length as your arm for this one, as shown in Figure 13-1). This action stretches your arm and shoulders. Now bend forward until your arm is horizontal. The forward movement stretches your lower back, one of the most important areas in your body when it comes to playing golf. If your back is stiff, you have a hard time making a full turn on the backswing. Hold this position for a few seconds and then switch arms; repeat this stretch until you feel loose enough to swing.

Another method of loosening up is more traditional. Instead of practicing your swing with one club in your hands, double the load by swinging two clubs (see Figure 13-2). Go slowly, trying to make as full a back-and-through swing as you can. The extra weight soon stretches away any tightness.

Holding the club like this, bend forward.

Then switch arms and do it again.

Figure 13-1:
Stretch before you swing.

Swing two clubs back...

and through.

Figure 13-2:
Double up for a smooth practice swing.

This next exercise is one that many players use on the first tee. Place a club across your back and hold it steady with your hands or elbows. Then turn back and through as if making a golf swing, as shown in Figure 13-3. Again, this action really stretches your back muscles.

Stand as if at address, a club behind your back. Then turn back...

and through.

Figure 13-3:
Watch your
back!

Warming Up Your Swing

Go to any pro tournament, and you'll see that most players show up on the practice range about an hour before they're due to tee off. Showing up early leaves them time to tune their swings and strokes before the action starts for real.

I'm one of those players who likes to schedule about an hour for pre-round practice. But half that time is probably enough for you. You really need to hit only enough balls to build a feel and a rhythm for the upcoming round. Don't make any last-minute changes to your swing.

Start your warm-up by hitting a few short wedge shots. Don't go straight to your driver and start blasting away. That's asking for trouble. You can easily pull a muscle if you swing too hard too soon. Plus, you probably aren't going to immediately hit long, straight drives if you don't warm up first. More than likely, you'll hit short, crooked shots. And those are hazardous to the golfer's mental health.

The following steps and Figure 13-4 lead you through a good swing warm-up. *Remember:* You're just warming up. Focus on rhythm and timing — not on the ball.

1. Before each round, hit a few wedge shots...

2. and then a few 6-irons...

Figure 13-4: A sensible warm-up.

3. and then a few drivers...

4. and finish up with a few long putts.

1. Start with the wedge.

Focus on making solid contact. Nothing else. Try to turn your shoulders a little more with each shot. Hit about 20 balls without worrying about where they're going. Just swing smoothly.

2. **Move to your midirons.**

   I like to hit my 6-iron at this point. I'm just about warmed up, and the 6-iron has just enough loft that I don't have to work too hard to get the ball flying forward. Again, hit about 20 balls.

3. **Hit the driver.**

   Now you're warmed up enough for the big stick. I recommend that you hit no more than a dozen drivers. Getting carried away with this club is easy, and when you go overboard, your swing can get a little quick.

4. **Before you leave the range, hit a few more balls with your wedge.**

   You're not looking for distance with this club, only smoothness. That's a good thought to leave with.

5. **Finally, spend about ten minutes on the practice putting green.**

   You need to get a feel for the pace of the greens. Start with short uphill putts of two to three feet. Get your confidence and then proceed to longer putts of 20 to 30 feet. After that, practice putting to opposite fringes to get the feeling of speed. Focus on pace rather than direction. You're ready now — head for the first tee!

First-Tee Tactics

The best players start each round with a plan for how they'll play the course. They know which holes they can attack and which holes are best to play safely. So should you.

Many people say golf is 90 percent mental. You're wise to take that statement to heart. The fewer mental errors you make, the lower your score is. And the great thing about bad thinking is that everyone at every level of play can work on eliminating it.

Think of golf as a game of chess. You have to plan two or three moves in advance. Over every shot, you should be thinking, "Where do I need to put this ball in order to make my next shot as easy as possible?"

I could write a whole book on the countless situations you can find yourself in on the course. Trouble is, I don't have the space for that in this book, and you don't need all that information yet. So what follows is a brief overview of tactical golf. I've selected three common situations; you'll come across each one at least once in almost every round you play. You can apply your approach for each one to many other problems that you encounter. So don't get too wrapped up in the specifics of each scenario — think big picture.

Tactic 1: Don't be a sucker

You're playing the 170-yard par-3 hole in Figure 13-5. As you can see, the hole is cut toward the left side of the green, behind a large bunker. If your first inclination is to fire straight at the flag, think again. Ask yourself

1. What are my chances of pulling off such a difficult shot?

2. What happens if I miss?

3. Is the shot too risky?

If the answers are 1. Less than 50 percent, 2. I may take 5 to get down from the bunker, or 3. Yes, play toward the safe part of the green (shown by the solid line in Figure 13-5). Only if you happen to be an exceptional bunker player should you go for the flag (using the dotted path in Figure 13-5).

Think of it this way: Golf is a game of numbers. If you shoot at the pin here, you bring the number 2 into play: If you hit a great shot, you have a great opportunity for a deuce. That's the upside. The downside is that missing the green makes the numbers 5, 6, and maybe even 7 possibilities, especially if you aren't too strong from sand or if you're unlucky enough to get a really bad lie. You want to eliminate your chances of making anything worse than a bogey.

If, on the other hand, you play for the middle of the green, your range of likely results is narrower. Say you hit the putting surface with your first shot. In all likelihood, the most you'll take for the hole is 4, and that's only if you 3-putt. You'll get a lot of 3s from that position, and once in a while you'll hole the long putt — so a 2 isn't impossible.

Even if you miss the green on that side, you'll probably be left with a relatively simple chip or pitch. So unless you mess up terribly, 4 is again your worst score for the hole. I like those numbers better, don't you?

You should follow this policy more often than not. If you decide to be a middle-of-the-green shooter, practice your long-putting a lot. You're going to have a lot of 30- to 40-foot putts, so be ready for them.

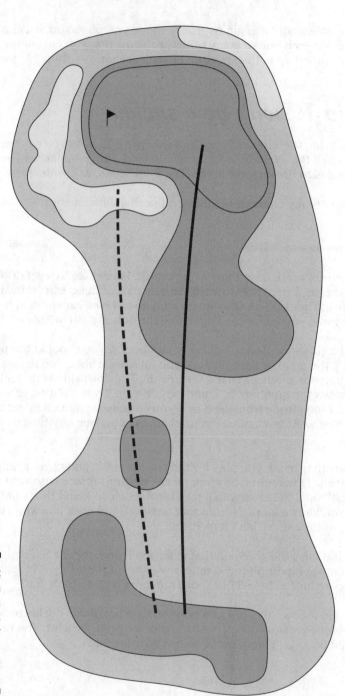

Figure 13-5:
Don't aim
for the flag
(dotted line);
the safer
path (solid
line) is
farther right.

Tactic 2: Think before you drive

You're on the par-4 hole of just over 400 yards shown in Figure 13-6. But the actual yardage isn't that important. All you have to do is pay attention to the layout of the hole and plan accordingly. The key to this hole is the narrowing of the fairway at the point where your drive is most likely to finish. When this situation comes up, tee off with your 3-wood, 5-wood, or whatever club you can hit safely into the wide part of the fairway. Even if you can't quite reach the green in two shots, that's the best strategy. Like in the preceding section, it's a question of numbers. If you risk hitting your driver and miss the fairway, you'll probably waste at least one shot getting the ball back into play — maybe more than one if you get a bad lie. Then you *still* have a longish shot to the green.

Now follow a better scenario: You hit your 3-wood from the tee safely down the fairway. Then you hit your 5-wood, leaving the ball about 25 yards from the green. All you have left is a simple chip or pitch. Most times, you'll make no more than 5 on the hole. Indeed, you'll nearly always have a putt for a 4. Most golfers don't follow this path, but it makes sense, doesn't it?

Tactic 3: It's easy as one, two, three

This par-5 hole is long, just over 500 yards (see Figure 13-7). Your first inclination is again to reach for your driver. Most of the time, that's probably the correct play — but not always. Look at the hole: You can break it down into three relatively easy shots with a single club! Say you hit your 4-iron 170 yards. Three of those 4-irons can put you on the green. To me, that's easier for the beginning player than trying to squeeze every possible yard out of the driver and getting into trouble. (Disclaimer: I know you gorillas out there won't consider this strategy. You'd rather flail away. But flailing often leads to failing.)

No law says that you must use your driver from the tee. If you don't feel comfortable with your driver, go with your 3-wood. If your 3-wood doesn't feel right, go to the 5-wood. And if you still aren't happy, try your 3-iron or a hybrid club. Don't swing until you're confident that you can hit the ball into the fairway with the club that's in your hands. I'd rather be 200 yards from the tee and in the fairway than 250 yards out in the rough.

Being in a spot where you can hit the ball cleanly is better than being in a tough spot, even if the clean shot is longer. If you don't believe me, try this test. Every time you miss a fairway from the tee, pick your ball up and drop it 15 yards farther back but in the middle of the fairway. Then play from there. Bet you shoot anywhere from five to ten shots fewer than normal for 18 holes.

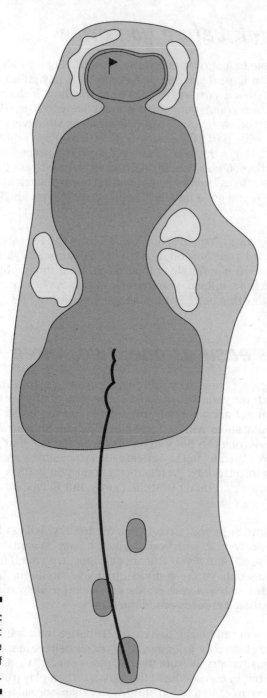

Figure 13-6:
Safety first:
Go for the
wide part of
the fairway.

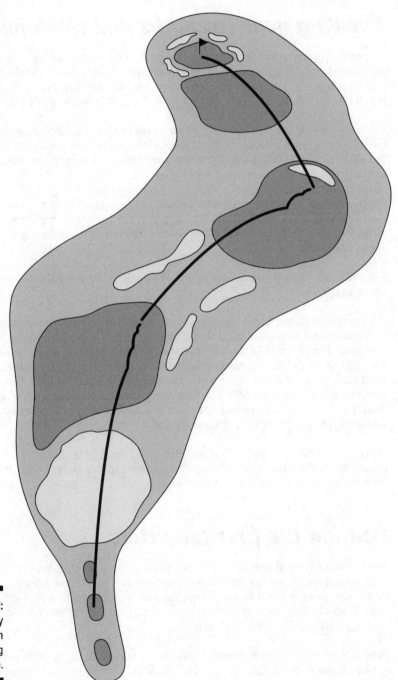

Figure 13-7:
Three easy
shots can
tame a long
hole.

Knowing your strengths and weaknesses

To really employ good strategy, you have to know your tendencies. For example, on the par-4 hole described earlier in this chapter (see "Tactic 2: Think before you drive"), a really accurate driver of the ball can take the chance and try to hit the ball into the narrow gap. She's playing to her strength.

But how do you know what your pluses and minuses are? Simple. All you have to do is keep a close record of your rounds over a period of time. By "a close record," I don't simply mean your score on each hole. You have to break down the numbers a bit more than that.

Keep a record of your scores that details various aspects of your game: how many fairways you hit, how many times you hit the green, and how many putts you take on each green. That record can tell you which parts of your game you should work on.

For example, look at the scorecard in Figure 13-8, where John has marked his score in detail.

If John tracks these items over, say, ten rounds, trends soon appear. Assume that this round is typical for John. Clearly, he isn't a very good putter. Forty-two putts for 18 holes is a poor statistic by any standard, especially when he isn't hitting that many greens — only one in three. If John were hitting 12 or 13 greens, you'd expect more putts because he'd often be near the edge of the green. But this card tells another story. John's missing a lot of greens and taking a lot of putts. So either his chipping and pitching are very bad, or his putting is letting him down. Probably the latter.

On the other hand, John isn't a bad driver, at least in terms of accuracy. He's hitting more than half the fairways. So, at least in the short term, John needs to work on his short game and putting.

Beating the first-tee jitters

The opening shot of any round is often the most stressful. You're not into your round yet. Even the practice shots that you may have hit aren't the real thing. And people are almost always nearby watching when you hit that first shot. If you're like most golfers, you're intimidated by even the thought of striking a ball in full view of the public.

How a player reacts to first-tee jitters is an individual thing. You just have to get out there and do it and see what happens. Common symptoms: Blurred vision. A desire to get this shot over and done with as soon as possible. Loss of reason.

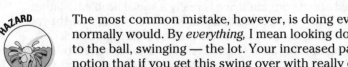

Blue Tees	White Tees	Par	Hcp	JOHN				HOLE	HIT FAIRWAY	HIT GREEN		NO. PUTTS	Hcp	Par	Red Tees
Men's Course Rating/Slope — Blue 73.1/137, White 71.0/130													Women's Course Rating/Slope — Red 73.7/128		
377	361	4	11	4				1	✓	✓		2	13	4	310
514	467	5	13	8				2	✓	0		3	3	5	428
446	423	4	1	7				3	0	0		2	1	4	389
376	356	4	5	6				4	0	0		2	11	4	325
362	344	4	7	5				5	0	✓		3	7	4	316
376	360	4	9	6				6	✓	0		2	9	4	335
166	130	3	17	4				7	0	✓		3	17	3	108
429	407	4	3	5				8	✓	✓		3	5	4	368
161	145	3	15	5				9	0	0		2	15	3	122
3207	2993	35		50				Out	4	4		22		35	2701
Initial													**Initial**		
366	348	4	18	5				10	0	0		2	14	4	320
570	537	5	10	7				11	✓	0		3	2	5	504
438	420	4	2	5				12	✓	0		2	6	4	389
197	182	3	12	4				13	0	0		2	16	3	145
507	475	5	14	5				14	✓	✓		2	4	5	425
398	380	4	4	5				15	0	✓		3	8	4	350
380	366	4	6	5				16	✓	0		2	10	4	339
165	151	3	16	4				17	0	0		2	18	3	133
397	375	4	8	5				18	0	0		2	12	4	341
3418	3234	36		45				In	3	2		20		36	2946
6625	6227	71		95				Tot	7	6		42		71	5647
Handicap													Handicap		
Net Score													Net Score		
Adjust													Adjust		

Scorer _____ Attested _____ Date _____

Figure 13-8: Keep track of more than your score.

The most common mistake, however, is doing everything twice as fast as you normally would. By *everything*, I mean looking down the fairway, standing up to the ball, swinging — the lot. Your increased pace is due to the misguided notion that if you get this swing over with really quickly, no one will see it. It's the hit-it-and-go syndrome, and you should avoid it.

Be cool, dude

When you show up at the course, being a little late is okay. (That is, you don't have to show up exceptionally early; if you've got a 9 a.m. tee time, get there about 8:30.) Your partners may be starting to panic a bit about where you are, but they'll get over it. Always change your shoes while sitting on the trunk of your car. That's cool. Always have a carry bag and never a pull cart. Pull carts aren't cool. Get one of those stand bags with prongs that keep it upright when you set it down. Very cool.

Never tie your shoelaces until you reach the tee. On the tee, bend down to tie them while complaining about all the things that hurt. Bursitis in your right shoulder. That pesky tendonitis in your left knee. The sore elbow you sustained while carrying an old lady's groceries. Whatever. Elicit sympathy from your companions. Get up very slowly. Adjust yourself. Grab your back. Then get into *stroke negotiations* — how many strokes the other side (or player) is giving or getting from your side (or you). This dance is an art. If your opponent's handicap is 5 and yours is 10, for example, you don't have to settle for five strokes. Not with your back *killing you!* That's got to be worth a couple of shots.

Then there's the flu you had last week, and the fact that you couldn't sleep last night . . . you get the idea. By the time you tee off, you may be getting ten strokes instead of five.

What's also very cool is having your own turn of golfing phrase. Make up your own language. Don't say stuff like "wow" or "far out." Keep your talk underground. Use stuff that no one else can understand. For example, Fairway Louie refers to the local denizens of our golf course as "herds of grazing hack" because they're always looking for balls in the rough. If you come up with something memorable, others will start using your language. It's a domino effect.

At first, though, I recommend that you do more listening than talking. It's like when you go to a foreign country. You have to listen before you start spouting off. Listen to how golfers express themselves during moments of elation, anger, and solitude. After you pick up the lingo, you can add your own touches. There's no right or wrong as long as you respect your fellow golfers and the game.

I remember when my golf swing wasn't where I wanted it to be. I had a bad grip, a bad takeaway, a bad position at the top. I wasn't comfortable with myself, so how could I be comfortable with others watching? I'd get up there, hit the ball as soon as I could, and get out of the way. After I understood the mechanics of my swing, that dread went away. All of a sudden, I stood over the ball as long as I wanted to. I thought about what I was doing, not about what others were thinking. I *wanted* people to watch, to revel in the positions in my golf swing, because they were good positions. I didn't mind showing off.

Being too concerned about your audience is really a social problem. Rather than taking refuge in your pre-shot routine and whatever swing thought you may favor, you're thinking about what others may be thinking. (Check out Chapter 6 for more on utilizing swing thoughts.) The secret to overcoming this problem is to immerse yourself in your routine. Say, "Okay, I'm going to start behind the ball. Then I'm going to look at my line, take five steps to the ball, swing the club away to the inside and turn my shoulders." Whatever you say to yourself, just remember to focus internally. Focus on *you* and forget about *them*.

Deciding Which Format You Should Play

GARY SAYS

The best format I know of for the beginning golfer is a *scramble*. In that format, you're usually part of a team of four. Everyone tees off, and then everyone plays another shot from where the best shot lies. And so on. A scramble is great for beginners because you have less pressure to hit every shot well. You can lean on your partners a bit. Plus, you get to watch better players up close. And you get to experience some of the game's camaraderie. Scrambles are typically full of rooting, cheering, and high-fives. In short, they're fun.

You can also play in games where the format is *stableford*. In this game, the scoring is by points rather than strokes. You get one point for a *bogey* (score of one over par); two for a par; three for a *birdie* (one under par); and four for an *eagle* (two under par). Thus, a round in which you par every hole reaps you 36 points. The great thing is that in a stableford, you don't have to complete every hole. You can take your 9s and 10s without irreparably damaging your score. You simply don't get any points for a hole in which you take more than a bogey. That's with your handicap strokes deducted, of course. (For more on golf handicapping, see Chapter 14.)

You may well find that you play most of your golf with three companions. That's known as a *foursome* in the United States (a *four-ball* elsewhere). The format is simple. You split into two teams of two and play what is known as a *best-ball* game. That is, the best score on each team on each hole counts as the score for that team. For example, say we're partners; if you make a 5 on the first hole and I make a 4, our team scores a 4 for the hole.

Keeping Score

Don't get too wrapped up in how many shots you're taking to play a round, at least at first. For many golfers, the score doesn't mean that much anyway. Most of the guys I grew up with never kept score. That's because they were always playing a match against another player or team. In a match like that, all that matters is how you compare with your opponents. It's never "me against the course;" it's always "me against you." So if I'm having a really bad hole, I simply concede it to you and then move on to the next one.

Believe me, that's a totally different game from the one that you see the pros playing on TV every week. For them, every shot is vital — the difference between making the cut or not, or finishing in or out of the big money. That's why the pro game is better left to the pros.

Practice Makes Better

It's amazing, but nearly half of golfers who score poorly don't practice. Are you one of them? You can't expect to improve if you don't put some time in. Now, I can already hear you griping, "I don't have time!" Well, stop whining, because I've made it easy for you. I've put together a sample practice schedule that you can easily work into your weekly routine. You may want to tone it down at the office (you look bad if your boss walks in while you're practicing your putting), although you may be able to multitask during those long conference calls.

Practice can be fun. If you don't want to take strokes off your game, skip this part, but if you're a weekend warrior who wants to improve, here's a shortcut to success:

- ✔ **Practice your swing whenever possible.** You can practice most of the suggestions in Part II in your basement, living room, or backyard. Place old clubs in various locations around your house so that you're prepared to swing when the spirit (or schedule) moves you.

- ✔ **Make imaginary swings in front of a mirror or window with your arms and hands in the proper position (see Part II).** If you don't have a club handy, that's okay. Visualize and feel the correct position.

- ✔ **Grip a club when you watch television.** You're not doing anything else! Try swinging a club during commercials — unless it's one of my commercials. In that case, put your club down and turn up the volume.

- ✔ **Build a practice area in your house or office where you can work on your short game.** Use those plastic practice balls. Set up a small obstacle course in your yard. (Your kids can help you with this part.)

- ✔ **Where and when possible, hit a bucket of balls during lunch.** If it's a hot day in July, you may want to hit the showers before you head back to the office.

Here's a sample practice schedule:

- ✔ **Monday:** Health-club workout (1 hour); putt on rug (15 minutes).

- ✔ **Tuesday:** Swing a club in front of a mirror or window (30 minutes).

- ✔ **Wednesday:** Health-club workout (1 hour); read a golf magazine or golf book or watch a golf DVD (30 minutes). Chapter 3 gives you some good options for study materials.

- ✔ **Thursday:** Swing a club or chip (1 hour).

- ✔ **Friday:** Health-club workout (1 hour); practice range, including golf drills (1 hour).

✔ **Saturday:** Practice range (1 hour); play 18 holes.

✔ **Sunday:** Watch golf on TV; practice range (30 minutes); play 9 holes.

Getting older — and better

On the Champions Tour for golfers 50 and over, I get to tee it up with some of the same guys who used to beat the pants off me on the PGA Tour. I still love to play, but as I've aged, my game has changed. I can deal with it. We all have to. If you've become a senior golfer since the last edition of this book came out, or if you're taking up the game for the first time as a senior, you need to know some things to keep your game young.

As you may know already (or will find out soon enough), you just don't hit the ball as far as you used to. Four basic problems cause this discrepancy:

✔ **Poor posture:** Bad posture can stop you from turning properly. Be careful how you hold your head; keep it off your chest. Maintain good posture by standing in front of a full-length mirror and holding a club out in front of you. Keep looking in the mirror as you lower the club into the hitting position. Don't let your head tilt or move forward. When you master this technique, you can make that turn and swing your arms.

✔ **Lack of rotation on your backswing:** You probably aren't turning your hips and shoulders enough on the backswing. You can increase your range of motion by increasing your flexibility. See Chapter 4 for stretching exercises. They can be a huge help! Then review the elements of the swing in Chapters 6 and 7, get out to the driving range, and work out those kinks.

✔ **Lost strength:** As you grow older, you lose strength in your hands and forearms, which makes keeping your wrists in the proper position on the downswing harder. This weakness reduces clubhead speed, so the ball doesn't go as far. Simple drills to combat loss of strength include squeezing a tennis ball, doing forearm curls with light barbells, and Harvey Penick's drill: Swing a club back and forth like a scythe 20 or 30 times a day. I don't recommend doing this one anywhere near your priceless new HDTV.

✔ **Lack of rotation in the follow-through:** You may be so intent on hitting the ball that you're not finishing your swing. This short shot causes the club to stop three or four feet beyond the ball and the arms to stop somewhere around your chest, with your belt buckle pointing to the right of your target. As you can imagine, this swing results in an unsightly shot. The ball flies to the right and is, well, weak.

To correct such a problem, repeat the following drill each day until it feels natural: While looking in a full-length mirror, go to the top of your backswing (see Chapter 6) and then mirror-image that position on the follow-through, with your belt buckle facing to the left of your target. To make this happen, you must transfer 90 percent of your weight from your right foot to your left foot.

I can't stress this point enough: If you don't exercise, start (see Chapter 4). Consult your local golf pro for suggestions, too. A good program coupled with a stretching routine improves your flexibility and strength, your golf game, and your life in general.

Chapter 14

Rules, Etiquette, and Keeping Score

In This Chapter

▶ Knowing the rules, past and present

▶ Respecting other golfers

▶ Keeping score

▶ Surviving penalty shots

Golf is a beautifully structured game, rife with rules of play, etiquette, and scoring that have evolved through its long history. You don't have to memorize all 182 pages of the USGA's latest *Rules of Golf*, but you must know the essentials, and this chapter helps you do just that.

Beware of Dog — and Watery Filth! Perusing Golf's Original Rules

The Honourable Company of Edinburgh Golfers devised the original 13 Rules of Golf in 1744, over a *wee dram* (whisky) or 12, no doubt. Anyway, those Rules are worth recounting to show you how little — and how much — golf play has changed over the centuries.

1. You must tee your ball within a club's length of the hole.

2. Your tee must be upon the ground.

3. You are not to change the ball which you strike off the tee.

4. You are not to remove any stones, bones, or any break club, for the sake of playing your ball. Except upon the fair green, and that's only within a club's length of your ball.

5. If your ball comes among watter, or any watery filth, you are at liberty to take out your ball and bringing it behind the hazard and teeing it, you may play it with any club and allow your adversary a stroke, for so getting out your ball.

6. If your balls be found anywhere touching one another you are to lift the first ball, till you play the last.

7. At holling, you are to play honestly for the hole, and not to play upon your adversary's ball, not lying in your way to the hole.

8. If you should lose your ball, by its being taken up, or any other way you are to go back to the spot, where you struck last, and drop another ball, and allow your adversary a stroke for the misfortune.

9. No man at holling his ball, is to be allowed, to mark his way to the hole with his club or any thing else.

10. If a ball be stopp'd by any person, horse, dog, or any thing else, the ball so stopp'd must be played where it lyes.

11. If you draw your club, in order to strike and proceed so far in the stroke, as to be bringing down your club; if then, your club shall break, in any way, it is to be counted a stroke.

12. He whose ball lyes farthest from the hole is obliged to play first.

13. Neither trench, ditch or dyke, made for the preservation of the links, nor the scholar's holes or the soldier's lines, shall be counted a hazard. But the ball is to be taken out, teed and play'd with any iron club.

As you can tell from the language and terms used in 1744, these rules were designed for match play (see "Match play" later in this chapter). My particular favorite is Rule 6. It wasn't that long before the rule was redefined from "touching" to "within 6 inches" — which in turn led to the *stymie rule*. The stymie has long since passed into legend, but it was a lot of fun. Basically, *stymie* meant that if your opponent's ball lay between your ball and the hole, you couldn't ask him to mark it. You had to make do. Usually, that meant chipping over his ball, which is great fun, especially if you're close to the hole.

Understanding the Rules Today

Take a look at a rulebook today (you can pick one up from almost any professional's shop, or order one directly from the United States Golf Association [USGA]), and you find a seemingly endless list of clauses and subclauses — all of which make the game sound very difficult and complicated.

In my opinion, the Rules are too complex. For a smart, enjoyable look at them, pick up a copy of *Golf Rules & Etiquette For Dummies* (Wiley) by John Steinbreder. You can also check out an excellent book by Jeffrey S. Kuhn and

Bryan A. Garner, *The Rules of Golf in Plain English,* 2nd Edition (University of Chicago Press).

Even if you're too busy to track down those two fine tomes, you can get by with about a dozen simple rules. Common sense can help, too. You can't go too far wrong on the course if you

- ✔ Play the course as you find it.
- ✔ Play the ball as it lies.
- ✔ Do what's fair if you can't do either of the first two things.

Although the Rules of Golf are designed to help you, they can be a minefield. Watch where you step!

To demonstrate just how crazy the Rules of Golf can get and how easily you can commit an infraction, look at the cases of Craig Stadler and Paul Azinger.

Stadler was playing the 14th hole at Torrey Pines in San Diego during a PGA Tour event. Because his ball was under a tree, he knelt on a towel to avoid getting his pants dirty as he hit the ball.

Think that sounds harmless? Think again. Some smart guy out there in TV land was watching all this (the next day, no less) and thought he was part of a new game show called *You Make the Ruling.* He called the PGA Tour and said that Stadler was guilty of *building a stance.* By kneeling on top of something, even a towel, Stadler was technically changing his shot, breaking Rule 13-3: "A player is entitled to place his feet firmly in taking his stance, but he shall not build his stance."

The officials had to agree, so Stadler was disqualified for signing the wrong scorecard — 24 hours after the fact. Technically, an event isn't over until the competitors have completed 72 holes. At the time the rules infraction came to light, Stadler had played only 54 holes. Madness! He clearly had no intent to gain advantage. But it was adiós, Craig.

The same sort of thing happened with Paul Azinger. At Doral's famed "Blue Monster" in 1991, Azinger played a shot from the edge of the lake on the final hole. Just before he started his swing, he flicked a rock out of the way while taking his stance. Cue the Rules police. Another phone call got Azinger busted for "moving loose impediments in a hazard." Common sense and the Rules parted company again.

Another incident occurred at the LPGA's Samsung World Championship in 2005, when Michelle Wie unintentionally took a drop several inches closer to the hole than allowed. A *Sports Illustrated* writer noticed the infraction, and Michelle was disqualified — in her first event as a professional!

Ten rules you need to know

By Mike Shea, PGA Tour Rules Official

Rule 1: You must play the same ball from the teeing ground into the hole. Change only when the rules allow.

Rule 3-2: You must hole out on each hole. If you don't, you don't have a score and are thus disqualified.

Rule 6-5: You are responsible for playing your own ball. Put an identification mark on it.

Rule 13: You must play the ball as it lies.

Rule 13-4: When your ball is in a hazard, whether a bunker or a water hazard, you cannot touch the ground or water in the hazard with your club before impact.

Rule 16: You cannot improve the line of a putt before your stroke by repairing marks made by the spikes on players' shoes.

Rule 24: Obstructions are anything artificial. Some are moveable. Others are not, so you must drop your ball within one club length of your nearest point of relief — no penalty.

Rule 26: If your ball is lost in a water hazard, you can drop another behind the hazard, keeping the point where the ball last crossed the hazard between you and the hole — with a one-stroke penalty.

Rule 27: If you lose your ball anywhere other than in a hazard, return to where you hit your previous shot and hit another — with a one-stroke penalty.

Rule 28: If your ball is unplayable, you have three options (each carries a one-stroke penalty):

- Play from where you hit your last shot.

- Drop within two club lengths of where your ball is now, no closer to the hole.

- Keep the point where the ball is between you and the hole and drop your ball on that line. You can go back as far as you want.

Source: *The Rules of Golf* as approved by the United States Golf Association (USGA) and the Royal and Ancient Golf Club of St. Andrews, Scotland

In each case, the Rules of Golf were violated. But the players weren't cheating; they broke the Rules accidentally. And what got them thrown out of those tournaments weren't the original infractions, but signing incorrect scorecards. In all three cases, tour officials did what they felt they had to do. I still think it was cruel and unusual punishment.

Marking a scorecard

Scorecards can be a little daunting when you first look at them (see Figure 14-1). All those numbers and little boxes. But fear not — keeping score is actually simpler than it looks.

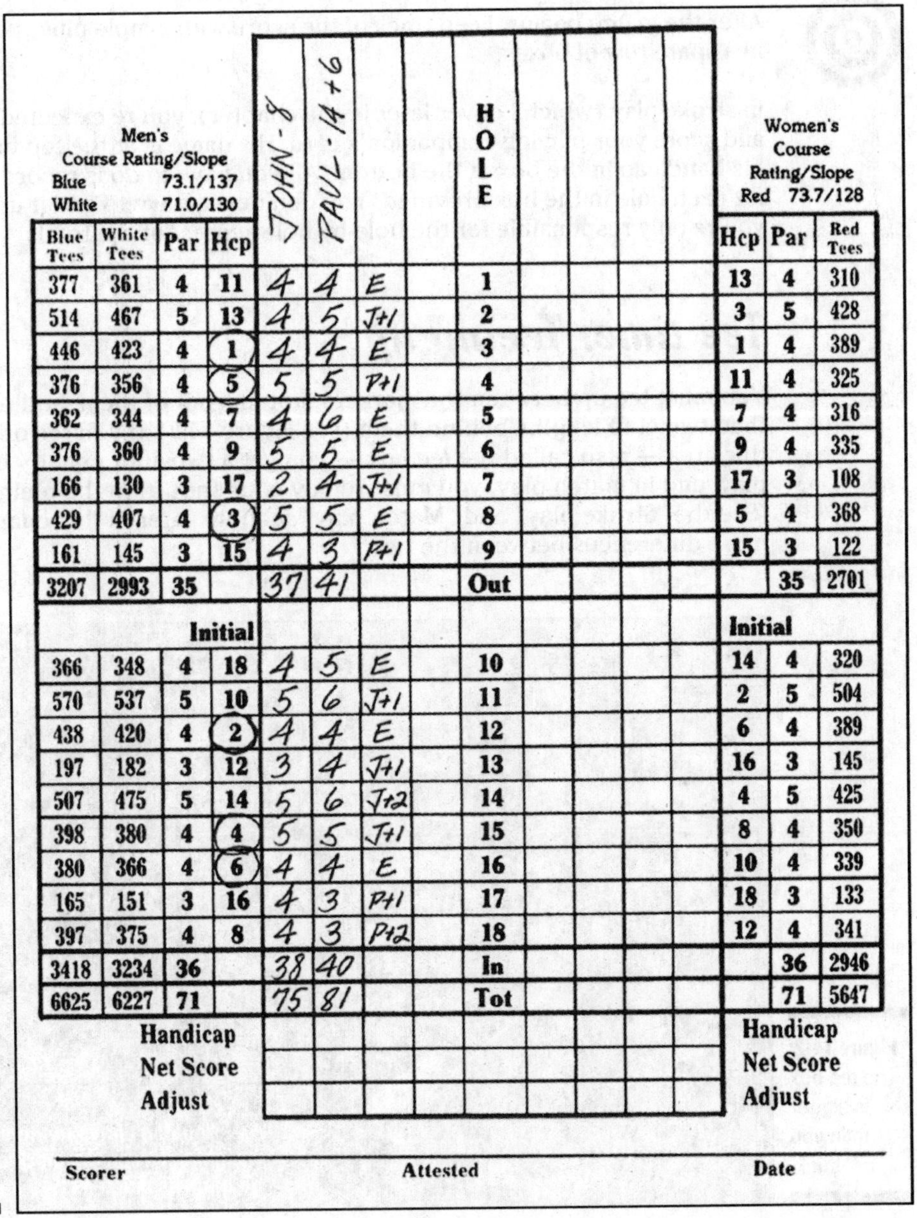

Blue Tees	White Tees	Par	Hcp	JOHN - 8	PAUL - 14 + 6		H O L E					Hcp	Par	Red Tees
												Women's Course Rating/Slope Red 73.7/128		
377	361	4	11	4	4	E	1					13	4	310
514	467	5	13	4	5	J+1	2					3	5	428
446	423	4	(1)	4	4	E	3					1	4	389
376	356	4	(5)	5	5	P+1	4					11	4	325
362	344	4	7	4	6	E	5					7	4	316
376	360	4	9	5	5	E	6					9	4	335
166	130	3	17	2	4	J+1	7					17	3	108
429	407	4	(3)	5	5	E	8					5	4	368
161	145	3	15	4	3	P+1	9					15	3	122
3207	2993	35		37	41		Out						35	2701
		Initial										**Initial**		
366	348	4	18	4	5	E	10					14	4	320
570	537	5	10	5	6	J+1	11					2	5	504
438	420	4	(2)	4	4	E	12					6	4	389
197	182	3	12	3	4	J+1	13					16	3	145
507	475	5	14	5	6	J+2	14					4	5	425
398	380	4	(4)	5	5	J+1	15					8	4	350
380	366	4	(6)	4	4	E	16					10	4	339
165	151	3	16	4	3	P+1	17					18	3	133
397	375	4	8	4	3	P+2	18					12	4	341
3418	3234	36		38	40		In						36	2946
6625	6227	71		75	81		Tot						71	5647
		Handicap										**Handicap**		
		Net Score										**Net Score**		
		Adjust										**Adjust**		

Men's Course Rating/Slope Blue 73.1/137 White 71.0/130

Scorer   Attested   Date

Figure 14-1: Marking your card.

Say your handicap is 9 and mine is 14. That means you're going to give me five strokes over the course of the round. I get those strokes at the holes rated the most difficult. That's logical. Equally logical is the fact that these holes are handicapped 1 through 5. So mark those "stroke holes" before you begin. (I explain scoring and handicaps later in this chapter.)

After the match begins, keep track of the score with simple pluses or minuses in a spare row of boxes.

In stroke play (which I cover later in the chapter), you're expected to keep and score your playing companion's card. His name is at the top of the card, his handicap in the box at the bottom. All you have to do is record his score for each hole in the box provided. You don't even have to add it up because you're only responsible for the hole-by-hole score, not the total.

Tee time: Teeing up

You must tee up between the markers, not in front of them, and no more than two club lengths behind them (see Figure 14-2). If you tee off outside this area — also called the *tee box* — you get a two-shot penalty in stroke play, and in match play, you must replay your shot from the teeing area. (See the "Stroke play" and "Match play" sections later in this chapter for more differences between the two.)

Figure 14-2: The tee box is bigger than you think.

You don't have to tee up your ball right between the markers; you can go back as much as two club lengths.

You don't have to stand within the teeing area; your feet can be outside it. This knowledge is helpful when the only piece of level ground is outside the teeing area or if the hole is a sharp dogleg. You can give yourself a better angle by *teeing up wide* (standing outside the teeing area).

Finding a lost ball

At this stage of your golf life, you're going to hit your share of errant shots. Some will finish in spots where finding a deer, bear, or Keebler elf seems easier than locating a golf ball. And sometimes you can't find the ball at all.

You have five minutes to track down your ball. If you can't find the ball in the five minutes you're allowed, you must return to the tee or to the point where you last hit the ball and play another ball. With penalty, stroke, and distance, you're now hitting off the tee with three strokes under your belt. (The later section "Out-of-bounds" gives you more details on penalty, stroke, and distance.) One way to avoid having to walk back to the tee after failing to find your ball is to hit a provisional ball if you think the first one may be hard to find. If the first ball can't be found, you play the second.

Be sure, however, to announce to your playing partners that you're playing a provisional ball. If you don't, you must play the second ball — *with* the penalty — even if you find the first ball.

Ain't this game full of surprises?

Looking for a ball is a much-neglected art form. I see people wandering aimlessly, going over the same spot time after time. Be systematic! Walk back and forth without retracing your steps. That's how search parties work. You double or triple your chances of finding the ball.

You have five minutes to look for your ball from the moment you start to search. Time yourself. The game is often too slow as it is — don't take a second over your allotted time hunting for a lost ball.

Taking a drop

In some situations, you have to pick up your ball and drop it. Every golf course has places that allow you to take a free drop. A cart path is one — you can move your ball away from the path with no penalty. *Casual water* (such as a puddle) is another. Here's how to do it:

1. **Lift and clean your ball.**

2. **Find the nearest spot where you have complete relief from the problem and mark that spot with a tee.**

   You have to get not only the ball but also your feet away from the obstruction. So find a spot where your feet are clear of the obstruction, and then determine where the clubhead would be if you hit from there. This spot is the one you want to mark. The spot you choose can't be closer to the hole.

3. **Measure one club length from that mark.**

4. **Drop the ball.**

   Stand tall, holding the ball at shoulder height and at arm's length, as shown in Figure 14-3. Let the ball drop vertically. You aren't allowed to "spin" the ball into a more favorable spot. Make sure the ball doesn't end up nearer the hole than it was when you picked it up. If it does, you have to pick up the ball and drop it again.

First, find the spot where your feet are clear of the obstruction.

You get one more club length from there.

Now drop your ball.

Figure 14-3: Dropping your ball.

How you drop the ball makes no difference; however, you always have to stand upright when dropping. I once had to drop my ball in a bunker where the sand was wet. The ball was obviously going to *plug* when it landed (that is, get buried in the sand), so I asked whether I could lie down to drop it. A clever idea, I thought. And the rules official agreed — if you replace the word "clever" with "totally wrong." Oh, well . . . .

Avoiding advice

The advice issue has two sides in golf. First, you can't give advice or receive it from anyone but your caddie. That means you can't ask your playing companion what club he or she hit. Neither can you say anything that may help in the playing of his or her next stroke.

This rule is a toughie, and even the best have been caught breaking it. In the 1971 Ryder Cup matches in St. Louis, Arnold Palmer was playing Bernard Gallacher of Scotland. Arnold hit a lovely shot onto a par-3, whereupon Gallacher's caddie said, "Great shot, Arnie. What club did you hit?" Arnold, being Arnold, told him. Gallacher never heard the exchange, but the referee did. Arnold, despite his own protestations, was awarded the hole. That was in match play; in stroke play, it's a two-shot penalty. So take care!

Second, you're going to find yourself playing with people, *lots* of people, who think of themselves as experts on every aspect of the golf swing. These know-it-alls may mean well, but they're dangerous to your golfing health. Ignore them. Or, if that proves too difficult, listen, smile politely, and then go about your business as if they'd been speaking Martian.

Keeping lost balls to a minimum

How can you keep lost balls to a minimum? Here are a couple of suggestions:

✔ **When your ball is in midair, watch it like a hawk.** That sounds pretty obvious, but not watching the shot is perhaps the number-one reason (after bad technique) why balls get lost. Temper gets the better of too many players. They're too busy slamming the club into the ground to watch the ball. Don't make that mistake.

✔ **Pay attention when the ball lands, too.** Give yourself a reference point — like a tree — near the landing area so that you can easily remember the location. You should also put an identifying mark on your ball before you begin play so you can be sure that the ball you find is the one you hit.

Etiquette: Knowing the Right Way to Play

Golf, unlike the trash-talking sports you see on TV, still prizes sportsmanship. Golf is an easy game to cheat at, so every player is on his or her honor. But there's more to it than that. Golf has its own code of etiquette: semiofficial "rules" of courtesy that every player is expected to follow. Here are the main ones:

- **Don't talk while someone is playing a stroke.** Give your partners time and silence while they're analyzing the situation, making their practice swings, and then making their swings for real. Don't stand near them or move about, either, especially on the greens. Stay out of their peripheral vision while they're putting. Don't stand near the hole or walk between your partner's ball and the hole. Even be mindful of your shadow. The *line* of a putt — the path it must follow to the hole — is holy ground.

  Easygoing types may not mind if you gab away while they're choosing a club, but that isn't true for everyone. When in doubt, stand still and shut up. If you're a problem more than once, you'll hear about it.

- **Be ready when it's your turn — when your ball lies farthest from the hole.** Make your decisions while you're walking to your ball or while waiting for others to hit. And when it's your turn, don't delay. You don't have to rush; just get on with it.

- **The *honor* (that is, the first shot) on a given tee goes to the player with the lowest score on the previous hole.** If that hole was tied, the player with the lowest score on the hole before that retains the honor. In other words, you have the honor until you lose it.

- **Make sure everyone in your foursome is behind you when you hit.** You don't hit every shot where you're aiming it. When in doubt, wait for your playing partners to get out of your line of play. The same is true for the group in front; wait until they're well out of range before you hit. Even if it would take a career shot for you to reach them, hold your fire. Lawyers love golfers who ignore this rule of thumb.

- **Pay attention to the group behind you, too.** Are they waiting for you on every shot? Is there a gap between you and the group ahead of you? If the answer to either or both is yes, step aside and invite the group behind you to play through. This move is no reflection on your ability. All it means is that the group behind plays faster than you do.

  The best place to let a group behind play through is at a par-3 (it's the shortest hole and, therefore, the quickest way of playing through). After hitting your ball onto the green, mark it, and wave to them to play. Stand off to the side of the green as they hit. After they've all hit, replace your ball and putt out. Then wait for them to finish, and let them go to the next tee ahead of you. Simple, isn't it?

Sadly, you see this piece of basic good manners ignored time and again by players who don't know any better. Do what's right: Let a faster group play through.

✔ **Help out the greenskeeper.** A busy course takes a major pounding — all those balls landing on greens, feet walking through bunkers, and divots of earth flying through the air. Do your bit for the golf course. Repair any ball marks you see on the greens. (You can use your tee or a special tool called a *divot fixer,* which costs about a dollar in the pro shop.)

Here's how to repair ball marks:

1. **Stick the repair tool in the green around the perimeter of the indentation, starting at the rear, and gently lift the compacted dirt.**

2. **Replace any loose pieces of grass or turf in the center of the hole and then take your putter and tap down the raised turf until it's level again (see Figure 14-4).**

Now you're a good golf citizen.

You also want to smooth out or rake any footprints in bunkers, as shown in Figure 14-5 (but only after you play out). And replace any divots you find on fairways and tees.

✔ **If you must play with a golf cart (take my advice and walk if you can), park it well away from greens, tees, and bunkers.** To speed up play, park on the side of the green nearest the next tee. The same is true if you're carrying your bag: Don't set the bag down near any of the aforementioned items; leave it in a spot on the way to the next tee.

✔ **Leave the green as soon as everyone has finished putting.** You see this situation a lot: You're ready to play your approach shot to the green, and the people in front are crowding around the hole marking their cards. That's poor etiquette on two counts: It delays play, and the last thing the greenskeeper wants is a lot of footprints around the cup. Mark your card on the way to the next tee!

When a ball lands on a soft green, it often leaves a *pitch mark.*

Lift the back edge of the hole... and then flatten it out.

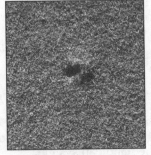

Figure 14-4: Take care of the green.

Nine perfect excuses for a bad shot

Try some of these convincing lines the next time your shot doesn't go where you wanted it to:

✔ "I only had an hour to loosen up."

✔ "I looked up and the sun got in my eyes."

✔ "I just had a lesson, and the pro screwed me up."

✔ "I borrowed these clubs."

✔ "These new shoes are killing my feet."

✔ "This new glove cuts off my circulation. I have the hand of a mummy."

✔ "I kept expecting your cellphone to go off."

✔ "I can't play well when the temperature is over 80. Or under 79."

✔ "I'm Gary McCord."

Figure 14-5:
Be rakish and restore the bunker.

Getting a Handle on the Handicap System

If you, as a beginner, are completing 18-hole rounds in fewer than 80 shots, you're either a cheat or the next Jack Nicklaus. In all probability, your scores are considerably higher than par. Enter the handicap system.

The USGA employs the handicap system to level the playing field for everyone. The association has an esoteric system of "course rating" and something called "slope" to help compute exactly how many strokes everyone should get. In all my years in golf, I have yet to meet anyone who understands or can explain how course rating and slope are computed, so I'm not going to try. Be like everyone else — accept both and go with the flow.

The handicap system is one reason I think that golf is the best of all games. Handicapping allows any two players, whatever their level of play, to have an enjoyable — and competitive — game together. Try to compete on, say, a tennis court. I can't go out with Rafael Nadal and have any fun. Ditto for poor, bored Nadal, who may at least get the excitement of doing CPR on me. The disparity in our abilities makes competitive play impossible. But in golf, if you play a little better than usual, your handicap may help you beat Phil Mickelson and Tiger Woods.

The following sections explain how to figure out your handicap and how it impacts your game.

Getting a handicap

You probably don't have a handicap yet. No worries — you've got plenty of time. When you can consistently hit the ball at least 150 yards with a driver, you're ready to play a full 18-hole round of golf.

When you reach the stage where you can hit the ball a decent distance on the range, you're ready to do the same on a real course. You want to test yourself and give your progress a number. Make that two numbers: your score and your handicap.

The first thing to do is keep score. Get a golfer friend to accompany you for 18 holes. This person must keep score and sign your card at the end of the round. To be valid, a card needs two signatures: your own and that of the person you're playing with. That way, all scores are clearly valid, and nobody fudges his or her total.

You need to play at least ten rounds before you're eligible for a handicap. Don't ask why; those are the rules. After ten rounds in a pre-handicap cocoon, you emerge as a beautiful, full-fledged, handicap golfer.

At first, your handicap will probably drop quite quickly. Most new golfers improve by leaps and bounds at first. After that, the real work starts.

Of course, the handicap system is easy to abuse, and some people do. Interestingly, most abuse occurs when players want their handicaps to be higher. They either fabricate high scores or don't record their better rounds so that their handicaps rise. Thus, they get more strokes from other players in betting matches. A few golfers go the other way; they want a lower "vanity" handicap to make people think they're *sticks* (championship-level golfers). Find these vanity handicappers and gamble with them for everything they own!

Don't get too cynical, though. Any abuse of the system is confined to a tiny minority of players. That's another reason golf is such a great game: Golfers can generally be trusted. The few cheats are soon identified and ostracized.

Calculating your handicap

Okay, you're wondering how you get a handicap. It's easy: All you do is report your scores at the course where you normally play. Then you're off and running. You can calculate your handicap at any one time by finding the average of the best 10 of your previous 20 scores (see Figure 14-6) and subtracting the par for the course from that average. Technically, it's 96 percent of that number — another wacky golf quirk — but I'll let the math whizzes handle that wrinkle.

Most country clubs and public courses make things easy for you. They have computers that take your scores and do all the work to update your handicap throughout the golf season, about twice a month.

Suppose your ten scores average out at exactly 100. In other words, for your first ten rounds of golf, you hit 1,000 shots. If par for the 18-hole course you played is 72, your average score is 28 over par. That figure, 28, is your handicap.

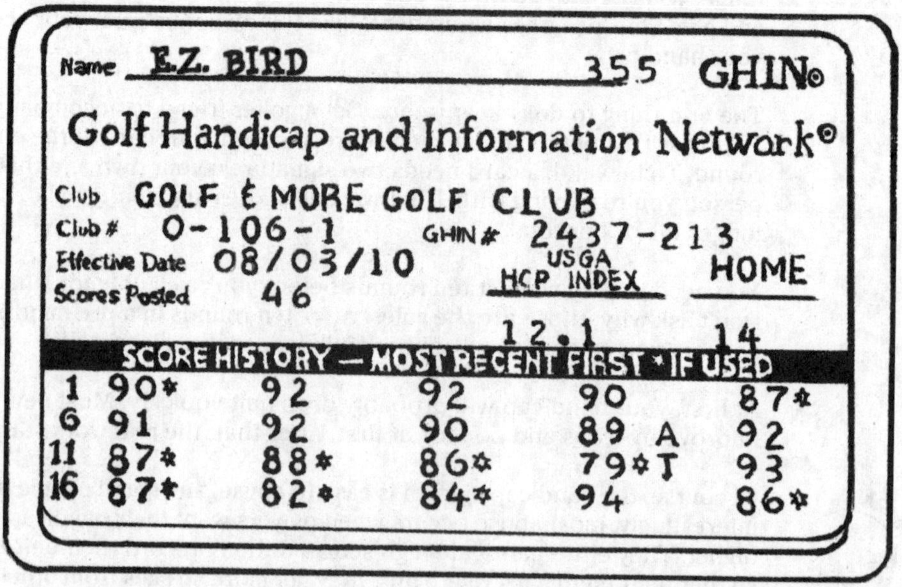

Figure 14-6:
Your
handicap
card.

Name **E.Z. BIRD**		355 GHIN©		
Golf Handicap and Information Network©				
Club **GOLF & MORE GOLF CLUB**				
Club # **O-106-1**		GHIN # **2437-213**		
Effective Date **08/03/10**		USGA HCP INDEX		HOME
Scores Posted **46**		**12.1**		**14**
SCORE HISTORY — MOST RECENT FIRST * IF USED				
1	90*	92	92	90	87*
6	91	92	90	89 A	92
11	87*	88*	86*	79*T	93
16	87*	82*	84*	94	86*

Every time you play from then on, your handicap adjusts to account for your most recent score. Suppose your 11th round is a 96. That's only 24 over the par of 72. So your *net score* — your actual score minus your handicap — is 68, four under that magic number of 72. Nice round! When you feed that 96 into the handicap computer, you'll probably find that your handicap drops.

Understanding what your handicap means

The lower your handicap is, the better golfer you are. Thus, if your handicap is 6 and mine is 10, you're a better player. On average, four strokes better, to be exact.

Assume that par for the 18-hole course we're going to play is 72. You, as someone with a handicap of 6, would be expected to play 18 holes in a total of 78 strokes, six more than par. I, on the other hand, being a 10-handicapper, would on a normal day hit the ball 82 times, ten more than par. Thus, your handicap is the number of strokes over par you should take to play an 18-hole course.

When you're just starting out, you don't want to team up with three low-handicap players — that's just discouraging. Play with golfers of your own ability at first. After you get the hang of the game, start playing with people who are better than you so that you can learn from them.

Put It on the Card: Keeping Score

Scoring is another unique part of golf. You can easily see how you're doing because your score is in black and white on the scorecard. Every course has a scorecard that tells you each hole's length, its par, and its rating relative to the other holes (see Figure 14-7).

The relationship of the holes is important when you're playing a head-to-head match. Say I have to give you 11 shots over 18 holes because of our handicap difference (check out the earlier section "Getting a Handle on the Handicap System" for more on handicap). In other words, on 11 holes during our round, you get to subtract one shot from your score. The obvious question is, "Which holes?" The card answers that question. You get your shots on the holes rated 1 through 11. These holes, in the opinion of the club committee, are the hardest 11 holes on the course. The 1-rated hole is the toughest, and the 18-rated hole is the easiest.

Most of your golf will typically be matches against others. That's why each hole's rating is important.

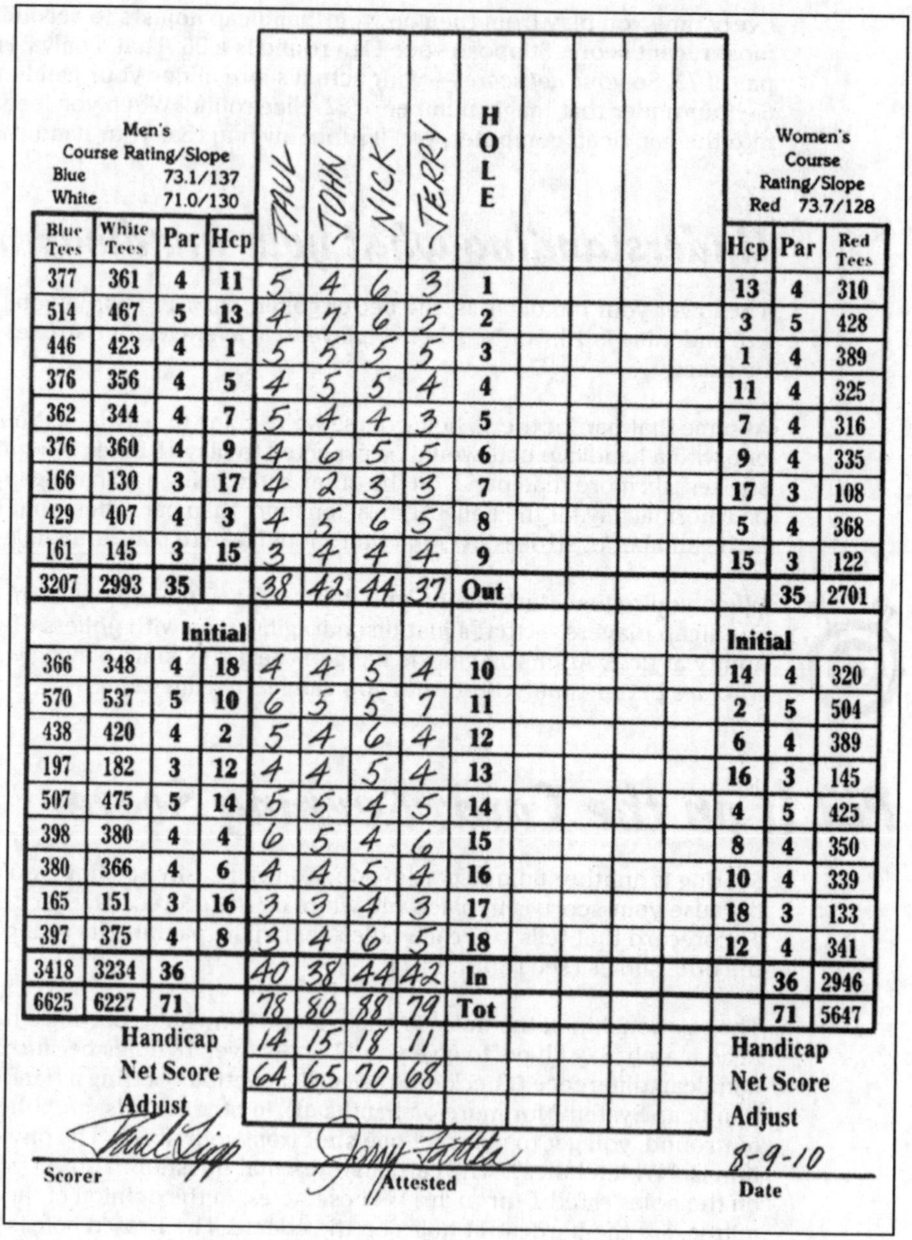

Men's Course Rating/Slope
Blue 73.1/137
White 71.0/130

Women's Course Rating/Slope
Red 73.7/128

Blue Tees	White Tees	Par	Hcp	PAUL	JOHN	NICK	TERRY	HOLE				Hcp	Par	Red Tees
377	361	4	11	5	4	6	3	1				13	4	310
514	467	5	13	4	7	6	5	2				3	5	428
446	423	4	1	5	5	5	5	3				1	4	389
376	356	4	5	4	5	5	4	4				11	4	325
362	344	4	7	5	4	4	3	5				7	4	316
376	360	4	9	4	6	5	5	6				9	4	335
166	130	3	17	4	2	3	3	7				17	3	108
429	407	4	3	4	5	6	5	8				5	4	368
161	145	3	15	3	4	4	4	9				15	3	122
3207	2993	35		38	42	44	37	Out					35	2701
			Initial									**Initial**		
366	348	4	18	4	4	5	4	10				14	4	320
570	537	5	10	6	5	5	7	11				2	5	504
438	420	4	2	5	4	6	4	12				6	4	389
197	182	3	12	4	4	5	4	13				16	3	145
507	475	5	14	5	5	4	5	14				4	5	425
398	380	4	4	6	5	4	6	15				8	4	350
380	366	4	6	4	4	5	4	16				10	4	339
165	151	3	16	3	3	4	3	17				18	3	133
397	375	4	8	3	4	6	5	18				12	4	341
3418	3234	36		40	38	44	42	In					36	2946
6625	6227	71		78	80	88	79	Tot					71	5647

Handicap	14	15	18	11				Handicap
Net Score	64	65	70	68				Net Score
Adjust								Adjust

Scorer *(signature)* Attested *(signature)* Date 8-9-10

Figure 14-7: Keeping score.

Match play

In *match play*, you don't have to write down any score. The only thing that matters is the state of the game between you and your opponent.

In match play, the score is recorded as holes up or holes down. Say my score on the first hole was 4, and your score was 5, and you received no strokes on that hole. I'm now one up. Because each hole is a separate entity, you don't need to write down your actual score; you simply count the number of holes you've won or lost. In fact, if you're having a particularly bad time on a given hole, you can even pick up your ball and concede the hole. All you lose is that hole. Everything starts fresh on the next tee. Such a head-to-head match ends when one player is more holes up than the number of holes remaining. Thus, matches can be won by scores of *four and three*. All that means is that one player was four holes ahead with only three left, the match finishing on the 15th green.

Stroke play

Stroke play (or *medal play*) is different. It's strictly card-and-pencil stuff. Now you're playing against everyone else in the field — or against that elusive standard, par — not just your playing companion. All you do is count one stroke each time you swing at the ball. If it takes you five strokes to play the first hole, you write *5* on your card for that hole. Well, your opponent does — your playing partner keeps your official score, although you can track it as well if you want. The card in your pocket has your playing companion's name on it. At the end of the round, he signs his name to your card and gives it to you; you do the same with his card. After you've checked your score for each hole, you also sign your card. Then, if you're in an official tournament, you hand your card to the scorers. If you're playing a casual round, you record your score on the computer.

Take care when checking your card. One Rules of Golf quirk is that you're responsible for the accuracy of the score recorded under your name for each hole — your companion isn't. Any mistakes are deemed to have been made by you, not him. And you can't change a mistake later, even if you have witnesses. Take the case of Roberto DeVicenzo at the 1968 Masters. Millions of spectators and TV viewers saw him make a 3 on the 17th hole in the final round. But the man marking his card, Tommy Aaron, mistakenly marked a 4. Checking his score after the round, DeVicenzo failed to notice the error and signed his card. The mistake cost him the chance to win in a playoff with Bob Goalby. DeVicenzo had to accept a score one higher than he actually shot and lost by that one stroke. Tragic. After realizing his mistake, poor DeVicenzo said, "What a stupid I am!"

DeVicenzo's misfortune shows what can happen when the score on your card is higher than the one you actually made on the hole. You're stuck with that score. If the opposite is the case and the score on the card is *lower* than it should be, the result is even worse: You're disqualified.

One last thing: Don't worry about the addition on your card. You aren't responsible for that part. As long as the numbers opposite each hole are correct, you're in the clear.

Dealing with Penalty Shots

Penalty shots are an unfortunate part of every golfer's life. Sooner or later, you're going to incur a penalty shot or shots. I can't cover all the possible penalty situations in this book, but in the following sections, I run you through the most common of them.

Out-of-bounds

Out-of-bounds is the term used when you hit your ball to a spot outside the confines of the golf course — over a boundary fence, for example. Out-of-bounds areas are usually marked with white stakes that are about 30 yards apart. If you're outside that line, you're out-of-bounds (often abbreviated with the dreaded initials *O.B.*).

Okay, so it's happened; you've gone out-of-bounds. What are your options? Limited, I'm afraid. First, you're penalized *stroke and distance*. That means you must drop another ball (or tee up if the shot you hit out-of-bounds was from a tee) as close as possible to the spot you just played from. Say that shot was your first on that hole. Your next shot counts as your third on that hole. Count 'em:

- ✔ The shot you hit
- ✔ The stroke penalty
- ✔ The distance

So now you're *playing three* from the original spot.

Unplayable lies

Inevitably, you're going to hit a ball into a spot from which further progress is impossible. In a bush. Against a wall. Even buried in a bunker.

When the unplayable lie happens (and you're the sole judge of whether you can hit the ball), you have three escape routes.

- You can pick up the ball and drop it — no nearer the hole — within two club lengths (take your driver and place it end-to-end on the ground twice) of the original spot under penalty of one shot.

- You can pick up the ball, walk back as far as you want (keeping that original point between you and the hole), and then drop the ball. Again, it's a one-stroke penalty.

- You can return to the point where you hit the original shot. This option is the last resort because you lose distance, as well as adding the penalty shot. Believe me, nothing is worse than a long walk while you're burdened with a penalty stroke!

Water hazards

Water hazards are intimidating when you have to hit across one. "Watery graves," the English TV commentator Henry Longhurst used to call them.

Whenever you see yellow stakes, you know the pond/creek/lake in question is a water hazard. If you hit into a water hazard, you may play the ball as it lies, with no penalty, if the ball's only half-submerged or otherwise hittable. (If you do, you may not *ground your club* — touch it to the ground or water before swinging.), Or choose from these options:

- Hit another ball from the spot you just hit from.

- Take the point where your ball crossed into the water hazard and drop another ball (you can go back as far as you want, keeping that point between you and the hole).

Either way, it's a one-shot penalty.

Follow the iRules

Just recently, the USGA introduced the first Rules of Golf app for the Apple iPhone and other mobile devices. Now, I'm the first to discourage more cellular use on the golf course, but this app (and a few similar ones you can find) is pretty cool. To find out more, go to usga. org. I also mention some other golf apps in Chapter 19.

Lateral water hazards

If you're playing by the seaside, the beach is often termed a *lateral water hazard*. Red stakes indicate a lateral hazard. Your options are to play the ball as it lies (no penalty, but risky) — as with regular water hazards, you may not ground your club — or as follows, with a one-stroke penalty:

✔ Drop a ball at the point where the ball last crossed the boundary of the hazard — within two club lengths, no nearer the hole.

✔ Drop a ball as close as possible to the spot on the opposite margin of the water hazard, the same distance from the hole.

✔ Hit another ball from within two club lengths of the spot you just hit from.

✔ Take the point where the ball crossed the water hazard and drop another ball as far back as you want, keeping that point between you and the hole.

Strike one! The dreaded whiff

It's the beginner's nightmare: You make a mighty swing and miss the ball. The penalty? None, actually. But you must count that swing as a stroke.

If you swing at a ball with intent to hit it, that's a shot regardless of whether you make contact. You can't say, "That was a practice swing." If you meant to hit the ball, your swing counts as a stroke.

Airballs can be highly embarrassing, but they're part of the journey of golf.

Chapter 15

Gamesmanship and Sportsmanship

Gambling can be a touchy subject. Being the type of game that it is — easy to handicap, played at a leisurely pace — golf lends itself to betting. So you'll probably find yourself playing for money before long. At first the money isn't much — if you have any sense, that is. But money games can get out of hand if you're not careful.

Fortunately, this chapter covers the rules of thumb for gambling on the course — and for handling other sportsmanship situations that golfers encounter. But I'm betting you can handle them all.

Wanna Bet?: Gambling on Your Golf Match

GARY SAYS

In my experience, golfers come in two types: those who want an even match and those who want to give you an evil beating. I recommend playing with the first group, at least in your early days. Those folks won't take advantage of your inexperience. They want a good, close match, so they give you the shots you need to make a good showing. The winner is the one who plays his or her best that day. Nothing wrong with that, of course. If someone is going to win, someone has to lose — sometimes that loser will be you.

Unfortunately, the nice people I just described sometimes seem as rare as four-leaf clovers. That second group constitutes the majority of gambling golfers. They don't play for the sunshine, the exercise (unless getting in and out of a cart qualifies as exercise), or the relaxation. They play golf for one reason: to bet and win. The following sections guide you through the golf bets you may encounter and help you keep from getting a raw deal when the betting begins.

Never play for more than you can afford to lose. Keep the bets small when you're a new golfer learning the ropes. Golf is a great game to bet on, but if you lose so much money that it starts to hurt, the game's no fun. Be careful and bet at your own risk.

Knowing common bets and how to win them

Following are the most common types of golf bets and what you can do to increase your chances of winning:

✔ **Nassau:** This bet was named for New York's Nassau Country Club, where it's said to have originated. Players bet a certain amount on the front nine, the same on the back nine, and the same on their overall score. So if you play a $5 nassau and win every hole, you pocket $15. The tricky part comes when players *press,* conceding the bet and doubling it for the rest of the round. You can even find an *aloha press,* in which you press everything on the last hole. By pressing, you can lose the first 17 holes and still come out ahead by winning the 18th.

Even pros are familiar with nassaus. Lee Trevino, in his early days as one of golf's great hustlers, once said, "Pressure is $5 on the front nine, $5 on the back, and $5 for the 18 when you've got $2 in your pocket."

✔ **Skins:** Players bet a certain amount each hole — a *skin* — but if two tie, all tie, and the money is added to the pot for the next hole. If a four-some plays skins and no golfer beats the other three on any hole, you can wind up five or six or even more skins riding on a later hole. To win at skins, relax early in the round and focus on playing your best when the chips (well, skins) are down. And don't be afraid to take risks. Remember, you have to win the hole outright to claim the skins.

✔ **Wolf:** Golfers take turn being the wolf, who takes on everyone else in the group. For a set price each hole, the wolf can either choose one of the others as his partner (before anyone tees off) or *go wolf* and try to win the hole himself. If a wolf partners up and his team wins, he and his partner split the money on that hole. If he goes wolf and wins, he gets it all for himself, but if he loses, he has to pay everyone else. In this game, you're smarter to partner up if you're a consistent player and to be the lone wolf if you're the type who can make a pressure putt.

- ✔ **Snake:** *Snake* is a fun side bet that makes putting more pressure-packed than ever. The first player who three-putts a green gets a snake that sticks with him until somebody else three-putts. If the snake is worth $5 and no one three-putts for five holes, he owes each other player $25. To win snakes, remember that most players leave their first *lag putts* (long putts meant to end up close to the hole) short. Hit your lag putts hard enough to reach the hole, and you'll dodge more snakes.

- ✔ **Sixes:** *Sixes* are a *best-ball match* (where players partner up and take the best score) with a twist: Golfers switch teams every six holes. That means that a foursome will feature three different best-ball battles in an 18-hole round. In sixes, every member of the foursome plays six holes with every other member. Try to play the first six with your group's best golfer as your partner. That way, you can establish momentum — and relaxation — that can last all day.

- ✔ **Bingo Bango Bongo:** Three points are up for grabs on each hole. One goes to the first golfer on the green (bingo), one to the golfer closest to the hole after everybody's on the green (bango), and one to the first in the cup (bongo). If a point's worth $5, you can win $15 on a good hole. Or steal a bango on a bad hole by chipping your sixth shot close.

Many golfers add bets for *greenies* (anyone hitting the green in one shot wins a predetermined sum from everyone else) or *sandies* (ditto for anyone who gets from a bunker into the hole in two shots). Such wagers are called *junk,* but everyone agrees they're fun. You can add *barkies* — you win if you hit a tree and still make par or better on a hole — or even bets of your own invention. Years ago, an Arnold Palmer fan invented a bet to honor his hero's talent for saving par from under trees, behind snack bars, and so on; you win an *Arnie* if you make par on a hole without ever hitting the fairway.

If you think all those wagers make golf betting seem dizzying, you're not alone. I've seen scorecards so marked up with bets and presses that they looked like modernist paintings. Fortunately, modern technology can help. Apps such as GolfMoolah for the Apple iPhone keep track of all your bets and side bets — all you have to do is hit the ball.

Negotiating strokes at the first tee

Common convention says that most golf bets are won on the first tee — the arena of negotiation, I call it. This spot is where golfers fight over and agree upon bets. The key to first-tee negotiations is determining the number of strokes you'll give or receive over the course of a round.

As a beginning golfer, you typically play with people whose handicaps are lower than yours, which essentially means they spot you some strokes to make the game a little more even. Say your handicap is 30 and your opponent's is 18. That's 12 strokes to you, right?

Not if Mr. Cutthroat has his way. He's not interested in improving your win chances when money is on the line. He'll moan that his wife just left him. Or that he hasn't played in weeks because of his workload at the office, that his old football injury is acting up again, or that he's worried sick about the value of the euro. In any case, he'll try to cut your strokes down by at least three. That, he figures, is the edge he needs to beat you. (Check out Chapter 14 for more on handicapping.)

You have a couple of options here: You either (a) nod sympathetically or (b) spin more tall tales than he just did. What you do *not* do is give up even a single stroke. Not one. European economy aside, you don't owe him anything; do you think he'd help you if you were the one with the excuses?

If you find yourself in the position of giving strokes to a player with a higher handicap, never *net* the strokes so that you're playing with zero. For example, if your handicap is 12 and your opponent's is 18, netting gives you 0 strokes and your opponent 6. Take all your strokes, because they'll be on the toughest holes.

Conceding putts: "That one's good"

The green is one place where a little tactical planning can pay dividends when you're playing for money. No one, from a first-time beginner to the most famous pro, likes short putts, especially when they mean something. That's why they're called *knee-knockers*. For this reason alone, you shouldn't be too generous in conceding short putts to your opponents. Always ask yourself whether you'd fancy hitting the same putt. If the answer is "no" or even "not really," say nothing and watch.

That's the hard-nosed approach. If you're playing a friendly round or you're with your boss, you can be a bit more generous. The conventional rule has long been that any putt *inside the leather* — that is, any putt closer than the length of the grip on your putter (or in some places, between the grip and the clubhead) to the hole is deemed to be unmissable and therefore a *gimme*. Such a policy is still applicable today, although those long putters some players use have pretty long grips, so watch out!

If, like Goldilocks, you don't like either of the extreme approaches in this section, you can consider the middle ground favored by the great Walter Hagen, the best match player of his day. In the 1920s, when the PGA Championship was a *match-play* event (in which each hole is a separate contest), "The Haig" won it four times in a row. So he had to know a thing or two about psychology. One of his ploys was to concede a few shortish putts early in the match. That way, two things happened: His opponent got used to being given putts and, perhaps more importantly, was deprived of the practice of knocking a few in. Then later in the round, old Walter wasn't so generous. The opponent would suddenly be faced with a knee-knocker, the sort of putt he hadn't hit all day.

I don't really recommend Walter's strategy. You can lose friends in a hurry if they miss that short one on the 17th. And your strategy may not work. *Remember:* A short putt missed on the third green counts the same as one on the 17th or 18th.

Choosing Up Sides

As with betting, picking partners for a round of golf can be as cutthroat or as casual as you like. If you're just playing for fun or for a few dollars, who your partners are doesn't really matter. If you play with the same guys every time, everything pretty much evens out in the end, anyway.

But if things are a little more serious, you need to put some thought into your partners. Here are the rules I try to follow in "money" games:

- ✔ My partner always has a perma-tan and callused, leathery hands.

- ✔ He has more than 37 tags hanging from his bag — preferably from Pebble Beach, PGA West, TPC Sawgrass, Harbour Town, and other famously difficult courses.

- ✔ Caddies at the course we're playing treat him like royalty.

- ✔ He has used the same putter since he was 5 years old.

- ✔ If he tells me about his marital problems on the practice range, he's gone!

Showing Off Your Match-Play Smarts

Stroke play has a simple premise: Score the best you can over 18 holes. Match play is equally simple: Win more holes than the other golfer. As you can probably guess, match play generally involves more strategy and thinking than stroke play. Here are my match-play tips:

- ✔ **Don't be too bold too soon.** Play conservatively on the first few holes to avoid making big numbers at the outset. Handing a couple of early holes to your opponent only hurts your confidence and boosts his.

- ✔ **Never lose your temper.** Nothing gives your opponent more heart than watching and listening as you blow a gasket.

- ✔ **Pay attention to where your opponent's ball is at all times.** Your opponent's situation dictates your tactics on any given shot. For example, if he's deep in the woods, you may want to play it safe.

✔ **Figure that your opponent will hole every putt he looks at.** Then you aren't disappointed if he does make one. And if he misses, you get a boost.

✔ **Observe and contradict your opponent's patterns.** Watch how fast he walks, for example. If he's slow, go fast; if he's fast, slow down. Anything to break his natural rhythm.

✔ **Try never to hit two bad shots in a row.** Easier said than done, of course! But trying to hit a great shot to make up for a bad one is tempting. Instead, try to follow up a clunker with a *decent* shot — you avoid more train wrecks (golf talk for disasters) that way. Sometimes mediocrity pays.

✔ **Never second-guess yourself.** If you're playing it safe, don't suddenly get aggressive halfway into your downswing. And if you're going for it, don't hold back. Even if you miss, you'll feel better because you tried! Take it from me, someone who played pro golf for 28 years before he won a tournament!

✔ **Only concede a hole when the situation is hopeless.** Make your opponent win the hole instead of gift-wrapping it for him. The more shots he has to hit under pressure, the more likely he is to make a mistake.

Being a Grinder

Here's the exception that proves the rule: In the 1972 British Open at Muirfield, Lee Trevino and Tony Jacklin were tied standing on the 17th tee in the final round. Distracted by a spectator, Trevino hooked his drive on the par-5 into a deep bunker, while Jacklin drove perfectly. After splashing out only a few yards, Trevino then hooked his third shot into heavy rough to the left and short of the green. Jacklin hit his fairway wood into the perfect spot, about 50 yards from the hole.

At that point, Trevino gave up. He quit. He told Jacklin that the championship was all his and did everything but shake his hand right there. Trevino's fourth shot flew right over the green halfway up a grass bank. Jacklin hit a so-so pitch to about 15 feet.

Barely glancing at the shot, Trevino then hit a lazy, give-up chip that rolled right into the cup for par! Jacklin then three-putted for a six. Trevino won.

I tell this story because it's so unusual — quitters never win! The moral is: Never give up, as Lee did that day. Don't be a quitter, because anything can happen in this game. Be a *grinder* — that's what golfers call a player who gives his all on every single shot of every round.

HAZARD

How to spot a golf hustler

As a relatively new golfer, you're going to be a prime target for hustlers. They'll figure you're not talented or savvy enough to beat them. And they'll be right — at least until you've played a while. So avoid them. Here's what to look for:

✔ **Does he have a 2-iron in his bag?** If so, don't play him. Only good players can hit those things. (And in these days, when even expert players have traded long irons for hybrid clubs, you may wonder about anyone with a 3-iron, too.)

✔ **If a stranger wants to bet serious money, beware.** If you do make the bet, make it a straightforward nassau (see the "Common bets and how to win them" section in this chapter for more on nassau bets). Don't get bamboozled with lots of side bets.

✔ **If he uses a ball that isn't new, say good-bye.** Bad players don't have old balls; they lose them too quickly.

✔ **As legendary teacher Harvey Penick used to say, "Beware of the golfer with a bad grip."** Why? Because he's found a way to make it work.

✔ **Another thing about the grip — look at your opponent's left hand.** If he has calluses, he's either played or practiced a lot. *Adios.*

✔ **If that left hand is less tan than the right, the same applies.** Anyone who's spent that much time wearing a golf glove has probably practiced more than you have.

Minding Your Manners When Golf Is All Business

Sure, golf is a game, but sometimes it's serious business, too. Hitting the links on a sunny day sure beats working in an office, and it's a great way to get to know the folks in your industry — and sometimes that means some high-level types, not just the ones you run into at the water cooler. Believe me, I've been to enough corporate outings to know what a major business schmoozefest the links can be. (Just to give you an idea, my smiling face appeared at 41 corporate golf outings last year. Whew!) Corporate golf outings have become an industry in themselves. And for every official company event, countless informal foursomes are taking it to the links. If you play golf, sooner or later a business round is bound to come your way. Maybe the chance to do a little networking is why you took up golf in the first place. So you need to know some basic rules when you mix business banter with the back nine.

✔ **Don't show off.** Golf is business — an extension of the workplace. You wouldn't yell and punch the air after a presentation or a well-made copy in the office, so don't do it on the fairway either. By all means play your best, but save the showboating for casual rounds with friends.

✔ **Watch the raunchy humor.** Sure, you want everyone to have a good time. But unless you know your partners' attitudes and outlooks well, you risk not only offending them but also losing their business.

✔ **Let your group get settled into its game before talking business.** Never talk about business before the fifth hole — or better yet, the back nine.

✔ **Don't try to squeeze profit out of every minute.** If all your companions wanted was to negotiate business, they'd have come to the office. At the very least, keep up the pretense that you're all out for good fun and good company — even if your companions couldn't sink a putt to save their mother's mortgage.

✔ **Be prepared to stop talking business.** No matter how seriously businesspeople take their work, they may be even more fanatical about their golf games, especially on that one difficult shot. Let your sense of the other person dictate when to lay off business conversation.

✔ **Watch the wagers.** You may choose to bet in the interest of being a good sport, but raising the stakes is probably unwise. If you lose a bet, do it gracefully — and pay up pronto. If you win, stay humble: "That was a lucky shot I hit."

✔ **Never, ever cheat or fudge your or anyone else's score in any way.** However tempting cheating may be, it sends the wrong message. Do you want potential business partners to see you as a corner-cutter or, worse, dishonest? Don't cheat even if no one else can possibly know. You'll know.

Playing with your boss

When playing with your boss (or with anybody, really), you want to do your best. If you're just starting to play golf, you don't have to worry about beating the boss and feeling bad. He or she has probably played a lot longer than you have and just wants to get to know you on the course. The golf course is a great place to find out a person's true personality. The game leaves you psychologically naked in front of your peers.

As your game develops and you become a better player, your boss may recognize your golf game as an asset to the company. Millions of dollars in business deals have been negotiated on the golf course.

Play your best at all times and be helpful to people who don't play as well as you do. You'll reap the benefits for many years to come.

Surviving a Pro-Am

> *I was sent off to war, a young man still slobbering from the fright. There were going to be people wearing camouflaged plaid, shooting at me, toward whom I had no ill will; would I be man enough to fight back? I was going to learn a lesson about life; the cruel nature of this odyssey was upon me. I was going to play in my first pro-am.*
>
> —Gary McCord, circa 1974, as he embarked without hesitation toward the first tee and certain death

One tradition in pro golf is called a *pro-am,* where professional players partner with amateurs. If you're armed with a sizable amount of cash (around $5,000), you can tee it up with Tiger Woods, Phil Mickelson, or Rory McIlroy and tell your friends for the next 300 business lunches how you enthralled these guys with your prowess on the links and your witty banter between shots. In no other sport can a layman go on the playing field and get this close to the action, except perhaps by streaking at a nationally televised game. The shortcomings of the latter, in most cases, are obvious.

Pro-ams are played every Wednesday, or on the *Champions Tour* (the tour for PGA golfers 50 and over) on Wednesdays and Thursdays. Each team consists of four amateurs and a pro. Corporations pay handsomely for the opportunity to put their names on tournaments and entertain their clients. This setup is unique in sports, and it's the pros' duty to see that corporate clients have a good time and want to come back for more.

Since 1998, the *Saturday Series* has been a pro-am for the budget-minded. It pairs amateurs with pros who have *missed the cut* (failed to score well enough to continue) in the current week's PGA Tour event, on a course near that week's tour venue. Entry fees are often less than half that at traditional pro-ams. To find out more about the Saturday Series, check out www.saturday series.com.

Much has been written about the attitudes of the tour players in Wednesday pro-ams. As I know from experience, the difficulties of concentrating on the day before a tournament while playing with nervous amateurs are many. However, no one seems to offer the quivering victims any advice. I always try to imagine what I'd feel like if I were plucked out of my comfort zone and thrust into the spotlight — say, on the hardwood with LeBron James or in the boardroom with Bill Gates — and told not to make an idiot of myself. The truth is that neither LeBron nor Bill would expect me to be any good. I, on the other hand, would still like to give a decent account of myself, or at least limit the damage.

The first thing to keep in mind is that your pro requires one thing from you: Enjoy yourself. The reason we play for so much money these days is that you do enjoy the game, you do buy the equipment that you don't need, and you do love to watch us on TV. So don't be overawed: Chances are you do something for a living that we would be completely useless at doing. A good pro does his or her best to put you at ease on the first tee so that when your first swing makes contact with the planet nine inches behind the ball and induces significant seismographic readings, you can at least have a laugh at it, too.

The following sections spell out my "Eight Steps to Pro-Am Heaven" for pros and amateurs alike — a few do's and don'ts of playing with a pro and a road map through the purgatory of the pro-am. I hope that these guidelines help both you and your pro enjoy the day.

Get a caddie

Having a *caddie* to carry your clubs is the only way to play the pro-am game. You can walk free of hindrance and have clubs handed to you clean and dry. If possible, get one of the tour caddies whose player isn't in the pro-am. For $50 to $100, you can hire someone who is used to being screamed at and blamed for the weather, the rate of inflation, and some of those hard-to-explain skin rashes.

Mind you, the caddie can't help you choose clubs very well at first because he or she isn't familiar with your play. But as your round progresses, he or she will catch on and help you more and more. Your caddie can also regale you with bizarre caddying stories, or *looper legends.* These tales are worth the price of admission, and parental guidance is suggested.

Be ready to hit

You need to be ready to swing, even if it isn't your turn. Discuss with your partners the concept of *ready golf* before you tee off. This setup means forgetting who earned the right to tee up first from the last hole — if you're ready, hit the ball. Pro-am play can be hideously slow, and your pro really appreciates it if you keep things going.

Forget your cellphone

At the very least, turn it off. The surgical removal of a cellular phone from certain regions of the anatomy is painful and, to the best of my knowledge, not covered under most health-insurance plans.

Get a yardage book

A *yardage book* (a booklet showing distances from various landmarks on each hole that you often find for sale in the pro shop,) can help you contribute to your pro's mental health by being the first "ammy" in the history of his or her pro-am career not to ask the question "How far have I got from here?" You can hear this question only a certain number of times in your adult life before your spleen bursts. I have been spleenless for decades.

Don't insist on holing out a doomed ball

If you're up to seven or so strokes on a particular hole, pick up your ball instead of hacking away for several more strokes. Rest the ammo. Holster that bad boy. And be sure to tell your pro that you've done so. Not only do you contribute to the pace of play by picking up, but you also avoid the awkward situation of having the pro wait, expecting you to hit, while you rummage around in your bag looking for the source of that smell that has been emanating from there since you let the kids play with your rain gear.

This tip doesn't contradict the one earlier in this chapter telling you never to give up. You should *not* pick up your ball if you have any chance to help your team. But the moment that chance disappears, pocket that ball. In a pro-am, the only one thing worse than waiting around for no apparent reason is waiting around for a very bad apparent reason — for example, somebody who's holing out for a nine.

Don't sweat your score, or whether your pro sweats the score

Don't be upset if your pro doesn't know how your team stands. It's a Wednesday. He probably doesn't even know his own score, and, quite honestly, after the 26th pro-am of the year, he may not remember what his gender is.

Watch your step

I know, you're wearing soft spikes and it shouldn't matter, but stepping on somebody's putting line, regardless of what's on the bottom of your soles, is an invitation to a hissy fit. Even soft spikes leave indentations in the green that can send a putt veering off-line. Be very, very mindful of the line of your pro's putt. Look at TV coverage of a golf tournament and see how respectful the pros are of each other's lines. Stepping on another pro's line is close to stepping on Old Glory. I've pulled a groin muscle trying to mark my ball without stepping on the sacred line. But I think that, in my career, I've excelled at acrobatic markings of the ball because I was exceptional at the game Twister during my formative years.

Simply ask the pro where his line is, and he'll show you. If my ball isn't in another player's line, I actually leave it right next to the coin the entire time we're on the green so that my amateur partners know where my line is and (I hope) avoid stepping on it.

Don't coach the pro

If you're still interested in playing in a pro-am ever again, do *not* give the pro any advice on how to play the course, even if your family has owned the property since the planet started to warm and you can wander it in the dark without bumping into anything. Trust me, the pro thinks he knows more about it than you do just because he has his name on his bag.

Let the pro's caddie advise him. Even giving the occasional line off the tee ("Aim for the church steeple") can be dangerous, because you don't normally play two club lengths from the back edge of the back tee. I can't tell you how many times I've heard, "Oops, I could've *sworn* you'd carry that bunker!"

Chapter 16

Stepping Up Your Game

After you have a good sense of what kind of golfer you are, know your strengths and weaknesses, and get to the point where you can usually keep the ball in play with more fours, fives, and sixes on your scorecard than eights, nines, and Xs, you're ready to take the next step: improving your game. In this chapter, I show you how to set reasonable goals for your improvement, make smart stroke-gaining decisions, and emulate the attitudes of some great golfing pros.

Moving from Golf Novice to Golf Greatness (Okay, Goodness)

Golf is hard. Few master the game, and nobody perfects it. But one of the great things about this game is that it rewards a little effort almost as much as a lot of blood, sweat, and blisters. After you get over *the hump* — the initial period when everything is new and the club feels weird in your hand — your improvement can be rapid. Some beginners can go from shooting 120, 130, or more for 18 holes to shooting around 100 in a matter of months.

Of course, the better you get, the harder you have to work to whittle away the next ten strokes. Did I say ten strokes? How about one, or even less than one? Touring pros would gladly work like maniacs to save half a stroke off their per-round statistics. Matt Kuchar led the PGA Tour in 2010 with an average score of 69.59, while Charlie Wi tied for 12th with an average of 70.09, exactly half a stroke worse. Kuchar raked in $4.9 million, and Wi earned $1.5 million, or less than a third as much! That's an extreme example — Kuchar played more rounds and played his best at the right moments, winning $1.35 million for a single tournament victory. But it goes to show you how valuable each stroke can be at the game's highest level.

Keep in mind that you don't have to *break* 70 like Kuchar — that is, shoot 69 or better — to have a breakthrough on the course. You don't have to break 80, 90, or even 100. Depending on your experience and physical abilities, breaking 120 may be the achievement of a lifetime.

What matters more than the number is setting goals. If you set out to make par on every hole, you're pretty much guaranteed to spend the day grumbling. The great Annika Sorenstam had an approach she (and coaches Pia Nilsson and Lynn Marriott) called Vision 54. The idea was to birdie every hole. Because most courses have a par of 72, that would give her a "perfect" round of 54.

Annika got within five shots of that number, firing a historic 59 in a tournament in 2001. But I don't recommend shooting for perfection, at least until you're playing in front of thousands of fans. Give yourself a goal that's challenging but reachable:

- ✔ I'm going to break 110 (or 100) this year.
- ✔ I'm going to play a whole round without three-putting.
- ✔ I'm going to shoot my best score yet.
- ✔ I'm going to keep the ball in play, and finish a round with the same ball I teed off with.

I know one player who was so focused on improving that he taped the words *Break 100 — and celebrate* on his golf bag. He was 13 years old, and doing it took him all summer. One day, he finished a round of 98, tore the message off his bag, and set a match to it. He's enjoyed the game for 40 years since then, but still calls that his favorite day on the course.

Surveying Strategic Stroke-Savers

If your dream is to progress from beginner to intermediate golfer, remember one word above all: practice. May I reiterate the most important tip any golfer ever got? *Practice!*

Thank you. I feel better now. And if you promise to heed that crucial bit of advice, following the methods outlined in this book, I'll offer some tips that can help you get to the next level.

Minimizing trouble

Picture a hole with danger on the right: dense rainforest, with volcanoes, swooping pterodactyls, machine-gun nests, and probably vampires. I exaggerate, but you get the picture. And on the left, clean green fairway as far as the eye can see.

Now watch your typical amateur set up to hit his drive. Does he adjust? Noooo, he aims right down the middle, as if this hole were just like any other. And two times out of three, he slices his drive into the vampires.

When danger lurks, shirk it. On a hole where all or most of the trouble is on one side, change your aim. You should choose a target that keeps your shot safe even if you miss toward the trouble.

The same is true for shots with your irons. If you see a pond or bunker in front of the green but no trouble behind it, shift your target. Take more club and try to hit the ball to the back part of the green. (See the later section "Take one more club" for more on this suggestion.) You may be surprised how often you come up a little short — and the shot turns out to be perfect! You may even begin to notice how architects often bank the back of such a green to favor the smart shot.

If you tend to leave sand shots short, like most players do, quit trying to land the ball short of the hole. Visualize a longer shot, with the ball landing beyond the flagstick. You double your margin for error and wind up escaping more bunkers. (After you get more proficient, of course, you can do that less and less.)

The putting surface offers its own danger. If the hole is cut near a drop-off in the green, the greenskeeper may be inviting you to three-putt. Outsmart him by leaving your lag putt a few inches shorter than usual, for a safe tap-in.

The safer side of the hole is almost always the side below the hole. You'd much rather have an uphill two- or three-footer than a downhill slider of the same length.

Knowing when to be a hero

Golf is a game of risk and reward. It usually rewards those who limit risk, playing "within themselves." As Socrates once said (or was it Snead?), the race doesn't always go to the swift, or the golf match to the smart player, but that's the way to bet. That said, sometimes the smart golfer embraces risk. And those can be some of the most exciting, *fun* times of all.

Suppose you're playing a best-ball match, and your partner's ball is safely on the green. Or you're in a scramble, and one or more of your three partners has struck a good shot. (For information on various team formats, see Chapter 13.) You've got a next-to-impossible shot over water, trees, and a barn to a green the size of a sticky note. Or maybe it's only a tricky flip from rough to a slippery green, as in Figure 16-1. Now's the time to go for it! If you splash the shot or even *chili-dip* it (hit behind the ball), it's no loss. But if you succeed, you're a hero to your partners and yourself. What's more, you gain confidence for the next time you face such a shot.

Figure 16-1:
In some tricky cases, you can go for the heroic shot.

The same goes for a less glorious situation. In match play, if you're down by two holes with two to play, for example, and your opponent is safely on the green, you can't just match his or her score on the hole. You've got to win it. So hitch up your courage and fire at the flag.

When you encounter the occasional must-make putt, whether it's a 3-footer or a 20-footer like the one in Figure 16-2, don't forget the one cardinal rule: *Don't leave it short!*

GARY SAYS

The reds, whites, and blues

Just as you start to feel ready to advance in this game, it often grabs you and drags you, kicking and screaming, back to where you were last month — or last year.

So don't get ahead of yourself. Too many golfers hit a few good shots in a row or shoot a career round and believe they've reached a new level of play. They're often the ones you see at your local course, playing from the blue tees . . . and dribbling worm-burners that never reach the fairway. You'll be better off playing to your level of skill — and gaining confidence.

I mention the various tee boxes in Chapter 1. Closest to the green are the junior and/or women's tees. They're often red. Next come the regulation tees, often called the men's tees. They're usually white. Then come the blue tees,

for better players. Still farther back, you find the championship tees, often reserved for tournament play and black or gold in color. They're often called *the tips,* as in "I shot 66 from the tips today."

The blues are widely abused. And believe me, you don't want to be the drive-dribbling impostor in the blue-man group. That makes you unpopular with others in your foursome as well as those in groups behind you because you're the one holding up the pace of play. The *marshall,* whose job it is to keep each group moving at a reasonable pace, may even ask you to pick your ball up.

So unless you consistently shoot in the low 80s, stick to the white tees. It's healthier for your score, your psyche, and the pace of play.

Figure 16-2:
If it's a do-or-die putt, it absolutely, positively has to reach the hole.

Taking one more club

I've said it before, and you'll hear it again if we ever play together: Do yourself a favor and *take more club*.

Pro golfers are pessimists, or at least realists. That's because it's a humbling game. We know how easily things can go wrong on the course, so we guard against disaster — or even bogey — and usually aim for the wide side of the fairway or the fat part of the green.

Your typical amateur is the exact opposite. After he bombs one 250-yard drive, the longest of his life, he's convinced they're all going to go that far. After she hits a 6-iron to a green 150 yards away, she reaches for the same club every time she's got a 150-yard shot.

May I be diplomatic here? All right, please attend to these words of wisdom: *Don't be a dummy!* Smart golf is more about typical shots than career shots. That's why the pros spend so much time determining precisely how far they *usually* hit a particular club. It's why you should pay more attention to your average shot than to the laser beam you blasted over the dogleg at 15.

Say you're *between clubs* — a little closer to the target than you want for a shot with one of the clubs in your bag, a little farther than you want for a shot with a different club. For example, many players hit an 8-iron about 140 yards and a 7-iron about 150. What should they hit from 145?

You're way ahead of me here. As a rule of thumb, hit the longer club. You come out ahead in the long run because your less-than-perfect shots will turn out better. In fact, most amateur golfers score better when they try a simple test: Each time they'd usually hit a 7-iron, they hit a 6-iron, and each time they'd usually hit a 6-iron, they hit a 5-iron. Try it yourself, and you can see what I mean.

Just don't get discouraged if you catch one pure and knock it over the green. Enjoy the feeling of solid contact; store it in your muscle-memory bank. But remind yourself: This game is all about typical shots.

Seeking professional help

The time when you're setting new goals may be the perfect time for a lesson. A PGA professional can spot flaws that may have crept into your swing and offer tips to help you reach your next level. He or she can also provide invaluable advice on your equipment. Ask these questions (and check out Chapter 3 for more on lessons):

✔ Can I keep improving without major swing changes?

✔ Is my practice routine appropriate to my current game and to the level I want to reach?

✔ Are my clubs appropriate to my current game and to the level I want to reach?

As golf's glorious road leads you to lower scores, you may seek more technological assistance through launch monitors and high-tech swing analysis. It's all part of the never-ending pursuit of happiness, or at least a half-stroke improvement.

Channeling the Champs

If you're a weekend basketball player, you're probably not doing your own game much good to watch Kobe Bryant soar to the hoop for a thunderous dunk. As hard as you may try, you couldn't match that feat without a ladder or a jetpack. Heck, I'd need both.

Just as you likely can't dunk like Kobe, slug homers like Albert Pujols and A-Rod, or crush an overhead smash like Serena Williams, you'll probably never play a full round of golf like Tiger Woods or Phil Mickelson. But you can apply aspects of great golfers' games to your own as you work to improve.

If you're looking to step up toward the Promised Land where drives soar out of sight and putts disappear, emulate these exemplary players:

✔ **Ernie Els:** Ernie has been swinging like syrup for more than 20 years on tour. Despite some recent physical woes, he has one of the smoothest moves the game has ever seen. And under the most intense pressure, with the world watching, he seems to relax even more. A competitive fire lurks under that calm exterior, and probably at least some of the same terrors that beset all golfers. But the Big Easy doesn't show it, and that helps keep his swing nice and easy when it counts.

Before your next really important shot, step back. Take a deep breath and picture Ernie's smooth, unhurried swing.

✔ **Tiger Woods:** Tiger went through a personal and professional crisis in 2010, but I expect him to come back in a big way, winning more majors as he chases Jack Nicklaus's record of 18. That's due in part to his track record. Unlike most great athletes, Woods wasn't satisfied with being the best. Earlier in the decade, the already-top-ranked golfer decided he had to improve. So he rebuilt his swing and played even better. At his best, he's both the game's best player and its greatest *grinder* — a golfer who gives his absolute all on every shot whether he's tied for the lead or ten strokes behind.

During your occasional bad rounds, grind out a bogey that could have been a double- or triple-bogey. Even if your score that day is terrible, you'll have something to be proud of.

- **Phil Mickelson:** Phil was the modern Arnold Palmer, always taking chances and never laying up, until he realized he wasn't going to win majors that way. By banking his fires a little and choosing discretion over valor, he took a step to the very forefront of the game. Phil can still hit the heroic miracle shot when he has to; he just doesn't feel he always has to.

Play a practice round with two balls. Play it safe with one ball, and go for broke with the other. Compare your scores. And whatever happens with your hero ball, enjoy giving it a ride.

- **Christina Kim:** Christina is an LPGA star who wears her emotions on her colorful sleeves. A sharp dresser and fan favorite, she treats golf as a joy, not a job. Through 2010 she had two tour victories — no majors yet, but keep an eye on Christina and an ear out for her next highly quotable quip.

Try playing a round as if you didn't have a care in the world, as if just hitting the shot were the whole point, regardless of the outcome. You'll probably have a blast out there, and you may even play better.

- **Jim Furyk:** Jim had a weird swing when he was a kid, and he still does. My colleague David Feherty describes it as "like an octopus falling out of a tree." And Jim still has that unique swing because he and his father, Mike, resisted every attempt to change it when Jim was growing up. Jim actually delivers the club to the ball in near-perfect, classic fashion (that's why his swing works), and he plays with a belief in himself that owes a lot to the way he and his dad stuck to their guns.

When you play with golfers whose swings are prettier than yours, remind yourself that it's *how many* that counts in golf, not *how*. Picture 40-year-old Furyk playing with all those guys with picture-perfect swings in September of 2010. All he did was win the season-ending Tour Championship and its first prize of $1.35 million. Plus a little bonus for claiming the FedEx Cup: another $10 million.

- **Jack Nicklaus:** Jack was a master at just about everything, really, with six Masters championships among his all-time-record 18 major titles, but he was particularly brilliant at minimizing danger and at *course management* — moving the ball around the course in a way that optimized his chances. The Golden Bear *faded* the ball from left to right with great consistency, so he seldom had to worry about trouble on the left. And although the weakest part of his game was wedge play ("weak" only compared to the rest of his genius game), that didn't matter much: Jack would bomb the ball all the way to the green, or lay up so that he had a 9-iron shot.

Strategize like Jack by laying up once in awhile, leaving yourself a full shot to the green.

✔ **Erik Compton:** Erik, a Florida pro, has spent much of his career on the minor-league Nationwide Tour, one rung below the PGA Tour. Not bad for a former college star who has endured not one but two heart transplants. His health and strength are always a worry, but he doesn't complain, saying he's lucky to be playing the game he loves. Few people in any walk of life have shown more heart than Erik.

Step up, swing hard, and smile. Isn't it great to be alive?

Part V
How to Be a Smart Golf Consumer

The 5th Wave   By Rich Tennant

"The fans certainly seem to be enjoying following their favorite players around the course."

In this part . . .

I've been a touring pro since 1974. In this part of the book, I use my expertise to show you how to watch golf in person, which events to attend, and how to get the most out of your day as a spectator. This part also explores some of the wonders of golf on TV, the best golf sites on the Internet (all my favorite cyber-haunts), and the latest golf video games.

Chapter 17

Watching Golf in Person

Some golf-lovers spend years, even their whole lifetimes, without ever attending a live golf event. Madness, I say! Of course, I can understand wanting to play the game rather than watch others play. And when you find yourself in a spectating mood, tuning in to my colleagues and me on a CBS telecast can be easier than trekking to the event itself. But we don't cover every tournament on CBS; if it's on another network, head for the course!

Seriously, every golfer and golf fan should try to see live competition at least once a year. It doesn't have to be a PGA Tour or LPGA event. It doesn't have to be a professional tournament of any kind. You can find exciting golf action in your neck of the woods if you know where to look.

Seeking Out Live Golf

Where should you go to watch golf action live? The short answer: It doesn't matter. You can have a great day on the course and glean important information by witnessing golf at any level. Just pay close attention. You pick up more that way, and you can duck any dimpled missiles that may be coming your way.

High-school golf

It's fun, dramatic, and accessible. Your local high-school team tees it up at a nearby public or country-club course. If you go to watch, you're part of a very small gallery, along with a few parents and girl- or boyfriends, with no gallery ropes to keep you away from the action. You're close enough to see the terror and excitement in the players' eyes — and their appreciation if you clap politely after an excellent shot.

Ask at your home course to see whether local teams play there; the professional can tell you. You can also check the local school's Web site to see when and where the golf team plays or call the school and ask for the golf coach. Be sure to ask the coach whether you can come out and watch. He or she will probably be delighted to hear that you're interested. Explain that you're learning the game and ask whether you can learn from a certain player's swing (or whether you should avoid following a particular person, because some youngsters get unnerved by spectators). Before you know it, you may be an honorary assistant coach!

College tournaments

Collegiate competition is a big step up from high-school golf (see the preceding section). You may be surprised by how well (and how far) college players hit the ball. But don't just gape at the collegians' power. Study how precise they are around the greens. How *deliberate*. This meticulousness should drive home the crucial importance of the *short game* (chipping and putting). With rare exceptions, the best players are the ones who chip and putt better than the others.

College Web sites generally post schedules for their men's and women's golf teams. At the course, pairings are posted in or near the clubhouse. Galleries aren't much larger than at high-school matches, so don't sneeze at the wrong time! Pick a calm moment to introduce yourself to the coach (invariably a focused-looking person wearing a cap with the school logo). Praise one of his or her players, and you may make a new friend.

USGA events

Each year the United States Golf Association stages the prestigious U.S. Open, one of golf's four major championships (along with the Masters, British Open, and PGA Championship). The USGA also runs championships for women, seniors, amateurs, public-course players, and juniors. See USGA.org for details.

Galleries at these events are larger than at high-school and college events, but except for such premier tournaments as the U.S. Open, the Women's Open, and the U.S. Amateur and Senior Opens, you can still get up-close and personal with the golfers.

Here's a great chance to test your eye for the golf swing. What makes the typical player at a USGA event better than a good college golfer? Size, strength, power? Maybe. Maturity (that is, the ability to forget a bad bounce or bad hole and instantly refocus)? Probably. Consistency? Certainly! Consistency is the essential difference between good golfers and expert golfers. Watch closely, and you'll notice that competitors in USGA tournament play hit fewer bad shots than high-school and college players, and the bad ones they hit don't miss by as much.

Professional tours

If you live in Florida or Southern California, you can see professionals try to make a living the hard way, by teeing it up on the Gateway Tour, Emerald Coast Tour, NGA Hooters Tour, and other *minitours*. Minitours offer limited schedules and don't pay much compared to the riches on the PGA Tour. Hooters Tour leader Matthew Harmon earned $95,000 in 2010, but most minitour golfers struggle to make expenses. That's why these circuits are also called *developmental tours;* the players are developing their games under intense pressure.

Farther up golf's ladder, you find the Nationwide Tour, where future stars hone their craft just one rung below the PGA Tour. Nationwide Tour pros can earn more than $100,000 for a victory, and each year the top 25 on the money list (led in 2010 by Jamie Lovemark with $420,000) earn their *PGA Tour cards:* membership on the "big tour" for the following year. The women's version of the Nationwide Tour is the Duramed Futures Tour, led in 2010 by Cindy LaCrosse's $95,000. Each year the top ten Futures Tour players advance to the LPGA.

Then you have the Champions Tour for players 50 and over. After 27 winless years as a pro, I won this circuit's 1999 Toshiba Classic. These days, I've got my hands full with whippersnapper seniors like Fred Couples, Bernhard Langer, Nick Price, and newcomers Kenny Perry and Mark Calcavecchia. What can you discover from following graying veterans like us? Everything! We still drive the ball farther than 99.9 percent of the golfing population, but more important, we know our limitations. Follow a group of senior pros and you see plenty of strategy: drives on the favorable side of the fairway and lay-up shots that stay out of trouble. (See Chapter 12 for more on course management.)

We also stage our share of thrilling finishes, though we may not celebrate them quite as vigorously as the young pros do. You can throw your back out that way! But as good as we seniors are when we bring our A-games (*A* for ageless), we're not the main event. That's the PGA Tour, which I cover in the following section.

Ten ways to max out your day at a PGA Tour event

You'd be surprised how many spectators — particularly rookie spectators — are unprepared for their sojourn at a Tour venue. Take these tips, and you can be a superfan.

✔ Don't leave home without sunscreen, a hat, a portable chair, and binoculars.

✔ If you want to work inside the ropes, contact the tournament committee and offer to volunteer. The best volunteer jobs are walking scorer (keeping track of players' scores) and standard-bearer (carrying the sign that shows the scores). Either way, you're almost as close to the pros as their caddies are.

✔ If you're going as a fan, go early in the week and watch the players' practice rounds.

✔ Spend some time at the practice range, watching good swings.

✔ The best day for autographs is Wednesday, during the pro-am, when the pros sign between holes. Remember to bring your own pen!

✔ Arrive early on tournament days (usually Thursday through Sunday). Pick up a map of the course (you can usually find one on the pairing sheets you get free at the gate, as well as in souvenir programs). Choose a spot that's sure to see plenty of action, like a green guarded by water, and set up your portable chair right behind the gallery rope.

✔ Most tournaments offer XM PGA Tour radios for rent; they're a must for keeping track of what's going on.

✔ If you choose to walk along with a particular group, stay one shot ahead of the players; that way you can see their shots land.

✔ Don't yell "You're the man!" or "Go in the hole!" The pros can't stand gallery loudmouths.

✔ Be a proud host: Wear something that represents your city or local team.

The PGA Tour

The world's best golfers. The most beautiful courses. Golf's most dramatic moments. The PGA Tour can be expensive to watch — count on $100 a day for tickets, parking, and refreshments (kids 15 and under usually get in free with a paying adult) — but what you see is priceless. When the Tour with a capital *T* comes to a venue near you, you get to feast your eyes on Tiger, Phil, and the rest of the world's finest as they make a cruelly difficult game look easy. At least until the old game jumps up and bites them, of course. And then you get to enjoy the world's finest trouble shots!

Check out pgatour.com for the current year's schedule. (You can also find homepages for the Nationwide and Champions tours there.) Then pack up the car and get ready for a day you'll never forget. You may not get close enough to hear the players breathe at a PGA Tour event, but at least once or twice the level of play will leave you breathless.

Getting the Most out of Your Tour Spectating

Before you make plans to spend a great day at the course, in the festive atmosphere that attends any Tour stop, decide what you want to get out of your day. Do you want to find out more about the game? Do you want to get close to the players? Or do you want to feel the unfolding drama of a top-tier sporting event?

If you're after a learning experience, take in a Tuesday practice round. You save on your ticket and avoid the big weekend crowds. You can also take your camcorder on practice days — a definite no-no during tournament rounds. Go to the range, watch players warm up, and get a feel for how focused and disciplined they are. To see even tighter focus, stop by the practice putting green. Watch for a putting drill or two that you may want to try yourself.

On the course, film a few swings. When you get home, compare your own swing to the pros' swings. Not to make you feel inadequate, but to see where you can improve!

Wednesdays are *pro-am* days, when the pros team up with amateurs, and are generally best avoided. Play often slows to a crawl, and the pros are itchy for the next day's action to start.

After the tournament begins, Thursdays and Fridays offer better views because the crowds are smaller. You can also be sure to see your favorite player (assuming he entered the tournament) because the cut isn't made until the first two rounds are complete. *The cut* removes about half the players from the tournament after two rounds of play. They're considered too far behind to contend on the weekend, and they earn $0 for their efforts that week. Players who make the cut get a paycheck; those who don't, don't.

For those who survive the cut, Saturday is often called *moving day*, because a good round can move them into position to win on Sunday. If you don't mind the bigger crowds, Saturday can be a great choice. You can follow your favorites in the flesh, and then see them on TV the next day.

Whatever day you choose, be sure to spend some time watching the top twenty-somethings: young stars such as Rickie Fowler, Dustin Johnson, and Anthony Kim. They're fearless!

I can advise you all day about the importance of strategy and caution on the course. Never forget it! But sometimes seeing these youngsters going full-throttle, firing at flags, and playing like their hair is on fire is good. They prove that even at the highest level, golf's supposed to be fun!

Knowing How to Interact with Players

Professional golfers love their jobs, and who makes pro golf possible? That's right: golf fans! Most professionals recognize this crucial truth, and we try our best to be courteous to the thousands of gallery members we meet in the course of our job.

Want to have a great moment with a tour pro? It's as easy as one, two, three:

1. **Choose your moment.**

   Between holes during a Tuesday practice round can be a good time to say hello. Another is in the designated Autograph Area, which is usually behind the 18th green, after a tournament round. Players expect to meet fans and sign autographs at these times and places.

2. **Remember your manners.**

   You wouldn't shout "You da cop!" at a police officer, would you? You wouldn't demand a movie star's autograph, shoving a cap or program at her face. Fortunately, most golf fans would never do that stuff, either, but a few bad apples can spoil a great day for players and fans alike. Ask nicely, and you'll probably get that autograph you want.

3. **Make a connection.**

   It's easy. All you have to do is say something the pro hasn't already heard 100 times. Maybe you saw him or her pull off a great shot: "That was a beauty from the rough at 16." Maybe you read about him online or in the newspaper: "I hope your wrist is feeling better." Or maybe you just want to share the moment: "I like the way you play and just want to shake your hand."

What do pro golfers *really* think of the fans — at least the polite fans who approach us the right way? We think of them as friends.

Avoiding Fan Flubs

Interfering with a ball in play is a capital crime at any tournament. (But I know you'd never do that.) Getting struck by one is just a pain. Sometimes, especially at PGA Tour events where fans are packed like toothpicks along fairways and around greens, a shot gets away and a fan gets plunked.

This incident can leave the fan with a bump or bruise, as well as a few potential benefits, such as a moment on national TV, a handshake from the embarrassed pro who hit the ball, and an autographed cap and ball from said pro.

Just remember: The pros are playing for their livelihoods out there. Don't ask the Tour player whose ball hit you — or the one you spot in the parking lot or near the practice green — to shake hands with all your buddies and wave to your cousins watching at home.

A few more reminders:

- ✔ **Don't ask for autographs before or during a tournament round.** During tournament play (usually Thursday through Sunday), PGA Tour players will sign only after their rounds.

- ✔ **Don't try to sneak a cellphone through the gate.** You'll get caught and either lectured or kicked out.

- ✔ **Don't get dehydrated.** Following the pros can entail miles of walking in heat and blazing sun. Drink plenty of water!

Chapter 18

Golf on TV

. . . .

In This Chapter

▶ Understanding golf's TV success

▶ Getting into the nitty-gritty of broadcasting golf

▶ Improving your game by watching top players on TV

. . . .

Golf's growth over the past 25 years is clear in the amount of coverage the game gets on television. Back in '86, nobody dreamed of a 24/7 golf channel. Now you can see me on Golf Channel. Television has helped make golf a major spectator sport, to the point where today's top players are as well known as their counterparts in baseball, basketball, and football. In this chapter, I show you why.

My Auspicious Start in Broadcasting

The year was 1986, and my career needed a makeover. "Limited success" was a nice way of describing my playing years. The Tour was a vast, empty wasteland of setbacks and spent money. I was serving out the rest of my sentence with no chance of parole. Golf sucks. But then, a golf miracle in three acts.

Act 1: Breaks on a plane

As I boarded a plane for Columbus, Ohio, nothing was on my mind other than the two fat vacuum-cleaner salesmen I was going to be sitting between in the coach section. I was in my customary haze when I was jarred by harsh criticism from the first-class section. It was the CBS golf broadcast crew, already enjoying the amenities of first class (although in a plastic cup) before takeoff.

Frank Chirkinian, the executive producer and director for CBS at the time, Pat Summerall, and Ben Wright: All of them were basking in the knowledge that I was to be wedged in the coach section between two obese and slightly pungent salesmen. They said I could come up and use their restroom if I could peel myself from between the two guys. I hoped that the front of the airplane would fall off.

We were all going to Jack Nicklaus's golf tournament, the Memorial, in Ohio. We had just left Fort Worth, Texas, where I had played in the CBS-televised Colonial Invitational. I had recently been elected to the *policy board* of the PGA Tour, which is a group of three player-elected Tour members, three officers of the PGA of America, and three independent business leaders that basically runs the PGA Tour. In fact, I wasn't actually playing the Memorial; as a policy board member, I'd be attending closed-door meetings Monday through Wednesday.

I was fighting for a position on the armrest of seat 28B when the flight attendant presented me with a bottle of champagne, compliments of the royal family in first class. Those guys really knew how to have a good time when the bubbly was free.

I started hesitantly toward the front of the plane to thank my benefactors and to get away from the sumo-sized bookends I was seated between. As I scurried to first class, I fell on an idea that could help solve my problem of having nowhere to go after the policy-board meetings ended on Wednesday. After some quick banter, I told Frank that I had nothing to do from Thursday to Sunday, and because I was on the policy board making decisions about TV contracts, I should watch how a televised event is produced. "Show up Friday for rehearsal at 11:00 and check into the Stouffer's on Thursday; we'll have a room for you," Frank said. "Now get back to the screaming kids in coach before I have you thrown off the plane for being up here." He had the bedside manner of Attila the Hun sporting a bad case of hemorrhoids, but at that moment I loved him.

Act 11: This isn't what I signed up for

I showed up promptly at 11:00, well fed from gorging on room service and weary-eyed from the menu of movies that I signed to the room. I was a pig, and I enjoyed the wallow. I opened the door to Frank's office, and he bellowed from the confines of his trailer for me to go out to the 16th hole. He didn't sound like he wanted to engage in light conversation, so I broke into a trot toward the 16th. I couldn't help but wonder why I wasn't going to sit in the truck with Frank to gain some insight into how a telecast is produced and maybe get him some snacks every once in a while. Why was I going to the 16th hole?

As I arrived, a voice came serenading down from high atop the tower, beckoning me to come up. It was Verne Lundquist, the veteran announcer. I managed to make my way up the tower. Verne then handed me a headset and told me to grab a chair. I asked what the headset was for, and he said, "Didn't Frank tell you that he wanted to try you as an announcer this week?" As I weighed the decision between wasting time with caddies who missed the cut and being on national television, the conversation with myself was, as usual, very short.

"Where do I sit, Verne, and what do I do?" I said.

The *tower* is a little enclosure surrounded with clear plastic, much like the front seat of a car, with the windshield surrounding the front and you looking out at the green. Two monitors in front of the announcer show the action taking place and a current leader board. The *spotter* is next to you, giving you the scores and the clubs the players are hitting. In this case, spotter Carl took up most of the room. Carl, who weighed 385 pounds, looked like he'd just eaten a sumo wrestler. I felt like I was back on the plane.

My seat was next to the cameraman. Looking down at the action for the first time was really interesting. Golf looks incredibly easy from way up there. How can those guys screw up so many shots?!? I was above the tension, up in the clouds. My, how this view changes your perspective on the game.

But I heard voices everywhere. The voice in my left ear was the director, Frank, and the other voices were all the announcers from their towers. Occasionally, I would hear a rogue voice, and I had no idea who it was. I found out later that a guy operating a CB unit in the neighborhood had come through on our headsets. Welcome to network TV.

The rehearsal went pretty smoothly. I found out two things:

- ✔ **Your conversation must be short.** The action jumps all over the place, and you can't get stuck in the middle of a story.

- ✔ **Never answer anything Frank says directly.** The viewers can't hear the director, so "What are you raving about, Frank?" means nothing to them.

Act III: The greatest story ever lucked into

The next day, my first on national television, was going smoothly. Verne and I were clicking like a Geiger counter. He would ask a question; I would answer. I was rolling.

Due to a starter's time that spread the field, we had a large gap between the group that had just walked off the 16th green and the next group that was approaching the 14th green. I had some free time, so I kicked back in the chair and read interesting tidbits on the personal lives of the golf pros.

I was awakened from my near-catatonic state by a combination of Frank throwing the action to Verne and Verne asking me what this putt was going to do. I looked down real fast and saw nobody on the 16th green. The next group was walking up the 15th fairway. What was going on?

Verne had a look of desperation as he asked me again, and Frank was saying, "Answer him, you culturally lost golf derelict!" I looked down at the green again and still didn't see anybody there. Were they seeing ghosts, or was it just a ruse to excite the poor rookie? After several more verbal barbs from Frank and the look of a desperate sheepdog on the face of Verne, I decided to play along. I said, "Verne, this putt should be fairly fast, because it's going down the hill toward the water." Verne met my response by saying, "Boy, you were right, Gary; that putt cruised by the hole and, if he'd hit it a little harder, it would've gone in the water."

Wait a minute!

The only water near the 16th green at Muirfield Village golf course is in the drinking fountain on the tee. I made the water stuff up because the boys were trying to get the rookie and I was trying to throw them a curve. It was a wild pitch.

I heard Frank say, "Throw it to 18, Verne." Then Verne looked at me with those screeching Scandinavian eyes and asked if I could respond a little quicker next time. Frank hit his button and began to blast me for my "fune-real response," which I took as my TV obituary.

At this point, I realized that they weren't kidding. Oh, no! "Verne," I said, "could you help me in my moment of conjecture and look down on the 16th green and tell me whether you see anybody? Or do I have to call a ghostbuster?

"Of course nobody's there," said Verne. Now I really was confused. "Verne, if nobody's there, why did you say the ball rolled seven feet by the hole when I made up the thing about the water being there in the first place? The 16th doesn't have any water," I replied, dumbfounded. "I know that, you idiot, but we were doing the 12th hole!" Verne answered.

"Wait a minute, we're doing the 12th hole too? I was told to go out to the 16th hole with you."

What had happened was that during rehearsal, we hadn't used a camera for our other hole, the 12th, because the camera was broken. I had no way of knowing that I was supposed to be looking at the 12th hole as well as the 16th, unless I had called my psychic. Confusing business, huh?

As life weaves its reckless mysteries, the 12th hole at Muirfield Village has water surrounding the green. The putt had come from the top tier really fast toward the water and gone seven feet past the hole. I totally made something up, and it happened to be a perfect call in this less-than-perfect business.

Recognizing Why Golf Makes Great TV

Golf is played all year long, from the first week in January through the second week in December. Golf on the tube has grown proportionately, from a few shows in the 1950s to nonstop golf on TV today. The places that TV takes you during the golf year are a vacationer's dream. Every Saturday and Sunday, you can do the couch thing and watch the various tours play from every corner of the globe. The golf is good, but the pictures are stunning. The viewing audience and the PGA Tour start to prepare themselves in the Florida swing for the first major of the year in early April, when Augusta and the Masters Tournament are in full bloom. Then the PGA Tour settles into normalcy for a while, as players start to prepare for the heat and the long rough of the U.S. Open in mid-June. The month of July is for the British Open and its storied past; plenty of plaid and windblown golf balls decorate the landscape. The last of the four majors, the PGA Championship, comes in August. And now the majors are followed by the FedEx Cup, a series that culminates at the season-ending Tour Championship.

Each fall also brings a great team event: the Ryder Cup (pitting U.S. greats against Europe's finest) in even-numbered years or the Presidents Cup (America versus the rest of the world) in odd-numbered years. If you like team play, the Ryder Cup is as good as golf gets.

During the first part of the year, many celebrities play in the AT&T tournament at Pebble Beach and in the Bob Hope Classic. If viewing the stars is your thing, you can see these would-be golfers hacking away inhibitions during these pro-am tournaments. Justin Timberlake, Kenny G, and Mark Wahlberg may never make a living playing golf, but they can play a little!

If Hollywood stars aren't your idea of role models, maybe professional golfers can fill the void. You don't see much trash talk or foul play on the golf course. In fact, golf may be the only game in which the players police themselves. Almost weekly, you hear an example of a player on the PGA Tour penalizing himself for some inadvertent Rules transgression. Can you imagine a basketball player turning down two points because he pushed someone out of the way en route to the basket?

Televising the Game

Sports and TV have become inextricably linked through the years. Back in 1946, fans were still providing their own images to the dramatic radio broadcast of that year's World Series.

Baseball proved to be perfect for a new tube technology that beamed rays of hypnotic light into everyone's home. But golf presented unique challenges to television coverage. Aside from playing on 150 acres as opposed to being surrounded by fences at a distance of 400 feet from home plate, golf features constant, ongoing action with many athletes competing independently at any given moment. What's a broadcaster to do?

Keep it simple — and that's exactly what early broadcasters did. The first broadcast of a golf event was the Tam O'Shanter Classic from Chicago on Sunday, August 22, 1953. The telecast had one camera fixed on the 18th hole. Perhaps as an indication of the excitement that golf would eventually bring to the tube, the moment for this particular coverage was opportune. Lew Worsham, a modestly successful pro, approached the 18th; the hole wasn't unlike many finishing holes that year, but this time Worsham produced a singular result: a hole-in-one.

The unbridled charisma of one man turned the nation's attention to the sport of captains and kings. Arnold Palmer, of the hitch-and-smile, go-for-broke style and unwavering charm, turned the viewing world on its ear and kept viewers glued to their sets. In 1960, Palmer began carrying an industry on his back as golf and television developed together to provide a foundation for a sport that would reap immense rewards in the great sports and television-rights derby.

Behind the screens

Many insiders tell you that golf is the hardest sport to cover. Think about it: The playing field is a park, a wide-open expanse covering acres of competitive challenges. Golf has no timeouts and no clock. Play begins at ten-minute intervals, and at any one time, 100 or more competitors may be playing on the same course, all on different holes.

To properly cover this unusual setup, golf courses first have to be technically prepped. That's just a fancy way of saying that you must run miles of cable in order to broadcast signals from the golf course to the television truck. A small army of engineers and cable-pullers invades on the Sunday or Monday preceding broadcast week. Tractor-trailers filled with several million dollars worth of cameras and technical equipment deploy. The average telecast requires two dozen or more cameras mobilized in a variety of ways, video-tape machines, digital recorders, character generators, spotters, high-tech graphics gizmos (for those great images of super-slo-mo swings, golf balls squished against clubfaces at impact, and towering arcs showing shot trajectories), and a control room staffed with producers and directors.

The staff is divided into two groups, known as *above the line* and *below the line*. Those with above-the-line duties are the folks who make production and story-line decisions. The following list spells out the important members of each group, starting at the top:

✔ **Producer:** The *producer* is responsible for creating the story line of the event. The better producers must have an intimate knowledge of the game itself and all the key players. Although the leaderboard dictates the story line, a dozen or more contestants may be newsworthy. The producer's task is to capture the players' shot-making efforts and to make a complicated drama coherent to the viewer.

✔ **Director:** The director is responsible for placing cameras at strategic spots around the course to capture the best possible angles of coverage. He or she communicates with the camera personnel, audio crew, and other technical people to provide insightful coverage of the action on the course. Although the producer may say, "Let's go to Rory McIlroy on the 9th green," the director is responsible for readying those cameras and operators and for framing the shots that most dramatically capture Rory's next shot. The director also oversees a complex array of audio tracks, graphics, and special effects.

✔ **Associate directors:** One associate director (A.D.) supports the producer and director. Although titles may change from network to network, standard coverage usually involves an *iso* truck in which an associate director records coverage of shots that are central to the story line but not shown live. You may hear an announcer say, "Moments ago . . . ." Taped coverage assures that viewers see as many shots as possible in a sensible sequence. Some producers favor using more taped shots than others.

A second associate director is known as the *sundial,* or timer. ("Sundial" is an inside joke, a nickname for one A.D. whose countdowns in and out of commercials were less than accurate.) About 12 times in a telecast, the network breaks for at least two minutes of commercials or promotional announcements. The second A.D. gives a count out of the program action into the commercial time to make the transition appear seamless to the viewer. The same is true coming out of a commercial back to the center of activity, the remote truck.

✔ **Talent:** The remaining critical element of the above-the-line team is the talent. That's us, the talking heads you hear on the air. The producers and directors provide the blueprint of the telecast, but we deliver it. The National Football League may employ up to four announcers per broadcast, and baseball maybe three, but the multiple broadcast booths in a golf telecast necessitate a team of announcers in this decidedly individual sport. Networks use up to eight on-air personalities to recite the golf action. Chemistry is key. Do you love Johnny Miller and Roger Maltbie? Jim Nantz and Nick Faldo? Mike Tirico? David Feherty? Maybe even me? Each network's team has a unique personality.

The 18th tower is the focal point where the host and key analyst hold forth. From there, networks differ. Some choose the analyst-per-green format à la CBS, erecting towers adjacent to the final few greens on the course. (Figure 18-1 shows you a shot of me in just such a tower.) From these vantage points, the announcers have bird's-eye views and can call the action of a particular hole or report on a neighboring hole within view of the tower. ABC uses a secondary studio in which the commentators view the monitor and report each shot played. All networks employ on-course personnel who walk with designated players and report on the action from the ground.

Figure 18-1: In the CBS booth, I get a bird's-eye view of the game.

 ✔ **Technical personnel:** The below-the-line folks are the technical people — camera and audio operators, engineers, and tech gurus. Of course, everyone involved in this tightly knit, interlocking puzzle is important, but one key individual brings it all together: the *technical director,* who presses the buttons that effectively determine which pictures and sounds go on the air. If you ever notice a glitch in moving from one shot to another or a graphic appearing and then disappearing hastily, chances are that the technical director made a mistake or got some bad information from the field.

All in all, when you add up all the above-the-line and below-the-line folks, the spotters, the runners, and the *craft-services personnel* (a fancy, entertainment-industry way of saying *caterers*), a network may roll into town with a production crew of more than 100 people — not to mention the satellite truck that beams signals from the remote broadcast site off a satellite, to the studio, and eventually to your TV set.

Deal or no deal?

Of course, none of this would happen without a demand for golf telecasts. The game remains popular for a variety of reasons, not the least of which is the steadfast support of corporate America. Why? Well, first by golf's very position in the world as a game played by the captains of industry. It's a game of tradition, honor, and integrity. The image of the game presented by the players is essential to the sponsors and magnified in importance by what has become an increasingly cluttered world of athletes whose mugs — and sometimes mug shots — are apt to be found on the front page of the newspaper rather than in the sleazy gossip on the back. Yes, Tiger Woods's tabloid travails in 2009 and 2010 hurt the image of the world's top golfer, but the game's image remains strong.

Golf forged its way to prominence as a major player in television sports in its own way. It began meekly in an effort to gain exposure on TV. Time buys, rights, and production deals were (and are) the principal forces that drive network coverage, and I cover them in the following sections.

Time buys

A network or cable channel places an hourly value on airtime — like a supermarket stocking shelves. Each hour of airtime represents a quantifiable asset for the network. In this case, a program buyer negotiates a date and airtime for a program. The buyer purchases time from a network or cable channel, arranges to sell the time to advertisers, and keeps the advertising revenue.

Here's an example: The McCord Group buys two hours of time from the Thrills Channel. McCord pays the network around $1 million. Network rules allow the McCord Group, now a program *packager,* to sell 18 commercial units per hour. So for its million dollars, the McCord Group gets 36 commercial units (18 times 2) to allocate to its list of sponsors or to sell.

The formula is fairly basic and not inexpensive because the packager bears the production costs, which can reach $1 million for reasonable golf coverage. With professional talent added, that's well over a $1.5-million investment from the outset. That's before the cost of a tournament prize and on-site event amenities from range balls to security to cookies in the players' locker room.

Infomercials work similarly, but instead of selling ads, of course, they *are* ads. After purchasing TV time, the buyer makes money by selling the latest golf gizmo online or by phone.

Rights and production

Here's where networks take a risk. The escalation in sports rights fees in recent decades resulted in billion-dollar TV contracts for the NFL, NBA, Major League Baseball, and NASCAR as well as golf. Network executives decide that they're willing to pay an upfront fee to the rights holders and provide production in exchange for the chance to maximize their investment in the advertising marketplace.

Ten things golf announcers shouldn't do

Good golf commentating requires announcers to keep a few pointers in mind:

✔ **Never talk to your director on the air.** No one else can hear the director; you don't want viewers to think you have an imaginary friend.

✔ **Don't get the sound guy mad at you.** He'll cut you off when you're making a witty comment and keep you on the air while you're mumbling.

✔ **Never tell the TV audience how good a player you used to be.**

✔ **Never say a shot is impossible.** The golfer may quickly prove you wrong.

✔ **Never talk down to the audience.** Viewers are smarter than a lot of TV-talkers think.

✔ **Don't get into long stories.** You may get cut off as the director switches to another hole.

✔ **Never use clichés.** It shows that you're lazy.

✔ **Never tell the audience what viewers can clearly see on the TV screen.**

✔ **Never assume that your audience is hardcore golf fans.** Millions of TV viewers may not know Tiger and Phil from Batman and Robin.

✔ **Never, ever assume that what you do for a living has any role in the elevation of humankind.**

Golf, through its growing popularity and the valuable image it provides for sponsors — the quality and virtually unmatched demographics (millions of affluent golf addicts) delivered — has taken its place among the major TV sports. The PGA Tour signed a contract worth nearly $1 billion with the three broadcast networks (CBS, ABC, and NBC) plus ESPN, USA, and the Golf Channel for 2003 to 2006. The money kept growing in the Tour's TV deal for 2007–2012, but the next deal may not be so lucrative. As 2012 approached, the game faced a double whammy: The economy was struggling and so was Tiger Woods, the game's marquee player.

Can golf retain its TV audience? It's about to find out.

Knowing What to Watch for on TV

By all means, enjoy the physical beauty of golf on television. But pay attention to the players, too. You can learn a lot from watching not only their swings but also their whole demeanor on the course. Listen to the language, the jargon, the parlance being used. If you read this or any golf book, you're sure to notice the complexity of the game's terms. This special vocab is especially prevalent when a TV commentator analyzes a player's swing: He uses terminology that you need to understand to become part of the golfing world.

Watch the players carefully. Pay attention to the rhythms of their swings and to their mannerisms — the way they *waggle* the club (make pre-shot miniswings), the way triggers set their swings in motion, the way they putt, the way they set their feet in the sand before they play from bunkers, the way they stand on uphill and downhill lies. In other words, watch everything! Soak it all in. Immerse yourself in the atmosphere and ambience of golf. You'll soon be walking the walk and talking the talk. And don't discount the importance of osmosis: You can improve your own game just by watching great golf swings.

That's the big picture. But what about you, specifically?

Watching the pros is a good idea for every golfer. But most people can only learn so much from certain players. Pay particular attention to someone like Michelle Wie if you happen to be tall and slim. But if you happen to be shorter and more heavyset, you need to look elsewhere. Find someone whose body type approximates your own.

Then watch how that person stands to the ball at *address* (the point right before the swing). See how his arms hang or how much she flexes her knees. Golfers who are taller have much more flex in their knees than their shorter counterparts.

Watch how "your pro" swings the club. Do his arms move away from his body as the club moves back? How much does she turn her shoulders? How good is his balance? Does she have a lot of wrist action in her swing, or does she unwind her torso for explosive power?

Catching What Most Viewers Miss

The players who get the most airtime are the leaders and the stars. No telecast is going to waste valuable minutes on someone who's 20 strokes out of the lead. (Unless, of course, it's Tiger Woods, Phil Mickelson, or Michelle Wie.) Viewers want to watch the tournament being won and lost, so those players shooting the lowest scores are the ones you see most on TV. Here's what to look for in some of the stars you'll see on TV.

- **Tiger Woods:** Look at his virtuosity in every aspect of the game. He has left no stone unturned in his pursuit of perfection. His stalking of Jack Nicklaus's record of 18 major wins is his driving force, providing his will to succeed. Plus, in 2010, personal strife and swing changes gave him new motivation.

- **Phil Mickelson:** With four major victories under his belt (as of this writing), look for Phil to take advantage of his precise short game and really focus on the majors for the rest of his career. He gives golf fans all over the country a role model they love to root for.

✔ **Ernie Els:** Now in his 40s, the Big Easy has a golf swing that still brings glimpses of the legendary Sam Snead, with a demeanor made for greatness. Burn that smooth swing into your memory banks the next time you see it on TV.

✔ **Dustin Johnson:** This young PGA Tour star came within a whisker of winning the 2010 U.S. Open and PGA Championship. Keep an eye on him, particularly his super-slo-mo replays that show how he generates power.

✔ **Fred Couples:** The Champions Tour's "young" star still has the easy motion that made "Boom-Boom" Couples the model of effortless power. Watch him walk down the fairway after a drive as if he didn't have a care in the world. Fred has had his share of troubles through the years, including a bad back that may have ended other careers, but he's still smiling . . . and winning.

✔ **Rory McIlroy:** Here's a story for you: Young Rory, born in 1989 in Holywood, Northern Ireland, may be the most exciting young player since Tiger. As of this writing, he hadn't won a major yet, but that was only a matter of time. Watch how he swings hard, believes every putt's going in, and radiates pleasure in playing the game.

✔ **Michelle Wie:** This young lady, who turned 21 in 2010, has the potential to dominate the LPGA. Michelle turned pro late in 2005, fought injuries and great expectations, and struggled. But she has more talent than anyone I've seen come up in a long time. Winless until 2009, Michelle worked hard with coach David Leadbetter on her long, fluid swing. She had two LPGA victories going into the spring of 2011, with many more to come.

Taking Your Punishment

You can learn the most from the players on TV by watching how they handle disaster. Professional players make most of their decisions with their heads, not their hearts. So pay close attention to the times when a player has to manufacture a weird and wonderful shot to extricate the ball from trouble. And don't forget to watch the more-frequent occasions when he accepts that a mistake has been made, takes the punishment, and moves on. That's when you know you're watching a real golfer, one who understands that everyone makes mistakes, and that he now has to make the most of the rest of his round.

That last point reminds me of a time when I let my heart — or my ego — rule my decision-making process. I was playing in Memphis, I think. Anyway, I had to birdie the last three holes during my second round in order to make the cut. After my drive at the 16th, I had 223 yards to the hole, which was cut dangerously close to a large lake. I chose a 4-iron, convinced that I had enough club. I didn't. Splash!

I turned to my caddie and told him to give me another ball. He did. I hit the next shot perfectly. Splash!

"Give me another ball." Splash!

"Give me another ball." Splash!

"Give me another ball." Splash!

By this time, I knew that I was using the wrong club. I knew it. My caddie knew it. Everyone in town knew it. But I wasn't going to give up. We were testing my manhood here.

Eventually, my caddie handed me another ball with a 3-iron. I said, "What's this?" He told me that I had only one ball left. So I took the 3-iron and hit my last ball onto the green. I holed the putt for, I think, a 15.

The moral of the story? If you do stuff this stupid, someone may make a movie of it. In this case they did — the movie was *Tin Cup,* and Kevin Costner re-enacted my disaster. Somehow, he looked better doing it.

The Masters and me

The entire CBS production crew was dining at the Tournament Players Championship two weeks before the 1987 Masters. The conversation turned quickly to who would be assigned to which holes during the telecast in Augusta. Everyone had his assignments except for me. I was left holding air.

I'd been working with CBS on a part-time basis for only a few months, but the announcing crew was excited that I would be going to Augusta. When producer Frank Chirkinian excluded me from the party, anarchy prevailed. Pat Summerall led the charge for my inclusion, and the others followed, but to no avail. It was late on Saturday when Frank, between commercial breaks, announced to everyone that I was going to the hallowed grounds of Augusta National after all.

I was told to be at Augusta by Tuesday for a meeting with Hord Hardin, the tournament director. Frank was waiting for me when I arrived. We proceeded to Hardin's office; I felt like I was going to the principal's office. Frank looked concerned as we went into the catacombs of the clubhouse at Augusta.

Jim Nantz joined us as we walked the narrow corridor toward the door at the end of the hall. I was dressed rather spectacularly in white Calvin Klein jeans and a bulky DKNY sweater ablaze in yellow, the whole outfit topped with a Panama straw hat. I was a walking rebuke to tradition.

As we approached the darkened door at the end of the hall, it creaked open as if willed by a higher power. A shadowy figure appeared, backlit against a ray of sun filtered through the lone window. Hord Hardin greeted us like Lurch of *The Addams Family.* Frank and Jim sat in the corner, and I proceeded to take residence on the big couch in front of Hardin's desk. I was the subject of discussion.

(continued)

(continued)

After introductions and small talk, Hardin proceeded to make a passionate speech about the flavor of this tournament. "We must maintain tradition; it is the cornerstone of the tournament," he said with conviction. The speech was beautiful and actually kept my attention, which is hard to do. But I couldn't help looking around and seeing the dimly lit pictures of Bobby Jones and the 13th hole that filled the room. It dawned on me that this place was Augusta National, home of the Masters, and that *it was a big deal*. At moments like these, when I'm truly moved, I do stupid things. I think I do them because they relieve tension. I waited until Hardin had made his closing remarks, and then abruptly stood up and asked him if he thought the clown outfit I had planned to wear on Saturday was out of the question. Frank immediately put his head in his hands, and Jim started to whistle.

Hardin looked at Frank, who wasn't about to look up, and then addressed me. "Probably not a good idea," he said.

"Darn, I'm gonna lose the deposit," I said.

As Hardin closed the oaken door of his office behind us, Frank grabbed the back of my neck and applied a pressure hold that would've choked a Burmese python. "Don't you ever just shut up and listen, you moron?" he asked. I couldn't respond because of the restriction of air in my esophagus, as Jim said, "Maybe it was a bad idea, bringing him here." Frank affirmed the notion with more pressure on my neck. But they let me join the broadcast.

My stint at Augusta didn't last long, though. In 1994, while trying to be articulate about a shot to the 17th green, I explained that Jose Maria Olazabal had better not hit it over the green because there were "body bags" down there, and no one ever recovers. That was the first strike against me. I paddled on down the river Styx and described a putt by Tom Lehman, also on the 17th green, as being so fast that I didn't think they mowed those greens, "I think they bikini wax 'em." Strike two, three, four — and I was off the Masters broadcast team forevermore.

Chapter 19

Getting Your Golf Online

You'd be amazed at the ways you can explore the world of golf without leaving your favorite chair. Or maybe you wouldn't. But I come from an age when we had three or four TV channels, not three or four hundred. We navigated the old swimmin' hole with inner tubes, not cyberspace with the Internet.

You get my cyberdrift: I'm a dinosaur who couldn't write a line of code if my Linux depended on it. But I know my way around cybergolf. With this chapter, let me be your guide.

Checking Out Cool Golf Sites

The Internet offers a nearly infinite array of golf stuff. Search for the word *golf,* and you get 646 million hits. That's more hits than Charles Barkley had in his last round. But if you surf the Net aimlessly, you'll only drown in a digital deluge. So here's a quick look at some of my favorite golf sites. Together, they offer 99 percent of what you need. You can thank me later.

PGATour.com

Millions of golf fans rely on the PGA Tour's site (pgatour.com) for news, stats, player profiles, and (perhaps most important of all) up-to-the-minute tournament coverage. At this site, you can follow your favorite players as they compete, drilling down into their stats and even looking at their scorecards. You can check out audio and video clips, too. And to the delight of hardcore fans, the site now offers Shot Tracker, an interactive feature that crunches stats and allows users to get an inside look at every shot by every player only nanoseconds after it happens.

You can do more than just follow Tiger Woods, Phil Mickelson, and friends at this site. It's also the home site of the Champions Tour — the one I play on — and the Nationwide Tour, golf's highest "minor league," where you can find the stars of tomorrow.

This site features fantasy golf, too. PGATour.com is home to the Tour's official fantasy golf game, in which you get to assemble a dream team of PGA Tour stars who'll play for *you* every week. It's free to play, and you can win golf goodies. Check out `pgatour.com/fantasy`.

LPGA.com

The official site of the women's tour, `lpga.com`, is similar to PGATour.com (see the preceding section), if not nearly as lavish. You can find stats, profiles, and live tournament updates from the Ladies Professional Golf Association. Want to follow Se Ri Pak and Juli Inkster as they make still more LPGA history or see stars like Yani Tseng and Cristie Kerr light up the leader board? Read a blog by one of the young players who are making women's golf so popular worldwide? Maybe you just want to follow Paula Creamer as she knocks her pink golf ball into the cup. Here's your chance — it's all at LPGA.com.

Golf.com

`Golf.com`, which combines the resources of *Golf Magazine* and *Sports Illustrated,* has become the industry leader it is by developing a potent mix of tour coverage, equipment reviews, travel features, and commentary from some of the game's best-known writers and personalities, including my fellow CBS golf commentator David Feherty — one of the funniest writers around. It also offers loads of instruction and a new club fitting feature called See-Try-Buy. With some of the best text and multimedia capabilities online, Golf.com has found the sweet spot at the intersection of two of humankind's greatest inventions: golf and the Web. Check out Figure 19-1 for an example of all this site has to offer.

GolfObserver.com

One of the sport's most addictive sites features an amazing amount of information and opinion every day, updated faster than you can say "Fore!" At `GolfObserver.com`, you find headlines, stats, smart columnists, tournament previews and reviews, and the invaluable Golf Notebook. I check this site all the time to make sure I haven't missed anything.

Figure 19-1:
The home
page for
Golf.com.

ESPN.com

What list of golf-related Web sites would be complete without something from the folks at ESPN? At the channel's golf page (ESPN.com/golf), you can check out schedules, statistics, and player rankings for the PGA, LPGA, Champions, Nationwide, and European Tours, along with the game's top headlines. And if that's not enough to keep you occupied, you also find extras like contests, polls, and columnists — such as sharp, funny Rick Reilly — that make this stop one of the hottest golf sites on the Web.

Thegolfchannel.com

The only TV network devoted to golf 24/7 has changed its name to Golf Channel — no *the* anymore — but its site, Thegolfchannel.com, is the same as ever. Only better. Check live leader boards, Golf Channel schedules, photo galleries, and video after video; play trivia games; and read up-to-date features from Golf Channel personalities. You can e-mail questions and opinions during some live TV shows, and get tweets from Golf Channel News. (If you're unfamiliar with the concept of *tweeting,* check out the later section "Twitter.com.") With these great free features, you almost don't need to pay for lessons!

PGA.com and other major destinations

PGA.com, the official site of the Professional Golfers' Association of America (not the PGA Tour; see the earlier "PGATour.com" section), features the headlines and industry news, as well as current tour schedules and standings. Plan a golf vacation, enter to win cool golf stuff, or check out other PGA-recommended golf links. This site is definitely the place to be during the annual PGA Championship.

While I'm at it, this is the place to mention three other sites you want to visit during the majors. Masters.org offers great coverage of the Masters every spring. You get wall-to-wall U.S. Open stuff at the United States Golf Association's Web site, www.usga.org, and you can follow each year's British Open at two related sites, Opengolf.com and Randa.org. The latter is worth a visit any time of year; it's the home cyber-sod of the Royal and Ancient Golf Club of St. Andrews, golf's home.

GolfDigest.com

In collaboration with its weekly sister publication, *GolfWorld,* America's premier golf magazine has created one of the best sites on the Web. GolfDigest.com is chock-full of insightful commentary, interesting stories, and professional instruction. You find inside stuff, opinions from notable writers, and reports from the tours. You can also find an equipment hotline, view swing sequences of great players, search for specific tips, browse back issues of the magazine, and sign up for instant instruction with a new feature, Golf Digest On Demand.

Twitter.com

You may not think Twitter.com, the social networking site that lets users fire off missives (called *tweets*) in 140 or fewer characters, would be a go-to spot for golf info. True, you don't find in-depth instruction or analysis on Twitter, but pro golfers such as Stewart Cink and Ian Poulter tweet their fans constantly, and more and more players are joining in. To see what all the fuss is about, check out Twitter.com/Golf_Tweets.

Hookedongolf.com

One of the richest sources of blogorrhhea (and I mean that in a good way), Hookedongolf.com is a popular source of instant opinion, podcasts, jokes, games, travel features, and just about everything else a golf fan could want.

Founded by San Francisco golf nuts John Abendroth and Mitch Juricich, it's fast becoming a national golf treasure.

Perusing Online Course Guides

As you can see, a whole virtual world is out there, just waiting for you. Don't be shy. Now's the time for a virtual tour of roughly one zillion golf courses.

If you don't have the time or money to play all the world's great courses, don't fret. The Web can take you to them for free. Web sites carry descriptions, layouts, and scorecards for countless courses around the world, from Alabama to Zimbabwe.

Take, for example, the Web site for golf's oldest and greatest course: the Old Course at St Andrews, Scotland (`Standrews.org.uk`). From this site, you can view historical information about the course, feast your eyes on a wonderful photo gallery, make hotel and tee-time reservations, and even play a virtual round.

Similar sites cover other famous courses and resorts — often with gorgeous photos — from Pebble Beach (`Pebblebeach.com`) to PGA West (`Pgawest.com`) to Bandon Dunes (`Bandondunesgolf.com`).

Many of the sites I discuss earlier in the "Checking Out Cool Golf Sites" section also feature golf courses. You can also find sites that specialize in giving golfers an up-close-and-virtual look at courses nation- and worldwide. Here's a look at some of the best.

About.com: The course-guide helper

This handy site provides links to several prominent Web sites devoted to courses. Start by visiting `golf.about.com`. Scroll down a bit to the *Browse Topic* area to the left of the page; click on *Golf Courses* and then *Find a Golf Course*. From there, you can make your way to just about any tee or green on earth.

Worldgolf.com

Whenever I feel like exploring the wide world of golf, I tootle on over to `Worldgolf.com`, an international golf and travel guide. It features numerous links that let you bounce easily from one continent to another. You can make reservations at St. Andrews in Scotland and then view pictures of desert courses in Palm Springs. Easy to navigate, with dozens of departments, Worldgolf.com lets you check worldwide weather and tap into links to a slew of local golf-course guides.

Golf.com's Courses and Travel Page

Rankings, a course-finder, travel blogs, satellite photos and more, all presided over by gallivanting guru Travelin' Joe Passov — that's what you find at one of the most popular golf-travel pages. Go to `Golf.com`, click on the *Courses & Travel* tab, and you're on your way.

Travelandleisure.com

The late, lamented magazine *Travel & Leisure Golf* is no more, but its spirit lives on at a site that boasts a unique blend of upscale travel and discount deals. It's not the easiest page to find from the Travel & Leisure home page, so go straight to `travelandleisure.com/ideas/golf`.

Fore! Reservations

Getting tee times just got a lot easier. The old information superhighway has an on-ramp called Fore! Reservations. To get there, go to `Teeitup.com`. This nationwide reservation system provides you with direct access to thousands of courses at the click of a button. Just choose a state, and a list of courses appears. Double-click the course you're interested in, and — voilà! — you're on your way. I can almost smell the fresh-cut grass.

Golfclubatlas.com

You don't find course discounts or a tee-time locator here — just the smartest, most passionate discussion of the merits of the world's golf courses you're likely to find anywhere. The brainchild of founder Ran Morrissett, `Golfclubatlas.com` is dedicated to all things having to do with golf-course design. Explore information about famous architects and their work, see photos of noteworthy holes, and spend hours online, kicking opinions around with some highly knowledgeable folks — including some of the architects themselves.

But be warned: When you click on *Discussion Group,* you may find an irresistibly addictive feature.

Virtual Pro Shops: Buying Golf Gear Online

I can't finish a tour of the Web without trying to sell you something. In addition to golfing hangouts and course guides, cyberspace offers a plethora of great pro shops. Every major manufacturer (and even some unusual minor ones) has a presence on the Web, so don't hesitate to check out such sites as CallawayGolf.com, NikeGolf.com, Ping.com, TaylorMadeGolf.com, and Titleist.com. Many of the cyber-hangouts listed earlier in this chapter offer links to their own pro shops as well. The sites mentioned in the following sections specialize in bringing you good prices on brand-name new and used products.

eBay

The giant Web marketplace has become one of the hubs of equipment sales. At eBay's golf section (shop.ebay.com/Golf), you find not only tons of golf balls and clubs (often at great prices) but also clothing, carts, games, and memorabilia, not to mention golf-themed humidors, candles, hip flasks, and plenty of other stuff you never knew existed. But act fast: The last time I looked, only 6 hours and 17 minutes were left to buy that Betty Boop putter cover I found . . . on page 1 of 5,907 pages of golf stuff.

Dick's Sporting Goods

Head to Dickssportinggoods.com and click on the *GOLF* tab for a vast array of golf gear, much of it at bargain prices, at the Web HQ of Dick's Sporting Goods. A full-service chain with stores in 40 states and counting, Dick's is where you may find a hot new driver for $100 less than you'd pay elsewhere or a dozen premium balls for half the sticker price.

GolfDiscount.com

With a home page so busy it may give you eyestrain, GolfDiscount.com practically shouts "Value!" For more than 30 years, this online bazaar has helped golfers buy equipment at low, low prices. The site even dedicates a blog page to feedback from satisfied customers. With great prices on all the top brands and an online golf expert for recommendations, questions, and prices, GolfDiscount.com is hard to beat.

Edwin Watts Golf

The site for the popular Edwin Watts stores in Texas and the southeastern United States (`Edwinwatts.com`) offers deals on all sorts of gear, including high-quality used clubs.

Breaking Down Golf Blogs: Welcome to the Golfosphere

Lately everybody seems to be talking golf, mainly online, where every tournament, shot, and golfer's quote is met by a thousand comments from Monday-morning caddies in the blogosphere. How can you filter the wisdom from the blather? Start by focusing on the blogs in this section.

Thegolfblog.com

Topical and opinionated, if a little heavy on the golf-hotties videos, this blog is one of the heavy hitters in a fast-changing e-landscape. If you like it, you can click on the Twitter icon for a steady stream of golfblog tweets (provided you have a Twitter account, of course. See the earlier section "Twitter.com" for more on Twitter and golf.)

GeoffShackelford.com

Shackelford has been called "the Herbert Warren Wind of golf bloggers" by no less than *Sports Illustrated,* the magazine that employed legendary golf writer Wind. `GeoffShackelford.com` isn't a fancy blog, but Shackelford isn't a bells-and-whistles blogger; he's a thinker, an expert at filtering out the noise of golf news and presenting the stuff that counts. He's particularly sharp about golf-course design . . . and pretty much everything else.

A Walk in the Park

Jay Flemma didn't start out as a golf writer. An entertainment lawyer who has represented bands including Bowling for Soup, he was a passionate golfer dying to write about the game. Which he does at `Jayflemma.thegolf space.com` with unparalleled panache. In addition to being a keen observer of golf trends and one of the best course-design bloggers out there — a contributor to the smart site Cybergolf.com — Flemma may be the game's best poet. If you don't believe me, do a Web search for "St. Padraig and the Monster."

Chapter 20

Screen Gems: Surveying the Best of Virtual Golf

In This Chapter

▶ Understanding why Tiger Woods PGA Tour is the top video game

▶ Trying golf simulators: Almost the real thing?

▶ Checking out the Golden Tee phenomenon

It's amazing but true: Video games are a bigger business than Hollywood. All those beeps and boings coming out of PCs, iPads, and gaming consoles like PlayStation, Xbox, and Wii rake in more money than all the movies made in any given year. Millions of consumers are introduced to golf through virtual versions of the game. I can't tell you how many kids have come up to me and said, "You're that dude on Tiger's EA Sports game!" What happened to the love for a CBS color analyst and legendary tour player? (Okay, "legendary" is a stretch.) Times have changed!

One possible downside to all this virtual golf: Electronic golf games tend to make the game seem pretty easy. You press a button or roll a trackball and — boom! — the ball flies 300 yards. Sadly, real golf is much harder. In real life, the ball has an annoying tendency to dribble sideways and stop where you don't want it to.

But golf gaming's popularity has an upside, too: Video golf is fun! And it's getting more realistic by the nanosecond. This chapter lets you in on some of the most popular golf games.

The Leader: Tiger Woods PGA Tour

Tiger Woods PGA Tour is the dominant game, an ever-evolving concoction of wizardry from the folks at EA Sports. Since its debut in the digital stone age back in 1999, Tiger's product has sold more than 25 million copies for Sony PlayStations, Microsoft Xboxes, and Nintendo Wii consoles. As often happens in real life, Tiger's game led the field, thanks to realistic action and more features than you can shake a balky putter at. It even replicates Tiger's real swing muscle-by-muscle.

In the latest edition, *Tiger Woods PGA Tour 11,* real tour pros (male and female), players out of history's mists, and fictional golfers all challenge Tiger. You can use one of them or build your own character by mixing and matching with EA Sports's Game Face technology. The action unfolds on dazzling digitized versions of more than a dozen famous courses. The latest incarnation features the *Ryder Cup* — international team play between American tour stars and their counterparts from Europe. The Wii version also boasts a cool new golfer's-eye-view mode.

Fore more video games

Tiger Woods PGA Tour may have lapped most of the field, but golf's video-game village offers no shortage of choices. Some games are more cartoonish than the EA Sports product, but that can be a plus, particularly for younger gamers.

Here's a list of games you may want to have a look at:

✔ *Mario Golf: Toadstool Tour:* This game from Nintendo stars the mustachioed character from Super Mario Bros. and his friends. It features several courses, from an easy par-3 circuit to some that could challenge any tour pro. I mean, not even Roy "Tin Cup" McAvoy had to hit over lava.

✔ *Hot Shots Golf: Out of Bounds:* This offering from Sony can get too off-the-wall for some folks, but others find its irreverence refreshing. If you've got a soul patch on your chin, this game may be the place to start. I've got a gray one; let's play!

✔ *Planet Minigolf:* From the makers of *Zen Pinball,* this game features some crazy landscapes, trick shots, and, best of all, the chance to design your own minigolf course.

✔ *Aqua Teen Hunger Force Zombie Ninja Pro-Am:* Many gamers hated this entry upon its debut, and why not? But with only nine holes, racing golf carts, bazooka battles, and characters named Meatwad and MC Pee Pants, it gained a cult following (and a mention here because I couldn't resist its name). I actually have a buddy named Meatwad!

But the most interesting wrinkle may be that you no longer have to buy the game to play it. A new online version allows you to experience Tiger Woods PGA Tour for free. Just go to `Tigerwoodsonline.ea.com`, fill out the free registration, and you can get started right away with striking graphics, gorgeous courses, and realistic game play. After you're hooked, though, you have to pay to get deeper into the game.

Every year, video golf games get better at replicating the game itself. You can actually learn a lot about course management by playing a game like Tiger's. In fact, Bubba Watson played the video version of Celtic Manor, the site of the 2010 Ryder Cup in Wales, to get an idea of how to play the course.

As in the real world, you discover humility as a beginner, and get increasingly addicted as you improve. You start out as a novice and get better slowly, gaining distance off the tee and dexterity around the virtual greens, until — with talent, determination, and practice — you get *good!* As one reviewer put it, "The game sucks you in through an alternately rewarding and maddening experience."

And if that ain't golf in a nutshell, what is?

Golf Simulators: Virtually Perfect?

Simulators have gotten so good that they're almost as much fun as the real thing; you can play Pebble Beach in 45 minutes! The one thing that sets them apart from all other virtual versions of the game is that you get to swing a real golf club. The graphics in such games may not match those in the video games I discuss in this chapter, but you get to use more muscles than just the ones in your thumbs.

Many great golf simulators are available, from the huge (and hugely expensive) to new, inexpensive models that can fit in a briefcase. Here's a sampling:

- **AboutGolf's PGA Tour** simulator (`Aboutgolf.com`), endorsed by Tour pro Luke Donald, employs excellent graphics, great courses, and heavy-duty science to produce the next generation of indoor golf. At a price of more than $50,000, these machines are too expensive for home use (unless you're Bill Gates); you find them in more and more golf shops nationwide. When you do, be sure to try the incredible "Infamous Eighteen," a fantasy course that lets you hit balls through the Grand Canyon and the skyscrapers of New York.

- ✔ **P3ProSwing** offers impressive graphics and plenty of other options for far less than AboutGolf, thanks to technology that turns 65 infrared bursts into data about your swing, instantly processed into virtual-golf reality. Find out more at P3proswing.com.

- ✔ **DeadSolid** simulators (Deadsolidgolf.com) let you swing full-out at a screen. The company's Ballflight Trajectory Sensor projects where your shot will go, and you putt right into the screen. The new version 3.0 offers online tournament play and reverse-angle views that let you watch your brilliant approach shot home in on the hole.

- ✔ **High Definition Golf** from Interactive Sports Technologies boasts photo-realistic courses and optional swing analysis, as well as testimonials from tour pros and swing guru Jim McLean. Like the AboutGolf and DeadSolid simulators, this one may be too expensive to own, but it's great fun to play if you find one in your town. Check out ISTgolf.com.

- ✔ **Launchpad** from Electric~Spin Corporation (Electricspin.com) bills its product as "the world's leading home golf simulator." A compact device that sells for a reasonable $199.99, it's a cut-down version of the bulky full-swing simulators. Using a short club and a ball on a tether, you play Pebble Beach, the Old Course at St. Andrews, Bethpage Black, and other storied tracks.

- ✔ **Optishot Golf Simulator** uses a small turf mat and up-to-date software to bring you a more-than-reasonable facsimile of the more expensive brands for $399.95. The only hitch is the goofy Web address: Dancindogg.com.

These golf simulators are getting so good that you may never get any work done. But that's okay as long as you get out to the real-world course, too!

Golden Tee Golf: Stand and Deliver

If you've been in a sports bar in the last 20 years, you've probably seen me and the arcade-style game called Golden Tee Golf. A couple of tech whizzes at Incredible Technologies, a small firm in Arlington Heights, Illinois, developed the game back in 1989. They packed almost as much info into the programming as NASA used to put a man on the moon and paired it with a trackball that let players wham the pixilated ball vast distances, with hooks, slices, and backspin. Veteran tour star Peter Jacobsen provided the voiceover — "He's on the dance floor!" — which soon sounded as familiar as "What'll it be?" in taverns everywhere.

Golden Tee was no overnight sensation, but over the next decade it became what the company calls "the most popular coin-op video game in history," with more than 5 million players worldwide. Most of today's play, however, is with five- and ten-dollar bills rather than coins, as well as with credit cards. Well over 100,000 Golden Tee machines are now in use around the world. Most may still be in bars and pool halls, but some players put them in their homes. The last time I checked on eBay, you could buy a full-size arcade-style console for as little as $99. You can buy Golden Tee visors, shirts, and even golden golf tees — all for a game that requires no tees!

Golden Tee is fun, addictive, and fairly realistic when you get used to the trackball. To score well, you need to hurl yourself at that trackball for 400-yard drives and figure out the shortcuts that are programmed into the game. Sometimes, for instance, you can drive the green on a par-4 hole by slicing the ball around a mountain. Less than a week after Golden Tee 2011 came out, an Illinois bar patron made what the company called a *super albatross* — he busted a drive through trees and over water and bunkers for an ace on a par-5 hole!

After you get to where you can average ten under par for an 18-hole round, you may be ready for Golden Tee tournament play. But beware: Some players out there routinely break 50 for a par-72 round. Some have more than 1,000 virtual holes in one, and some earn more than $75,000 a year playing Golden Tee tournaments. No matter how many beers you've had, do *not* bet with those guys.

Part VI
The Part of Tens

The 5th Wave   By Rich Tennant

"Betty, you're not going to embarrass me at the club by wearing that hat, are you?"

In this part . . .

This part is my favorite section of the book. I give you ten timeless tips so that you can avoid the common faults I see repeated on fairways and greens all over the world. I tell you about some of my favorite golfers and golf courses. I even give you my choices of ten immortal moments from the game's great history.

This Part of Tens was my therapy. I needed to write this stuff to keep my sanity. I hope you enjoy this section and remember: In golf, we all speak the same language — mutterings of the insane!

Chapter 21

Golf's Ten Commandments

Having been around golf for a while, I've noticed certain sins my friends commit on the course. Knowing not to repeat their errors can help you live a long and peaceful life on the links.

I've racked my feeble brain and jotted down ten tips to keep you from suffering the same cataclysms I see on golf courses all over the world.

Take Some Golf Lessons

If you really want to have fun playing this game, start off with a few lessons to get you on the right track. It's amazing what you can do with a clear concept of how to make a golf swing. And, of course, read this book in its entirety.

Use a Club That Can Get You to the Hole

I'm constantly playing with amateurs who come up short with their approach shots to the green. For whatever reason, they always choose a club that can get their shot only to the front of the green even if they hit the most solid shot of their lives. You can play smarter than they do: Take a club that you can swing at 80 percent and still get to the hole. Conserve your energy; you have a long life ahead of you!

If You Can Putt the Ball, Do It

Don't always use a *lofted* club (a wedge or other iron designed to hit the ball high) around the greens. I have a friend at home called Flop-Shot Fred who is always playing high sand-wedge shots around the green, regardless of what the shot calls for. I think his idol is Phil Mickelson, who can hit those shots straight up in the air. Leave this kind of shot to guys like Phil, who can handle them. My best advice is to use a less-lofted club that gets the ball rolling as soon as possible whenever you can.

Keep Your Head Fairly Steady

Your head should move a little during the swing, especially with the longer clubs. But try not to move it too much. Moving your head too much leads to all sorts of serious swing flaws. Have someone watch you — or film you — to see how much you move your head.

Be Kind to the Course

In fairways, replace your divot or fill it in with *divot mix,* the mixture of sand and grass seed you find in plastic jugs attached to golf carts. On the green, use a divot-repair tool to fix the mark your ball made when it landed. (Left untended, a ball mark can take two or three weeks to heal, while one that's fixed can be good as new in three or four days.) And for good measure, fix one other ball mark, too. You'll be a hero to other golfers and to the greens-keeper!

Bet Only What You Can Afford to Lose

You can lose friends by betting for more money than you have. Never bet what you can't afford to lose. My strategy was always to bet everything in my pocket except for $10 — enough to pay for the gas I'd need to get home. Check out Chapter 15 for more on betting etiquette.

Keep the Ball Low in the Wind

When the wind starts to kick up, you need to adapt. Play the ball back in your stance, put your hands ahead of the ball, and keep them ahead of the ball at impact. Keep the ball as low as you can, and you manage your game much more efficiently. You probably won't lose as many golf balls, either.

Don't Give Lessons to Your Spouse

Giving golf lessons to your spouse should be a federal offense. Don't try it! Doing so can only lead to disaster. Invest some money in lessons from a pro instead. Get your spouse good instruction and reap the benefit: peace of mind.

Always Tee It Up at the Tee Boxes

Whenever it's legal (in the teeing area), tee the ball up. This game is more fun when the ball is in the air. As Jack Nicklaus once said, "Through years of experience I have learned that air offers less resistance than dirt."

Keep Your Wits about You

If all else fails, if you lose your last golf ball, you can keep your sense of humor and survive. *Remember:* This game is hard enough without blaming yourself for everything. Or for anything! I like to blame my bad shots on magnetic fields from alien spacecraft. Which leads me to one of golf's eternal questions: What's *your* excuse?

Chapter 22

Gary's Ten Favorite Courses

In This Chapter

▶ Getting a feel for some of the best courses in the world

▶ Understanding what makes a great golf course

*T*he longer you play golf, the more courses you visit. Some are along the ocean, and others are in the desert. Many have trees that frame your every shot. Others have no trees and a horizon that seems to stretch on forever.

Some golf courses are fastened onto flat land, and others are borne by the hills and valleys of rural America. Limitless features attach themselves to each golf course — that's what makes each one a separate journey. Every tennis court, basketball court, or football field is pretty much the same, but every golf course is different from every other.

Many golf architects have put their fingerprints on the map of American golf. These folks employ different design philosophies, which keeps the look of every golf course unique. Robert Trent Jones incorporates large, undulating greens with enormous bunkers guarding the landing areas. Pete Dye uses railroad ties to reinforce the greens, giving his courses the "Dye" look. Jack Nicklaus uses wildly rolling greens and expansive fairways as his trademark. Tom Fazio works wonders with all sorts of land — he's a guy who could build you a terrific course on the moon. And Tom Doak is a minimalist, using natural terrain as much as he can. You see a wide variety of golf courses in your golfing life.

These ten courses are my favorites. I based my choices for this list on the courses' challenge and beauty. Royal Melbourne is one that I haven't even played. Greg Norman told me that Royal Melbourne is in his top three, so who am I to argue?

Four of these courses are private, but six are open to everyone who can pay their (steep) green fees: Pebble Beach, Royal County Down, Pinehurst No. 2, Pacific Dunes, Cape Kidnappers, and the Straits course at Whistling Straits.

Pebble Beach (Monterey, California)

Pebble Beach is an extraordinary place to do anything. Golf has made it popular, but the land has made it legendary. Robert Louis Stevenson called this stretch of shoreline "the greatest meeting of land and sea in the world." Pebble Beach is truly one of the most beautiful spots on earth, and it's blessed with two of my favorite courses in the world: Pebble Beach and Cypress Point, which I cover later in the chapter.

I've been playing Pebble Beach Golf Links since I was 15 years old. We used to play the California state amateur on these storied links. We'd round up ten guys and rent a motel room together. We based the sleeping arrangements on how well we'd played that day: Low round got his pick of the two beds. High round got the other bed — we figured he needed some sleep with all the swinging he did that day. Everybody else grabbed some floor. Those were the fun days, when golf was a twinkle in your eye, and innocence made the game seem easy.

Pine Valley (Clementon, New Jersey)

Pine Valley is the greatest course without an ocean view. If you have a week to hang with your friends and play golf, Pine Valley is the place. The grounds are spectacular. Cottages house overnight guests, and a great dining room is full of golf memorabilia. The walls are saturated with tall tales of Pine Valley's golf history. Best of all, most of the tall tales are true.

The course is one of the great designs in the world. Builder George Crump bought this stretch of New Jersey land in 1912 and got input on the course design from great architects including C. B. Macdonald, Harry Colt, Alister Mackenzie, Donald Ross, and A. W. Tillinghast. You measure a golf course by how many holes you can remember after playing one round on it, and this course is instantly etched in your mind — every hole, every tree, and every bunker. I'm in total fascination when I walk through Pine Valley's corridor of perfectly maintained grass. This course is a place that breathes with the true spirit of golf.

Cypress Point (Monterey, California)

Cypress Point is a course of such beauty and solitude, you'd think it had holy qualities. From the quaint pro shop to the confining locker room and dusty rooms that perch atop the clubhouse, Cypress Point is a memory-maker.

The course winds from the pines into the sand dunes. Deer caper everywhere, often dodging errant tee shots. You can see the turbulent Pacific on a few holes going out and then again on most of the back nine, including the famous 16th — a gorgeous and scary par-3 that must be seen to be believed.

I'll never forget Cypress Point, which was the site of my first tour event in 1974. I birdied seven holes in a row (holes 7 through 13) and posted an opening round of 65. My career tapered off after that.

Royal County Down (Newcastle, Northern Ireland)

In recent years, more and more golfers making pilgrimages to the game's ancestral home in Scotland have detoured to Ireland, where some of the best links in the world are starting to get the attention they deserve. First and foremost among these is Royal County Down. It's rugged, tricky (with blind shots all over the place), and altogether magnificent.

Originally laid out by Old Tom Morris in the 1880s and redesigned by immortals including Harry Vardon and Harry Colt, this place is one of the most beautiful, memorable courses on earth. No one who plays there ever forgets his or her day at County Down.

Pinehurst No. 2 (Pinehurst, North Carolina)

Pinehurst No. 2 is a masterpiece of design. Perhaps the most famous course designed by the great Donald Ross, it hosted the U.S. Open in 1999 and 2005. Hidden in the pines of Pinehurst, the course combines every facet of the game and boasts some of the best-designed greens in the world.

This entire complex at Pinehurst takes you back half a century with its rustic, Southern motif. Golf courses are everywhere — there are eight at the Pinehurst Resort and many others nearby — and golf is the central theme of the town.

We used to play a tour event at Pinehurst No. 2 every year, and we'd get into a golf frenzy weeks before our arrival. Pinehurst No. 2 is second to none in the Southeast, a challenge to be revered and enjoyed. And in 2014, the course gains a distinction no other venue has ever boasted: It plays host to the U.S. Open, followed a week later by the U.S. Women's Open!

Royal Melbourne (Melbourne, Australia)

My information about Royal Melbourne comes from the Aussies I know on tour. Greg Norman and Steve Elkington rave about the greens, which are said to be among the fastest in the world. The tournament course dates back to 1891, when the club hired Alister Mackenzie to come down from Scotland to oversee the design. The modern course is made up of 18 holes out of the 36 they have on site. I walked Royal Melbourne during the 2002 Presidents Cup and found that the Aussies were right: The course is gorgeous, with large eucalyptus trees standing sentinel over the scene.

Pacific Dunes (Bandon, Oregon)

In 1999, an exciting new golf course opened on a remote stretch of Oregon coastline. The architect was David McLay Kidd, a Scotsman who put a remarkable, seemingly all-natural layout on a bluff above the Pacific. In 2001, Pacific Dunes, a new course designed by Tom Doak, earned rave reviews, and 2005 brought a third natural beauty, Bandon Trails, designed by Ben Crenshaw and Bill Coore. A fourth course, called Old Macdonald in honor of pioneering player and architect Charles Blair Macdonald, opened in 2010.

Mentioning them here is my way of applauding all four courses. Still, if I had to choose just one of these jewels for my last round ever, I'd tee it up at Doaks' minimalist, magnificent Pacific Dunes.

Shinnecock Hills (Southampton, New York)

Eighty years after its founding, Shinneock is still America's premier Scottish-style links course. At this course, you play the game as it was designed to be played — along the ground when the wind blows. The world's best players saw how tough that could be during the 2004 U.S. Open at Shinnecock.

From the porch of the nation's oldest clubhouse all the way out to the Atlantic Ocean, Shinnecock Hills is an American-bred beauty. Wind and golf course are meshed into your being as you stroll through this green treasure.

Cape Kidnappers (Hawke's Bay, New Zealand)

Remote? Hey, it's only 1,000 miles from Tasmania!

Here's another Tom Doak course arrayed on a spectacular site: a stretch of New Zealand's North Island where fingers of land reach toward the South Pacific atop cliffs that plunge 500 feet to the surf. One of the most scenic venues any sport has ever seen, Cape Kidnappers is eye candy to golf photographers and a once-in-a-lifetime treat for golfers of any hemisphere.

Whistling Straits — Straits Course (Kohler, Wisconsin)

Whistling Straits opened in 1998 but really grabbed everyone's attention when it hosted the 2004 PGA Championship. Pete Dye took a flat wasteland on Wisconsin's lakefront and turned it into a rugged roller coaster of a course that evokes Scotland at every turn. You find grassy dunes and deep pot bunkers on the Straits Course, as well as stone bridges and even Scottish sheep standing almost sideways on hillsides.

Whistling Straits hosted another memorable PGA Championship in 2010. Germany's Martin Kaymer won the tournament after American Dustin Johnson got confused about one of Dye's myriad bunkers — he wasn't sure whether it was a bunker or not and he grounded his club.

When the wind whistles off Lake Michigan, this course can be a terror track. But the greens are large enough that if you play from the set of tees that matches your skill level, you have a chance to score.

Chapter 23

Gary's Top Ten Male Players

Some men exist at a whole 'nother level. The course turns into their canvas as they display their golfing artistry, playing the game as it was meant to be played. I have joined some of them on the course and heard stories about the others. Millions of mortals have tried to reach their level — these guys are the immortals.

Severiano Ballesteros

Nobody ever scrambled like Spain's brilliant, dashing Seve. He could — and did — save par from previously uncharted lands, like parking lots. A three-time British Open winner and two-time Masters champ, he was also one of the finest Ryder Cup players ever. Back problems slowed him down late in his career, and starting in 2008 he spent several years fighting a brain tumor while everyone in golf wished him well.

Fans have two lasting images of Seve. In the first, he's barely visible, out in the wilderness somewhere, swinging hard, trying an impossible recovery shot. In the second image a few minutes later, he's holding a trophy.

Walter Hagen

"Sir Walter" won the PGA Championship five times, the British Open four times, and the U.S. Open twice. While doing so, he redefined the role of the professional golfer. Before Hagen, the golf pro was low on society's food chain. He was never allowed to walk through the front door of the clubhouse and was certainly never seen socializing with members.

Hagen changed all that with his game and his flamboyant personality. He'd arrive at the course in a limousine, park next to the clubhouse he was barred from entering, and then have his chauffeur serve lunch in the back of the car. Not just any lunch: Full complements of wine and silver settings were the norm.

The silk-shirted Hagen played golf with kings and queens, dukes and duchesses. On one famous occasion, he asked King Edward VIII to tend the flag for him: "Hey, Eddie, get the stick, will you?"

Hagen elevated himself to full celebrity, and the golfing world was never the same again. Sir Walter really could play the game, and he was the first to make his living doing only that.

Fairway Louie

I went to school with this brilliant sage. He took seven years to get out of Riverside City College, a two-year school, but eventually got it right. Fairway Louie got his master's from some faraway outpost of academia and wound up managing an avocado orchard in the hills of Bonsall, California. He took me to my first rock concert, showed me how to cheat on tests, and came to my first wedding. I've known Fairway a long time.

He is the on-again, off-again president of a course where I grew up. That's the only way he can play for free. He advised me to quit the tour many years ago — a wiser man I do not know. We see each other rarely nowadays, and I miss him. His was a voice of reason in days of madness.

Phil Mickelson

For years, fans loved him for his go-for-broke style. They loved him even more after he worked like crazy to improve, learned to play the percentages under pressure, and won the 2004 Masters. That victory, Phil's first in a major, was one of the most popular in recent history. He claimed the 2005 PGA Championship, won the Masters again in 2006 and 2010, and looks poised to keep galleries cheering for years to come.

Jack Nicklaus

He simply was the one I grew up watching as he won and won and won.

Arnold Palmer

No one is more responsible for making golf the huge success it is today than Arnold Palmer. He came to the tour swinging hard at every shot, never laying up, and always (it seemed) getting out of trouble when it seemed he was doomed to fail. He was flamboyant and charismatic, with a swagger that galleries flocked to see. And he happened along in the early days of golf on television. The nation had a new hero. Arnie was responsible for all the attention that golf got in those early cathode-ray moments. He held our banner and set us on a new course for marketing. Golf — or any sport, for that matter — could not have had a better spokesman. He is, and always will be, the king.

Sam Snead

Sam started playing golf by carving an old stick to resemble a club and then whacking away at rocks on the West Virginia farm where he grew up. What came of that youthful folly was the most natural-looking golf swing ever devised. Sam's swing is still the gold standard today.

Samuel Jackson Snead won 81 tournaments on the PGA Tour (though he told everyone he'd won more). His flair for telling jokes and leaping up to kick the tops of doorjambs around the world's clubhouses are legendary. I had the opportunity to play and practice with Sam in his last years on tour. I'll never forget those moments.

Titanic Thompson

Golf has a way of attracting gamblers, and none is more legendary than Alvin "Titanic" Thompson. I have encountered very few of my peers who haven't heard of or played a long-ago round of golf with this famous king of the road gamblers. Titanic would make bets that he had no way of losing, no matter how ridiculous they seemed. He roamed with the rich and famous during the middle of the 20th century and supplied us with stories we'll tell deep into the 21st. He lived by his wits and imagination and added to the lore of golf.

If you have any mayhem and larceny in your bones, you'll want to read Kevin Cook's great look into the eyes of the greatest proposition man in history, *Titanic Thompson: The Man Who Bet on Everything* (W.W. Norton & Company).

Lee Trevino

In 1967, a 27-year-old Mexican American came out of nowhere to finish fifth in the U.S. Open. He didn't go back to El Paso, where he lived, but stayed to play a few more tournaments. He won enough money to stay on tour. "How long has this been going on?" he asked in jest.

He has been around ever since, and our lives have been richer for Lee Trevino's presence. A nonstop conversationalist, Lee talked his way through 27 tour victories, stopped off at NBC for a while to do some announcing, and then went on to the Champions Tour.

The man has an unequalled flair for words and shot making. He takes this sometimes-staid game and makes it fun. I hope we see his like again; our game can always use a good laugh.

Tiger Woods

Sure, he's been the game's biggest star for 15 years. Sure, he suffered through one of the most public scandals in tabloid history. But there's more to Eldrick "Tiger" Woods than the headlines. There's the competitive fire that makes him one of the hardest workers in the game. There's the brilliant short game that often escapes the notice of casual fans. And there's the will that makes him believe he can win every time out. Remember: Many pro golfers reach their peak in their mid-30s —Tiger, with 14 majors to his credit, turned 35 on December 30, 2010.

Chapter 24

Gary's Top Ten Female Players

In This Chapter

▶ Reminiscing about legendary golfers

▶ Honoring legends in the making

More than 20 percent of today's golfers are women, and they play an average of 17 rounds a year. The sport needs to do more to celebrate their contribution, so I'll start the trend by praising ten of the all-time best golfers who happen to be female (not just "female golfers").

Babe Zaharias is considered by some to be the greatest athlete — male or female — in sports history. Kathy Whitworth won more pro tournaments than anybody else who has ever played the game. They're the ones who blazed a trail for Michelle Wie and millions of others to follow. Now millions of even younger girls can look forward to a great future in the game.

JoAnne Carner

This charismatic Hall of Famer is one of the reasons LPGA golf became a popular major sport. "Big Mama," as she's called, is one of the greatest personalities the women's tour has ever known. She won 43 events and was the tour's leading money winner three times. In the long history of golf, she's the only player to win the U.S. Girls' Junior, U.S. Women's Amateur, *and* U.S. Women's Open — a feat that only Tiger Woods has matched among the men. The LPGA has long been enriched by Big Mama's performance as one of the game's true ambassadors.

Laura Davies

Laura was one of the dominant figures on the women's tour for years. Her enormous power reduced championship courses to mere pitch-and-putt status. She has an engaging way about her and is still a blast to watch as she goes all-out in an effort to destroy golf courses. She has won numerous LPGA titles, including four majors, and she lights up the faces of galleries worldwide.

Juli Inkster

Juli was inducted into the LPGA Hall of Fame in 1999, and she's still a star more than a decade later. In 1982, she became the first golfer, male or female, to win three consecutive U.S. amateur titles. The 1984 Rookie of the Year went on to win 31 times on tour, with 7 majors to her credit, including the U.S. Women's Open in 1999 and 2002 and back-to-back victories in the 1999 and 2000 McDonald's LPGA Championships.

Nancy Lopez

Nancy always has a smile on her face and plays the game with youthful zest. An outstanding representative of golf, she's one of the great putters in golf history. In her rookie year of 1978, she won nine tournaments, including five in a row, and brought worldwide attention to the LPGA. She went on to claim 48 tournament titles, including 3 majors, and although she isn't playing as much these days, Nancy still brings joy to all who meet her.

Lorena Ochoa

A national heroine in her native Mexico, Lorena dominated college golf before turning pro in 2002. Soon she was a two-time major champion with 27 LPGA crowns to her credit and the top-ranked female player on earth. The woman who friends called "Super Ochoa" did all that while charming everyone she encountered — and running the occasional triathlon! She retired in 2010 at the age of 28, saying she wanted to raise a family. Here's hoping we see this super player on the course again someday.

Se Ri Pak

An instant sensation who won two majors in her rookie year of 1998, Se Ri went on to a glittering career that featured three more majors and more than two dozen victories overall. The pride of South Korea inspired thousands of her countrywomen — and men — to take up golf. In 2007, Se Ri was inducted into the World Golf Hall of Fame. Still active on tour, she notched her 25th career victory in 2010. She's had fewer wins in recent years, partly because the "Seoul Sisters" who followed her lead are so talented, but no one can forget her contribution to the game.

Annika Sorenstam

This highly disciplined superstar was one of the hardest workers in our sport. A native of Stockholm, Sweden, Annika won 72 times with 10 majors before retiring in 2008 at the age of 38. In 2001, she shot a historic 59 in an LPGA event. The perennial Player of the Year was a perfectionist whose work ethic drove her peers to step up their own games. She inspired millions of girls to take up the game and is widely regarded as the finest female player of her time, if not all time.

Kathy Whitworth

Of all the people who have played this game — male or female — Kathy Whitworth won more times (88, to be exact, including 6 major championships) than anybody else. She dominated the LPGA tour from 1965 to 1973, topping the money list eight of those years and coming in second the other time. A seven-time player of the year, Kathy's another deserving Hall of Famer.

Mickey Wright

In the late 1950s and early 1960s, Mickey Wright raised women's professional golf to a new level. She helped put the LPGA on the map. I was fortunate enough to see her play an exhibition match many years ago. I had heard so much about her golf swing — and I wasn't disappointed. She may have the best swing of anybody who's ever played this game. An 82-time winner, Mickey ranks with Annika Sorenstam, Babe Zaharias, and a few others as one of the greatest players the LPGA has ever known. In her prime, she may have been the very best.

Babe Zaharias

Perhaps the most talented athlete of all time, Babe Didrikson Zaharias won two gold medals and a silver medal in track and field in the 1932 Olympics. Earlier that year, she took eight of ten events in the AAU's National Women's Track and Field Championship and won the meet for Employer's Casualty — as the only member of a one-woman team! Then she decided to take up golf. Among her achievements was co-founding the LPGA. In a brief LPGA career lasting eight years, she won 31 events and 10 major titles. The immortal Babe, who died of cancer at the age of 45, lives on as one of the legends of the game.

Chapter 25

Ten Immortal Golf Moments

*E*very year, this great old game generates unforgettable events. Picking only ten shining moments from the game's glittering history is hard — almost as hard as keeping your head, heart, and guts in perfect alignment for 18 holes in a round. Here's my best shot at pinning down the greatest of the great.

Young Tom Morris: It's in the Hole!

Where better to start a tour of immortal moments than with something all golfers strive for on every par-3 hole: the hole in one? And the honor of making the first of those goes to Young Tom Morris.

The son of Old Tom Morris, one of the game's original greats, Young Tom was already famous as the youngest-ever victor in a major, having won the 1868 Open Championship (also known as the British Open) at age 17. More than 140 years later, he still holds that distinction. But Young Tom wasn't done yet: Just to prove he was no flash in the pan, he won the next three Opens to make it four in a row — another record that still stands. He also made "the big shot" in 1869 at Prestwick's 166-yard 8th hole: the first hole-in-one ever recorded in tournament play!

Nice one, Tommy!

Bobby Jones Wins Golf's Grand Slam

The measure of any professional golfer is the number of majors won. That's why Tiger Woods is chasing Jack Nicklaus's record of 18 majors with such intensity. To win all four in one year seems just about impossible, but in 1930, the impossible happened when Bobby Jones completed the so-called impregnable quadrilateral, consisting then of the British Amateur, British Open, U.S. Open, and finally the U.S. Amateur. Even though the makeup of the Grand Slam has changed since then, Jones is still the only golfer in history to win four major titles in a single year!

Sarazen's Shot Heard 'Round the World

In the final round of the 1935 Masters, Gene Sarazen hit what is arguably the greatest shot in golf history. Four shots back of Craig Wood, who had just finished his round, Sarazen hit his Turf Rider 4-wood from 220 yards over a pond on Augusta National's par-5 15th hole, and holed the shot for a double-eagle 2 in front of 25 people, including tournament host Bobby Jones. The man they called "The Squire" went on to defeat Wood in a playoff the next day. Said Sarazen, "If I hadn't won, it would have been a double eagle without feathers."

Ben Hogan's Courageous Comeback

On a fog-shrouded bridge in Van Horn, Texas, in 1949, a Greyhound bus swerved into oncoming traffic and hit the car driven by professional golfer Ben Hogan. A split second before the head-on crash, Ben dove across the passenger seat to protect his wife, Valerie. The Hogans survived, but Ben had a broken collarbone, broken ankle, broken ribs, and a double fracture of his pelvis. Fifty-nine days later, he left the hospital in a wheelchair. Doctors told him he might never walk again.

Eleven months later, Hogan fought Sam Snead into a tie in the Los Angeles Open, only to lose in a playoff. Six months later he won the 1950 U.S. Open at Merion Golf Club in Ardmore, Pennsylvania, in a playoff against Lloyd Mangrum and George Fazio. Not bad for a guy whose career was supposed to be over!

Arnie's Charge at Cherry Hills

In 1960, they still played two 18-hole rounds on the last day — Saturday — for the U.S. Open title. During lunch between rounds, Arnold Palmer cracked that if he could drive the first hole at Cherry Hills Country Club in Denver, a 346-yard par-4, that afternoon, he may make up a seven-shot deficit and win the tournament. Nobody thought he could do it. Palmer promptly drove the first green, made birdie, shot 65, and held off an aging Ben Hogan and a youngster in the field, Jack Nicklaus, to claim his first and only U.S. Open.

That day was immortal not only for the best of Palmer's trademark final-round charges, but because it was a confluence of golf greatness: Palmer charging, Hogan's last stand, and Nicklaus's intro into professional golf's quest for major titles.

Watson and Nicklaus Duel in the Sun

On the 16th tee at Turnberry during the 1977 British Open, one of the combatants, Tom Watson, turned to the other, Jack Nicklaus, and said "This is what it's all about, isn't it?" It surely was, and when it was over both men had birdied the last hole; Watson shot 65 to Nicklaus's 66, neither man giving an inch in one of the most dramatic finishes in golf history.

The "Olden Bear" Prowls Augusta

Jack Nicklaus had already cemented his legend in the sport, winning 17 majors, before the 46-year-old Golden Bear tried to beat the kids at the 1986 Masters. A back-nine score of 30 left the entire field chasing the legend. I'll never forget that final nine holes. It was my first Masters in the broadcast booth, and in my perch near the 14th green I pulled my headset off one ear and listened to the roars that were engulfing the famed pines at Augusta National as Jack made his charge. He was carried to his 18th major victory that April Sunday by a fate that sealed his place at the head of the table in our sport's history.

Tiger Pounces at Pebble Beach

The site of the 100th anniversary of the United States Open: Pebble Beach. The gathering of talent: unprecedented. The problem was that more than 100 of the world's best golfers were also-rans that week in 2000, as they witnessed the finest performance ever seen by a competitor. Tiger Woods, already the number-one player in the world, put on a performance of super-golfer proportions, obliterating the field by 15 shots. He drove the ball longer, hit his irons closer, and putted better than anyone had ever seen, leaving the other pros wondering how they were going to compete with him in the future. This performance lasted longer, in the minds of his competitors, than just the four days it took Woods to win the 100th U.S. Open Championship. More like forever.

Annika Sorenstam's Magic Number

The finest player of her generation jolted the golf world by shooting a 59 in the second round of the 2001 Standard Register Ping tournament in Phoenix. By becoming the first player ever to break 60 in an LPGA event, Annika Sorenstam put the LPGA on her back and lifted it higher in public perception.

Phil Mickelson's Breakthrough

Coming into Easter Sunday, 2004, Phil Mickelson had won 22 PGA Tour events. And no majors. Chasing that first major title was starting to take a toll on the genial Californian. And then, as if possessed by the certainty that that was his day, he scorched the back nine at Augusta National, until at last he faced an 18-foot putt to win the Masters. Now the whole golfing world seemed to come together, pulling for likeable Lefty to hole that career-making putt. It dropped into the cup, and Mickelson made his famous spread-legged leap (to a height of an estimated four inches off the turf); the weight of his burden had been lifted with his first major win.

Part VII
Appendixes

The 5th Wave   By Rich Tennant

"Come on David, quit whining. You knew we enact stiff penalties for rule infractions at this club."

In this part . . .

Golfers have a language all their own. Appendix A lists phrases, terms, and slang you need to know as you learn the game. Appendix B lists some of the most popular golf organizations, plus selected golf schools and other resources.

Appendix A

Golf Talk

• •

Five minutes of listening to the conversation in any clubhouse in the world will tell you that golf has a language all its own. Here are the phrases, terms, and slang of that language. Hey, if you're going to be a golfer, you need to sound like one.

These terms are written with right-handed golfers in mind. Lefties will have to think in reverse!

A

A-game: The best a golfer can play. Sometimes you can shoot a good score with your B- or even C-game, but you always hope to bring your A-game to the first tee.

ace: A hole-in-one. Buy a round of drinks for the house.

address: The positioning of your body in relation to the ball just before starting your swing.

airball: When your swing misses the ball. Blame it on an alien spacecraft's radar.

albatross: British term for *double eagle,* or three under par on one hole. I've had only one.

amateur: Someone who plays for fun, not money. Playing golf for fun? What a concept!

angle of approach: The degree at which the clubhead moves either downward or upward into the ball.

approach: Your shot to the green made from anywhere except the tee. Sounds dangerous; really isn't.

apron: The grass around the edge of a green, longer than the grass on the green but shorter than the grass on the fairway. Often called the *fringe*.

attend: To hold and remove the flagstick as another player putts, usually from some distance.

away: Term used to describe the ball farthest from the hole and, thus, next to be played.

B

back door: The rear of the hole.

back lip: The edge of a bunker that's farthest from the green.

back nine: The second half of your round of golf.

backspin: When the ball hits the green and spins back toward the player. Galleries love backspin.

backswing: The part of the swing from the point where the clubhead moves away from the ball to the point where it starts back down again. I hope your backswing is smooth and in balance.

baffy: Old name for a lofted wood; short for *baffing spoon*.

bail out (hang 'em high): When you hit the shot, for example, well to the right to avoid trouble on the left.

balata: Sap from a tropical tree; the most popular cover for balls until high-tech plastics came along

ball at rest: The ball isn't moving. A study in still life.

ball marker: Small, round object, such as a coin, used to indicate the ball's position on the green.

ball retriever: Long pole with a scoop on the end used to collect balls from water hazards and other undesirable spots. If the grip on your ball retriever is worn out, get some lessons immediately.

ball washer: A device for cleaning balls; found on many tees.

banana ball: See *slice.*

bandit: See *hustler.*

barkie: Bet won by a player making par or better on a hole after hitting a tree.

baseball grip: To hold the club with all ten fingers on the grip.

best ball: A game in which two or more players form a team; the best net score for each team is recorded on the scorecard.

birdie: Score of one under par on a hole.

bisque: Handicap stroke given by one player to another. Receiver may choose which hole to apply it to.

bite (also vampire, bicuspid, overbite): A spin that makes the ball tend to stop rather than roll when it lands.

blade: Shot where the leading edge of the club rather than the clubface strikes the ball, resulting in a low, ugly shot that tends to travel way too far. Also a kind of putter or iron. See also *thin* or *skull.*

blast: Aggressive shot from a bunker that displaces a lot of sand.

blind shot: Shot where you can't see the spot where you want the ball to land.

block: See *push.*

bogey: Score of one stroke over par on a hole.

borrow: The amount of curve you must allow for a putt on a sloping green. Or what you need to do if you play a hustler.

bounce: The bottom part of a sand wedge, designed to slide through sand. Or what a ball does (usually in the wrong direction) when it hits the ground.

boundary: Edge of the course; it confines the space/time continuum. Usually marked by white stakes.

brassie: Old name for a 2-wood.

break: See *borrow.*

British Open: National championship run by Royal and Ancient Golf Club of St. Andrews — known in Britain as "the Open" because it was the first one.

bulge: The curve across the face of a driver or fairway wood (or fairway metal).

bump and run: See *run-up.*

bunker: Hazard filled with sand; should not be referred to as a *sand trap.*

buried ball/lie: Lie where part of the ball is below the surface of the sand in a bunker.

C

caddie: The person carrying your clubs during your round of golf. The person you fire when you play badly.

caddie master: Person in charge of caddies.

Calamity Jane: The great Bobby Jones's putter.

carry: The distance between a ball's takeoff and landing.

cart: Motorized vehicle used to transport lazy golfers around the course.

casual water: Water other than a water hazard on the course (such as a puddle) from which you can lift your ball without penalty.

center-shafted: Putter in which the shaft is joined to the center of the head.

character builder: Short, meaningful putt; only builds character if you make it.

charting the course: To walk each hole, noting distances from various landmarks, so that you always know how far you are from the hole.

chili-dip (Hormel, lay the sod over it, pooper scooper): A mishit chip shot, the clubhead hitting the ground well before it hits the ball.

chip: Very short, low-flying shot to the green.

chip-in: A holed chip.

choke: To play poorly because of self-imposed pressure.

choke down: To hold the club lower on the grip. *Choke up* means the same; don't ask me why.

chunk: See *chili-dip.*

claw: An innovative grip that takes wrist action out of the putting stroke.

cleat: Spike on the sole of a golf shoe.

cleek: Old term for a variety of iron clubs.

closed face: Clubface pointed to the left of your ultimate target at address or impact. Or clubface pointed skyward at the top of the backswing. Can lead to a shot that goes to the left of the target.

closed stance: Player sets up with the right foot pulled back, away from the ball.

clubhouse: Main building at a golf club.

club length: Distance from the end of the grip to the bottom of the clubhead.

collar: See *apron.*

come-backer: The putt after the previous putt finishes beyond the hole. Tends to get harder to make the older you get.

concede: To give an opponent a putt, hole, or match.

core: The center of a golf ball.

country club: A golf club open only to members and their guests.

course rating: The difficulty of a course, measured with some silly formula by the USGA.

cross-handed: Grip with the left hand below the right.

crosswind: Breeze blowing from right to left or from left to right.

cup: Container in the hole that holds the flagstick in place.

cuppy lie: When the ball is in a cuplike depression.

cut: Score that eliminates a percentage of the field (or players) from a tournament. Usually made after 36 holes of a 72-hole event. I've missed a few in my time.

cut shot: Shot that curves from left to right.

D

dance floor: Slang for *green*.

dawn patrol: The players who tee off early in the day.

dead (body bags, cadaver, on the slab, perdition, jail, tag on his toe, wearing stripes, no pulse — you get the idea): No possible way to pull off this shot!

deep: High clubface from top to bottom.

deuce: A score of 2 on a given hole.

dimple: Depression on the cover of a golf ball.

divot: Turf displaced by the clubhead during a swing.

dogleg: Hole on which the fairway curves one way or the other.

dormant: Grass on the course is alive but not actively growing. Also my hair.

dormie: In match play, being ahead by the same number of holes as there are holes left to play — for example, five up with only five holes left, or four up with four left.

double bogey: Score of two over par on a hole.

double eagle: Score of three under par on a hole. Forget it, they're nearly impossible. See also *albatross.*

down: Losing.

downhill lie: When your right foot is higher than your left at address.

downswing: The part of the swing where the clubhead is moving down toward the ball.

DQ'd: Disqualified.

drain: To sink a putt.

draw: Shot that curves from right to left.

drive: Shot from teeing ground other than par-3 holes.

drive for show, putt for dough: Old saying implying that putting is more important than driving. It happens to be true.

drive the green: When your drive finishes on the putting surface. Can happen on a short par-4, or when the brakes go out on your cart.

driving range: Place where you can go to hit practice balls.

drop: Procedure by which you put a ball back into play after it's been lifted and/or replaced in accordance with a rule.

dub: Bad shot or player.

duck hook (shrimp, mallard, quacker): Shot curving severely from right to left.

duffer: Bad player.

dying putt: A putt that barely reaches the hole.

E

eagle: Score of two under par for a hole.

embedded ball: Portion of the ball is below ground.

etiquette: Code of course conduct.

explode: To play a ball from a bunker by moving a large amount of sand. Or what you do if the ball *doesn't* get out of the bunker.

extra holes: Played when a match finishes even (is tied).

F

face: The front of a club or bunker.

face-on: A style of putting that may cure the yips.

fade: Shot that curves gently from left to right.

fairway: The closely-mowed turf running from tee to green.

fairway wood: Any wooden club that's not your driver. Nowadays, saying *fairway metal* is more accurate.

fat: To strike the ground before the ball.

feather: To put a delicate fade on a shot — don't try it yet!

first cut: Strip of rough at the edge of a fairway.

first off: Golfers beginning their round before everyone else.

flag: Piece of cloth attached to the top of a flagstick.

flagstick: The stick with the flag on top, which indicates the location of the cup.

flange: Projecting piece of clubhead behind the sole.

flat: Swing that is less upright than normal and more around the body than up and down.

flatstick: Slang for a putter.

flex: The amount of bend in a shaft. Also the amount of bend in your knees during a swing.

flier: Shot, usually hit from the rough, that travels way too far past the target.

flub: To hit the ball only a few feet.

fly the green: To hit a shot that lands beyond the putting surface.

follow-through: The part of the swing after the ball has been struck.

foozle: To make a complete mess of a shot.

fore: What to shout when your ball is headed toward another golfer.

forged irons: Clubs made one by one, without molds.

forward press: Targetward shift of the hands, and perhaps the right knee, just prior to takeaway.

foursome: Group of four golfers. In the United States, it's a group of four playing together. In Britain, it's a match between two teams of two, each hitting one ball alternately.

free drop: Drop for which no penalty stroke is incurred, generally within one club length of where the ball was.

fried egg: When your ball is partially buried in the sand.

fringe: See *apron.*

frog hair: Slang for *apron, fringe,* or *collar.*

front nine: The first half of your round of golf.

full swing: Longest swing you make.

G

gallery: Spectators at a tournament.

gimme: A short putt that your opponent doesn't ask you to hit, assuming that you can't possibly miss the shot.

G.I.R: Acronym for *greens in regulation* (greens hit in the regulation number of strokes).

glove: Usually worn on the left hand by right-handed players to help maintain grip.

Golden Bear: Jack Nicklaus.

golf widow(er): Your significant other after you get addicted to the game!

go to school: To watch your partner's putt and learn from it the line and pace that your putt should have.

good-good: Reciprocal concession of short putts. See also *gimme.*

grain: Tendency of grass to lie horizontally toward the sun.

Grand Slam: The four major championships: Masters, U.S. Open, British Open, and PGA Championship.

graphite: Lightweight material used to make shafts and clubheads; the same stuff that's called *lead* in pencils.

green: The shortest-cut grass, where you do your putting.

greenies: Bet won by player whose first shot finishes closest to the hole on a par-3.

green jacket: Prize awarded to the winner of the Masters Tournament in Augusta, Georgia.

green fee: The cost to play a round of golf.

greenside: Close to the green.

greensome: Game in which both players on a team drive off. The better of the two is chosen; then they alternate shots from there.

grip: Piece of rubber/leather on the end of a club. Also your hold on the club.

grooves: *Scoring* (the set of shallow notches) on the clubface.

gross score: Actual score shot before a handicap is deducted.

ground the club: The process of placing the clubhead behind the ball at address, generally touching the bottom of the grass.

ground under repair: Area on the course being worked on by the groundskeeper, generally marked by white lines, from which you may drop your ball without penalty.

gutta percha: Material used to manufacture golf balls in the 19th century.

H

hacker: Poor player.

half: Tied hole.

half shot: Improvised shot with ordinarily too much club for the distance.

halve: To tie a hole.

ham-and-egging: When you and your partner play well on alternate holes, forming an effective team.

handicap: Number of strokes over par a golfer is expected to score for 18 holes. For example, a player whose handicap is 16 is expected to shoot 88 on a par 72 course, or 16 strokes over par.

hanging lie: Your ball is on a slope, lying either above or below your feet.

hardpan: Very firm turf.

hazard: Can be either sand or water. Don't ground your club in hazards — it's against the rules!

head cover: Protection for the clubhead, usually used on woods.

heel: End of the clubhead closest to the shaft.

hickory: Wood from which shafts used to be made.

high side: Area above the hole on a sloping green.

hole: Your ultimate 4¼-inch-wide target.

hole-high: Level with the hole.

hole-in-one: See *ace.*

hole out: Complete play on hole.

home green: The green on the 18th hole.

honor: When you score lowest on a given hole, thus earning the right to tee up first on the next tee.

hood: Tilting the toe end of the club toward the hole. To hood a club lessens the loft and generally produces a right-to-left shot.

hook: Shot that curves severely from right to left.

horseshoe: When the ball goes around the edge of the cup and comes back toward you. Painful!

hosel: Curved area where the clubhead connects with the shaft.

hustler: A golfer who plays for a living. Plays better than he claims to be. Usually leaves your wallet lighter.

hybrid: A club similar to a fairway metal, designed to get the ball airborne quickly; many players prefer hybrids to 2-, 3- and 4-irons.

I

impact: Moment when the club strikes the ball.

impediment: Loose debris that you can remove from around your ball as long as the ball doesn't move.

Impregnable Quadrilateral: Slang for the Grand Slam.

improve your lie: To move the ball to make a shot easier. Illegal unless local rules dictate otherwise.

in play: Within the confines of the course (not out-of-bounds).

in your pocket: After you've picked up the ball! (Generally after you finish a hole without holing out.)

inside: Area on your side of a line drawn from the ball to the target.

inside-out: Clubhead moves through the impact area on a line to the right of the target. Most tour players do this. See also *outside in*.

intended line: The path on which you imagine the ball flying from club to target.

interlocking: Type of grip where the little finger of the right hand is entwined with the index finger of the left.

investment cast: Clubs made from a mold.

J

jail: Slang for when you and your ball are in very deep trouble. In golf jail, the bars are often made of bark.

jigger: Old term for a 4-iron. Also a great little pub to the right of the 17th fairway at St. Andrews.

jungle: Slang for heavy rough. See also *rough*.

junk: Enjoyable golf wagers on such things as hitting the green in one shot, getting up and down from a bunker, or making par after hitting a tree.

K

kick: See *bounce*.

kickpoint: The spot on a club's shaft that twists the most during the swing.

kill: To hit a long shot.

L

ladies' day: Time when a course is reserved for golfers of the female persuasion.

lag: A long putt hit with the intent of leaving the ball close to the cup.

laid off: When the club points to the left of the target at the top of the backswing.

lateral hazard: Water hazard marked by red stakes and usually parallel to the fairway.

lay-up: Conservatively played shot to avoid possible trouble.

leader board: Place where the lowest scores in a tournament are posted. I don't stay on the leader board too long. In fact, when the scorers are putting up the *d* in *McCord,* they're usually taking down the *M.*

leak: Ball drifting to the right during flight.

lie: Where your ball is on the ground. Also, the angle at which the club shaft extends from the head.

lift: What you do before you drop.

line: The path of a shot to the hole.

line up: To stand behind a shot to take aim.

links: A seaside course. Don't expect trees.

lip: Edge of a cup or bunker.

lip out: When the ball touches the edge of the cup but doesn't drop in.

lob: A short, high shot that lands softly.

local knowledge: What the members know and you don't.

local rules: Set of rules determined by the members, rules committee, or course professional.

loft: The degree at which a clubface is angled upward.

long game: Shots hit with long irons and woods. Also could be John Daly's game.

loop: Slang for *to caddy.* Also a round of golf or a change in the path of the clubhead during the swing.

low handicapper: Good player.

low side: Area below the hole on a sloping green.

LPGA: Ladies Professional Golf Association.

M

make: Hole a shot.

makeable: Shot with a good chance of being holed.

mallet: Putter with a wide head.

mark: To indicate the position of the ball with a small, round, flat object, such as a coin, usually on the green.

marker: Small, round object, such as a coin, placed behind the ball to indicate its position when you lift it. Also the person keeping score.

marshal: Person controlling the crowd at a tournament.

mashie: Old term for a 5-iron.

mashie-niblick: Old term for a 7-iron.

Masters: First major tournament of each calendar year. Always played at Augusta National Golf Club in Georgia. The one tournament I can't go to.

match of cards: Comparing your scorecard to your opponent's to see who won.

match play: Game played between two sides. The side that wins the most holes wins the match.

matched set: Clubs designed to look and feel the same.

medal play: Game played among any number of players. The player with the lowest score wins (also called *stroke play*).

metal wood: Driver or fairway "wood" made of metal.

miniature course: Putting course.

misclub: To use the wrong club for the distance.

misread: To take the wrong line on a putt.

miss the cut: To take too many strokes for the first 36 holes of a 72-hole event and be eliminated. I did that once or thrice.

mixed foursome: Two men, two women.

model swing: Perfect motion.

MOI: Abbreviation for *moment of inertia;* in putters, it means resistance to twisting at impact.

mulligan: Second attempt at a shot, usually played on the first tee. It's illegal.

municipal course: A course owned by the local government and, thus, open to the public. Also known as *munis,* municipal courses generally have lower green fees than privately owned public courses.

N

nassau: Bet in which a round of 18 holes is divided into three — front 9, back 9, and full 18.

net score: Score for a hole or round after handicap strokes are deducted.

never up, never in: Annoying saying coined for putts that finish short of the hole.

niblick: Old term for a 9-iron.

nine: Half of a course.

19th hole: The clubhouse bar.

O

O.B.: Slang for out-of-bounds.

off-center hit: Less than a solid strike.

offset: Club with the head set farther behind the shaft than normal.

one-putt: To take only a single putt on a green.

one up: Being one hole ahead in match play.

open face: Clubface aligned to the right of the target at address, or to the right of its path at impact. Can lead to a shot's veering to the right.

open stance: Player sets up with the left foot pulled back, away from the ball.

open up the hole: When your tee shot leaves the best possible angle for the next shot to the green.

order of play: Who plays when.

out-of-bounds: Area outside the boundaries of the course, usually marked with white posts. When a ball finishes out of bounds, the player must return to the original spot and play another ball under penalty of one stroke. He or she thus loses stroke and distance.

outside: Area on the far side of the ball.

outside-in: Swing path in which the clubhead moves into the impact area on a line to the left of the target. See also *inside-out.*

over the green: Ball hit too far.

overclub: To use a club that will hit the ball too far.

overcooked: An approach shot that zooms onto — and over — the green.

overlapping: A type of grip where the little finger of the right hand lies over the index finger of the left hand.

p

pairings: Groups of two players.

par: The score a good player would expect to make on a hole or round.

partner: A player on your side.

penal: Difficult.

persimmon: A wood from which wooden clubs were made before the age of metal woods.

PGA: Professional Golfers' Association.

piccolo grip: A very loose hold on the club, especially at the top of the backswing.

pigeon: An opponent you should beat with ease.

pin: See *flagstick.*

pin-high: See *hole-high.*

pin placement: The location of the hole on the green.

pitch: A short, high approach shot. Doesn't run much on landing.

pitch and putt: A short course. Or getting down in two strokes from off the green.

pitch-and-run: Varies from a pitch in that it flies lower and runs more.

pitching-niblick: Old term for an 8-iron.

pivot: The body turn during the swing.

plane: The arc of the swing.

playoff: Two or more players play extra holes to break a tie.

play through: What you do when the group in front of you invites you to pass.

plugged lie: When the ball finishes half-buried in the turf or a bunker.

plumb-bob: Lining up a putt with one eye closed and the putter held vertically in front of the face.

pop-up: High, short shot.

pot bunker: Small, steeply faced bunker.

practice green: Place for working on your putting.

preferred lies: Temporary rule that allows you to move the ball to a more favorable position because of abnormally wet conditions.

press: Way to get your bet money back after you've lost your match. This new bet takes place over any remaining holes.

private club: See *country club.*

pro-am: A competition in which professional partners team with amateurs.

professional: A golfer who plays or teaches for his or her livelihood.

pro shop: A place where you sign up to start play and can buy balls, clubs, and so on.

provisional ball: You think your ball may be lost. To save time, you play another from the same spot before searching for the first ball. If the first ball is lost, the second ball (the provisional ball) is in play.

public course: A golf course open to all.

pull: A straight shot that flies to the left of the target.

punch: A low shot hit with the ball back in the stance and a shorter-than-normal follow-through.

push: A straight shot that flies to the right of the target.

putter: A straight-faced club generally used on the greens.

Q

Q-school: An annual tournament in which aspiring players try to qualify for the PGA Tour. The ultimate grind: six rounds of fierce pressure.

quail high (stealth, skull, rat-high): Low.

quitting: Not hitting through a shot with conviction.

R

rabbit: A poor player.

rake: A device used to smooth the sand after you leave a bunker.

range: Practice area.

range ball: Generally, a low-quality ball used on a driving range. Range balls often have stripes painted on them; these are called *stripers.*

rap: To hit a putt firmly.

read the green: To assess the path on which a putt must travel to the hole.

regular: A shaft with normal flex.

regulation: The number of strokes needed to reach the green and have two putts left to make par.

release: The point in the downswing where the wrists uncock.

relief: Where you drop a ball that was in a hazard or affected by an obstruction.

reverse overlap: Putting grip in which the index finger of the left hand overlaps the little finger of the right hand.

rhythm: The tempo of your swing.

rifle a shot: To hit the ball hard, straight, and far.

rim the cup: See *lip out.*

ringer score: Your best-ever score at each hole on the course.

Road Hole: The 17th hole at St. Andrews — the hardest hole in the world.

roll: The distance a shot travels after landing.

rough: Area of long grass on either side of the fairway or around the green.

round: Eighteen holes of golf.

Royal and Ancient Golf Club of St. Andrews: The organization that runs the British Open.

rub of the green: Luck.

run: How far a golf shot travels after landing.

run-up: A type of shot to play when the ground is firm. You bounce the ball onto the green and let it roll to the hole.

S

sandbagger: A golfer who lies about his or her ability/handicap to gain an advantage.

sand trap: Undesirable term for a bunker.

sandy: Making par after being in a bunker.

scorecard: Where the length, par, and rating of each hole is recorded. Also holds your score.

scoring: The grooves on the clubface.

scramble: To play erratic golf but still score well. Also a game in which several players tee off, pick the best shot, and then all play their balls from that spot; play continues that way until the team holes the ball.

scratch play: No handicaps used in this type of game.

scratch player: A golfer with a 0 handicap.

second cut: Second level of rough, higher than first cut. Some courses have three cuts of rough.

semiprivate: A course with members that is also open to the public.

setup: See *address.*

shaft: The part of the club that joins the grip to the head.

shag: To retrieve practice balls.

shag bag: To carry practice balls.

shallow: Narrow clubface. Also a flattish angle of attack into the ball.

shank: Shot struck from the club's hosel; flies far to the right of the intended target.

shooting the lights out: To play very well.

short cut: Cut of grass on the fairway or green.

short game: Shots played on and around the green.

shut: Clubface aligned left at address or impact; looking skyward at the top of the backswing. Results in a shot that goes to the left of the target.

sidehill lie: Ball either above or below your feet.

sidesaddle: Putting style where a player faces the hole while making the stroke. See also *face-on.*

sink: To make a putt.

sit down (full flaps, pull a hamstring, develop a limp): A polite request for the ball to stop.

skins: Betting game where the lowest score on a hole wins the pot. If the hole is tied, the money carries over to the next hole.

skull: A low shot. See also *blade* or *thin.*

sky: Ball flies off the top of the clubface — very high and short.

sleeve of balls: Box of three golf balls.

slice: Shot that curves sharply from left to right.

slope: A measure of the difficulty of a golf course.

smother: To hit the ball with a closed clubface, resulting in a horrible, low, hooky shot.

snake: Long putt.

snap hook: Severe hook.

sole: Bottom of the clubhead.

spade-mashie: Old term for a 6-iron.

spike mark: Mark on the green made by a golf shoe.

spin-out: Legs moving too fast in relation to the upper body on the downswing.

spoon: Old term for a 3-wood.

spot putting: Aiming for a point on the green over which the ball must run if it is to go in the hole.

square: Score of a match is even. Equivalent to "all square." Also indicates the clubface and stance are aligned perfectly with the target.

square face: Clubface looking directly at the hole at address/impact.

square grooves: USGA banned them from clubfaces.

St. Andrews: The home of golf, located in Fife, Scotland.

stableford: Method of scoring by using points rather than strokes.

stance: Position of the feet before the swing.

starter: Person running the order of play from the first tee.

starting time: When you tee off at the first tee.

stick: The pin in the hole.

stiff: A shaft with reduced flex. Also a shot very close to the hole.

stimpmeter: Device used to measure the speed of greens.

stroke: Movement of club with the intent to hit the ball.

stroke hole: Hole at which a player either gives or receives a shot, according to her handicap.

stymie: Now-obsolete term for a ball obstructing your route to the hole.

sudden death: Form of playoff in which the first player to win a hole wins the match or tournament.

superintendent: Person responsible for the upkeep of the course.

surlyn: Material from which golf-ball covers can be made.

swale: Depression or dip in terrain.

sway: To move excessively to the right on the backswing without turning the body.

sweet spot: Perfect point on the clubface with which to strike the ball.

swing plane: Angle at which the club shaft travels around the body during a swing.

swing weight: Measure of a club's head weight relative to its length.

T

takeaway: Early part of the backswing.

tap-in: Very short putt, considered unmissable.

tee: Wooden peg on which the ball is set for the first shot on a hole. Also, the area from which that initial shot is hit.

teeing ground: Area in which you must tee your ball, between the tee markers and neither in front of them nor more than two club lengths behind them.

tee it up: To start play.

tee time: The time golfers start a round — a difficult thing to get at premier courses like Pebble Beach.

tempo: The rhythm of your swing.

temporary green: An alternate putting surface used when the permanent green is being renovated, or used in winter to save wear and tear on the permanent green.

Texas wedge: Term for a putter when used from off the green.

that'll play: A kind reference to a mediocre shot.

thin: To hit the ball around its equator — don't expect much height.

three-putt: To take three putts on the green, which is undesirable.

through the green: The whole course except hazards, tees, and greens.

Tiger tee: Slang for the back tee.

tight: Narrow fairway.

tight lie: The ball on bare ground or very short grass.

timing: The pace and sequence of movement in your swing.

titanium: Metal used in lightweight shafts, clubheads, and even inside a few golf balls.

top: Ball is struck on or above the equator.

torque: Twisting of the shaft at impact.

tour: Series of tournaments for professionals.

tradesman's entrance: Ball goes in the hole from the rear of the cup.

trajectory: Flight of the ball.

trap: See *bunker.*

triple bogey: Three over par on one hole. Not good.

turn: To make your way to the back nine holes. Also the rotation of the upper body during the backswing and forward swing.

U

uncock: See *release.*

underclub: To take at least one club less than needed for distance.

unplayable lie: Lie from which you can't hit the ball. A one-stroke penalty is your reward.

up: Ahead in the match. Also the person next to play or reaching the hole with a putt.

up and down: To get the ball into the hole in two strokes from off the green.

upright: To swing with a steep vertical plane.

urethane: Synthetic material used in making golf balls, including covers.

USGA: United States Golf Association. The ruling body for golf in the United States.

U.S. Open: National men's golf championship of America.

U.S. Women's Open: National women's golf championship of America.

V

Vardon grip: See *overlapping*.

W

waggle: Movement of the clubhead prior to the swing.

water hazard: Body of water that costs you a shot to escape.

wedge: Lofted club (iron) used for pitching.

whiff: See *airball*.

whipping: The string that fixed the head of a wooden club to the shaft in the old days.

whippy: A shaft more flexible than normal.

wind-cheater: Low drive.

winter rules: See *preferred lies*.

wood: Material that long clubs used to be made of.

wormburner: Low mishit.

Y

yips: When a golfer misses short putts because of nerves, reducing the afflicted unfortunate to jerky little snatches at the ball, the putterhead seemingly possessing a mind of its own.

Appendix B

Golf Organizations

●●

*T*his appendix lists selected golf associations, golf schools, and club-component firms. Some states are more golf-oriented than others, but you can find golf schools all over the country and the world. If you can't find one that suits you here, search for "golf schools" on the Internet.

Some of the addresses listed below are the headquarters for chains of schools. Many chain golf schools have seasonal instruction in the northern states; call their headquarters to find out which have programs near you.

Associations

American Junior Golf Association
1980 Sports Club Dr.
Braselton, GA 30517
Phone 877-373-2542 (toll-free) or 770-868-4200
Web site ajga.org

American Society of Golf Course Architects
125 N. Executive Dr., Suite 302
Brookfield, WI 53005
Phone 262-786-5960
Web site asgca.org

Golf Collectors Society
P.O. Box 2386
Florence, OR 97439
Phone 541-991-7313
Web site golfcollectors.com

Ladies Professional Golf Association
100 International Golf Dr.
Daytona Beach, FL 32124
Phone 386-274-6200
Web site lpga.com

Multicultural Golf Association of America
P.O. Box 1081
Westhampton Beach, NY 11978
Phone 631-288-8255
Web site home.earthlink.net/~pgd58/

National Amputee Golf Association
11 Walnut Hill Rd.
Amherst, NH 03031
Phone 603-672-6444
Web site nagagolf.org

National Association of Left-Handed Golfers
3249 Hazelwood Dr. SW
Atlanta, GA 30311
Phone 404-696-1763
Web site nalg.org

National Golf Foundation
1150 S. U.S. Hwy. 1, Suite 401
Jupiter, FL 33477
Phone 888-275-4643 (toll-free) or 561-744-6006
Web site ngf.org

Professional Golfers' Association of America
100 Avenue of the Champions
Palm Beach Gardens, FL 33410
Phone 561-624-8400
Web site pga.com

Royal Canadian Golf Association
1333 Dorval Dr., Suite 1
Oakville, Ontario L6M 4X7
Canada
Phone 800-263-0009 (toll-free) or 905-849-9700
Web site rcga.org

United States Golf Association (USGA)
P.O. Box 708
Far Hills, NJ 07931
Phone 908-234-2300
Web site usga.org

Golf Schools

Aviara Golf Academy
7447 Batiquitos Dr.
Carlsbad, CA 92011
Phone 800-433-7468 (toll-free) or 760-438-4539
Web site aviaragolfacademy.com

Barton Creek Golf Academy
Barton Creek Resort
8212 Barton Club Dr.
Austin, TX 78735
Phone 512-301-1054
Web site bartoncreek.com/golf/
academy.cfm

Ben Sutton Golf Schools
P.O. Box 9199
Canton, OH 44714
Phone 800-225-6923 (toll-free) or 330-548-0043
Web site golfschool.com

Boyne Super 5 Golf Week
Boyne Mountain Resort
600 Highland Dr.
Harbor Springs, MI 49740
Phone 800-462-6963
Web site boyne.com/golf/
Instruction/Adult.html

Classic Swing Golf School
1500 Legends Dr.
Myrtle Beach, SC 29579
Phone 800-827-2656
Web site classicswing.com

Dave Pelz Scoring Game School
20308 State Hwy. 71 W, Suite 7
Spicewood, TX 78669
Phone 800-833-7370 (toll-free) or 512-263-7668
Web site pelzgolf.com

David Leadbetter Golf Academy
1410 Masters Blvd.
Champions Gate, FL 33896
Phone 888-633-5323 (toll-free) or 407-787-3330
Web site leadbetter.com or david
leadbetter.com

Golf Digest Schools
7825 E. Redfield Rd., #E
Scottsdale, AZ 85260
Phone 800-875-4347 (toll-free) or 480-998-7430
Web site golfdigestschool.com

Grayhawk Learning Center
8620 E. Thompson Peak Pkwy.
Scottsdale, AZ 85255
Phone 888-506-7786 (toll-free) or 480-502-2656
Web site www.grayhawkgolf.com/gray
hawk_learning_center/

Hank Haney Golf Ranch
4101 Custer Rd.
McKinney, TX 75070
Phone 972-315-5300

Jim McLean Golf School
4440 NW 87th Ave.
Miami, FL 33178
Phone 305-591-6409
Web site doralresort.com/golf

John Jacobs' Golf Schools
6210 E. McKellips Rd.
Mesa, AZ 85215
Phone 800-472-5007 (toll-free) or 480-991-8587
Web site jacobsgolf.com

Kapalua Golf Academy
1000 Office Rd.
Lahaina, Maui, HI 96761
Phone 800-527-2582 (toll-free) or 808-665-5445
Web site kapalua.com/index.php/
kapaluagolf/kapalua-golf-academy-
instruction

The Kingsmill Golf School
The Kingsmill Resort and Spa
1010 Kingsmill Rd.
Williamsburg, VA 23185
Phone 800-832-5665 (toll-free) or 757-253-1703
Web site kingsmill.com/golf/
academy/

PGA Tour Academy Golf Schools
220 Ponte Vedra Park Dr., Suite 260
Ponte Vedra Beach, FL 32082
Phone 800-766-7939 (toll-free) or
(904) 285-3700
Web site pgatourexperiences.com

Phil Ritson–Mel Sole Golf School
P.O. Box 2580
Pawleys Island, SC 29585
Phone 800-624-4653 (toll-free) or 843-237-4993
Web site ritson-sole.com

Pinehurst Golf Academy
1 Carolina Vista Dr.
Village of Pinehurst, NC 28374
Phone 866-291-4427
Web site pinehurst.com/golf-
schools/about-golf-academies.php

Randy Henry's Dynamic Golf School
Coeur d'Alene Resort
115 S. Second St.
Coeur d'Alene, ID 83814
Phone 800-688-5253 (toll-free) or 208-765-4000
Web site www.cdaresort.com/golf

Sugarloaf Golf Club & School
Sugarloaf USA
5092 Access Rd.
Carrabassett Valley, ME 04947
Phone 800-843-5623 (toll-free) or 207-237-2000
Web site www.sugarloaf.com/
GolfSchool

U.S. Schools of Golf
718½ Promenade
Richmond, IN 47374
Phone 800-756-5052
Web site ussog.com

Vermont Golf School
Stratton Mountain Resort
R.R. 1, Box 145
Stratton Mountain, VT 05155
Phone 800-787-2886
Web site www.stratton.com/golf_at_
stratton_vermont

Wintergreen Golf Academy
Wintergreen Resort
Route 664
Wintergreen, VA 22958
Phone 434-325-8250
Web site wintergreenresort.com/golf/
golf_academy.aspx

Component Companies

Golfsmith
11000 N. 1H-35
Austin, TX 78753
Phone 800-813-6897 (toll-free) or 512-837-4810
Web site golfsmith.com

The GolfWorks
P.O. Box 3008
Newark, OH 43023
Phone 800-848-8358 (toll-free) or 740-328-4193
Web site golfworks.com

Hireko Golf
16185 Stephens St.
City of Industry, CA 91745
Phone 800-367-8912
Web site hirekogolf.com

Hornung's Pro Golf Sales, Inc.
815 Morris St.
Fond du Lac, WI 54936
Phone 800-323-3569 (toll-free) or920-922-2640
Web site hornungs.com

Wittek Golf Supply
3865 Commercial Ave.
Northbrook, IL 60062
Phone 800-869-1800 (toll-free) or 847-943-2399
Web site wittekgolf.com

Index

• C •

T

Apple & Macs

iPad For Dummies
978-0-470-58027-1

iPhone For Dummies,
4th Edition
978-0-470-87870-5

MacBook For Dummies, 3rd
Edition
978-0-470-76918-8

Mac OS X Snow Leopard For
Dummies
978-0-470-43543-4

Business

Bookkeeping For Dummies
978-0-7645-9848-7

Job Interviews
For Dummies,
3rd Edition
978-0-470-17748-8

Resumes For Dummies,
5th Edition
978-0-470-08037-5

Starting an
Online Business
For Dummies,
6th Edition
978-0-470-60210-2

Stock Investing
For Dummies,
3rd Edition
978-0-470-40114-9

Successful
Time Management
For Dummies
978-0-470-29034-7

Computer Hardware

BlackBerry
For Dummies,
4th Edition
978-0-470-60700-8

Computers For Seniors
For Dummies,
2nd Edition
978-0-470-53483-0

PCs For Dummies,
Windows
7 Edition
978-0-470-46542-4

Laptops For Dummies,
4th Edition
978-0-470-57829-2

Cooking & Entertaining

Cooking Basics
For Dummies,
3rd Edition
978-0-7645-7206-7

Wine For Dummies,
4th Edition
978-0-470-04579-4

Diet & Nutrition

Dieting For Dummies,
2nd Edition
978-0-7645-4149-0

Nutrition For Dummies,
4th Edition
978-0-471-79868-2

Weight Training
For Dummies,
3rd Edition
978-0-471-76845-6

Digital Photography

Digital SLR Cameras &
Photography For Dummies,
3rd Edition
978-0-470-46606-3

Photoshop Elements 8
For Dummies
978-0-470-52967-6

Gardening

Gardening Basics
For Dummies
978-0-470-03749-2

Organic Gardening
For Dummies,
2nd Edition
978-0-470-43067-5

Green/Sustainable

Raising Chickens
For Dummies
978-0-470-46544-8

Green Cleaning
For Dummies
978-0-470-39106-8

Health

Diabetes For Dummies,
3rd Edition
978-0-470-27086-8

Food Allergies
For Dummies
978-0-470-09584-3

Living Gluten-Free
For Dummies,
2nd Edition
978-0-470-58589-4

Hobbies/General

Chess For Dummies,
2nd Edition
978-0-7645-8404-6

Drawing
Cartoons & Comics
For Dummies
978-0-470-42683-8

Knitting For Dummies,
2nd Edition
978-0-470-28747-7

Organizing
For Dummies
978-0-7645-5300-4

Su Doku For Dummies
978-0-470-01892-7

Home Improvement

Home Maintenance
For Dummies,
2nd Edition
978-0-470-43063-7

Home Theater
For Dummies,
3rd Edition
978-0-470-41189-6

Living the
Country Lifestyle
All-in-One
For Dummies
978-0-470-43061-3

Solar Power Your Home
For Dummies,
2nd Edition
978-0-470-59678-4

Internet

Blogging For Dummies,
3rd Edition
978-0-470-61996-4

eBay For Dummies,
6th Edition
978-0-470-49741-8

Facebook For Dummies,
3rd Edition
978-0-470-87804-0

Web Marketing
For Dummies,
2nd Edition
978-0-470-37181-7

WordPress
For Dummies,
3rd Edition
978-0-470-59274-8

Language & Foreign Language

French For Dummies
978-0-7645-5193-2

Italian Phrases
For Dummies
978-0-7645-7203-6

Spanish For Dummies,
2nd Edition
978-0-470-87855-2

Spanish
For Dummies,
Audio Set
978-0-470-09585-0

Math & Science

Algebra I
For Dummies,
2nd Edition
978-0-470-55964-2

Biology For Dummies,
2nd Edition
978-0-470-59875-7

Calculus For Dummies
978-0-7645-2498-1

Chemistry For Dummies
978-0-7645-5430-8

Microsoft Office

Excel 2010 For Dummies
978-0-470-48953-6

Office 2010 All-in-One
For Dummies
978-0-470-49748-7

Office 2010 For Dummies,
Book + DVD Bundle
978-0-470-62698-6

Word 2010 For Dummies
978-0-470-48772-3

Music

Guitar For Dummies,
2nd Edition
978-0-7645-9904-0

iPod & iTunes For
Dummies, 8th Edition
978-0-470-87871-2

Piano Exercises
For Dummies
978-0-470-38765-8

Parenting & Education

Parenting For Dummies,
2nd Edition
978-0-7645-5418-6

Type 1 Diabetes
For Dummies
978-0-470-17811-9

Pets

Cats For Dummies,
2nd Edition
978-0-7645-5275-5

Dog Training For Dummies,
3rd Edition
978-0-470-60029-0

Puppies For Dummies,
2nd Edition
978-0-470-03717-1

Religion & Inspiration

The Bible For Dummies
978-0-7645-5296-0

Catholicism For Dummies
978-0-7645-5391-2

Women in the Bible
For Dummies
978-0-7645-8475-6

Self-Help & Relationship

Anger Management
For Dummies
978-0-470-03715-7

Overcoming Anxiety
For Dummies,
2nd Edition
978-0-470-57441-6

Sports

Baseball
For Dummies,
3rd Edition
978-0-7645-7537-2

Basketball
For Dummies,
2nd Edition
978-0-7645-5248-9

Golf For Dummies,
3rd Edition
978-0-471-76871-5

Web Development

Web Design
All-in-One
For Dummies
978-0-470-41796-6

Web Sites
Do-It-Yourself
For Dummies,
2nd Edition
978-0-470-56520-9

Windows 7

Windows 7
For Dummies
978-0-470-49743-2

Windows 7
For Dummies,
Book + DVD Bundle
978-0-470-52398-8

Windows 7 All-in-One
For Dummies
978-0-470-48763-1

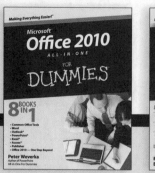
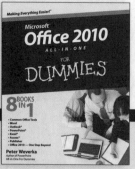
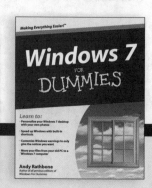

Staff
Development
Volume One

A CONTEMPORARY NURSING RESOURCE BOOK···

a reader
consisting of
nineteen articles especially selected
by The Journal of Nursing Administration
Editorial Staff.

CONTEMPORARY
PUBLISHING INC.